THE WINES OF FAUGÈRES

To Sheila & Roy

Hoping this leads
you to some good
bottles —

Best wishes

Rosemary George

avec toute,
mon amitié
Liliane

22/10/2016

THE WINES OF
FAUGÈRES

ROSEMARY GEORGE

infiniteideas

Copyright © Rosemary George, 2016

The right of Rosemary George to be identified as the author of this book has been asserted in accordance with the Copyright, Designs and Patents Act 1988.

First published in 2016 by
Infinite Ideas Limited
36 St Giles
Oxford
OX1 3LD
United Kingdom
www.infideas.com

A CIP catalogue record for this book is available from the British Library

ISBN 978–1–908984–71–5

Brand and product names are trademarks or registered trademarks of their respective owners.

Front cover image (top) of Château des Peyregrandes reproduced with permission of Patrice de Ginestet. Lower image © Dina Calvarese/Shutterstock.com
Photographs on pages 45, 46 and 60, and plates 3 (top) and 4 (bottom) © Jeanjean.
Photographs on pages 4, 6, 7, 9 and 11 courtesy of Domaine St Martin d'Agel.
Photograph on page 138 courtesy of Château Laurens.
All other photographs courtesy of Gary Macdonald.

Typeset by Suntec, India

Printed in Britain by 4edge Limited

CONTENTS

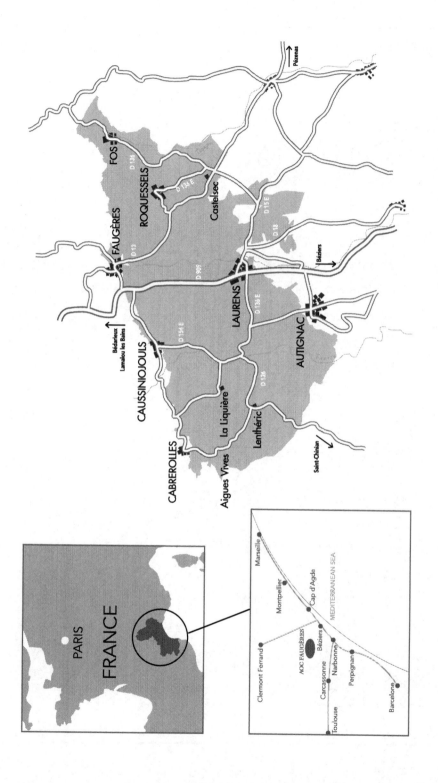

INTRODUCTION: SETTING THE SCENE

The vineyards of Faugères sit at the foot of the hills of the Espinouse. The perfect introduction to the area is to drive or, if you are feeling particularly energetic, walk up to the Pic de la Coquillade. Bernard Vidal of Château de la Liquière took me up there on a sunny spring afternoon and I had Faugères at my feet, with the village of Caussiniojouls in the immediate foreground, Cabrerolles and then Autignac and Laurens in the distance. I could just make out a silvery streak of the Mediterranean. It was breathtaking.

The other viewpoint is the site of Les Trois Moulins above the village of Faugères itself. It gives a wonderful idea of the topography of the vineyards and villages, the undulating hills and valleys that twist and turn as they fall away towards the sea. The term *balcons de schist* or balconies of schist is very apt. You can also see numerous examples of the *capitelles* – constructions that look rather like dry-stone igloos – for which Faugères is known. The tradition of *pierres sèches*, dry-stone walls, is strong in the region and being kept alive by an energetic woman, Claude Froidevaux, who encourages local people to learn the art of restoring walls and rebuilding the *capitelles*. Watching her work with amazing speed and dexterity, you sense how she can read the stones, knowing just which will fit where with unerring accuracy. Thanks to her efforts, some sixteen or seventeen *capitelles* around Faugères have been restored, but she laments the number of stone terraces that have disappeared.

The appellation of Faugères consists of seven villages and a couple of hamlets, all of which are rewarding to explore on foot. It is easy to overlook the charm of the village of Faugères itself as you drive past on the main road; you must stop and walk. The narrow streets of the village take you past little doorways and old houses as you turn away from the narrow main street, rue Droite, which climbs up through the village. The little café, the Dame Jane, is worth a stop for a *plat du jour* and some local produce, both liquid and solid, or just a cup of coffee. The village is at its most animated on the second Sunday in July, the Fête du Grand St Jean. Numerous *vignerons* have stands in rue Droite, upturned barrels from which they serve their wine – usually the most recent vintages. There are other attractions too, arts and crafts and things to eat. The members of the Confrérie in their tapestry robes and gold hats parade through the street, along with other *confréries* – not just for wine but also for olives, biscuits and paté – making a colourful pageant. Then they *intronise* (enrol, literally 'enthrone'!) a few people who they consider have helped the cause of Faugères. It was an honour that I was happy to accept.

Fos is one of the prettiest villages of the Faugérois. Its long and winding main street, with a small church and a bread oven, ends in Ollier-Taillefer's new cellar. Roquessels is dominated by its ruined castle; Cabrerolles too has the remains of a castle that you can climb up to. It is well worth it for the views of the surrounding countryside, and in the remains of the castle of Caussiniojouls you will find the tasting *caveau* of Château Chenaie. Laurens is a more substantial village; it once had a railway station and still has a marble quarry and, at the top of the village, hidden amongst the houses, is a château with an attractive green and yellow glazed tile roof. There are more substantial houses here. Autignac is a *circulade* village, built in a circle for defensive reasons, with an attractive little square and a café offering a satisfying *menu du jour*. However, you sense it has lost some of its former prosperity; there are some grand houses that are now sadly shuttered and neglected, vestiges of the former wealth of the village.

I spend part of each year in a village near Faugères but not within the appellation, and I find that I never tire of the scenery of my corner of the Languedoc. It changes with the seasons. In the winter the vines are silhouettes, some scraggy and waiting for pruning, others neat and trim. The almond trees are a gentle pink and the mimosa a brilliant yellow harbinger of spring. Then the green buds of the vines begin to appear and suddenly, if there is a warm spell, the vegetation will race, and the blossom on the trees and the yellow coronilla will add colour to the more muted scenery of green *garrigues* and brown vines and soil. The vines become verdant as the year advances, but you can easily miss the moment of flowering, so discreet are the tiny, pin-point, white flowers. As summer progresses and the grapes fill out the countryside takes on a sleepier note, with the leaves losing their vibrant freshness. And then in September, after the somnolence of August, everything bursts into life again with the harvest. You can see activity in the vineyards and find yourself stuck behind a trailer of grapes heading to a nearby cellar; you pass cellar doors from which emanate that intoxicating aroma of fermenting grape juice. Then the year draws in, but the winter days can sometimes be the most invigorating, for Faugères can be at its finest on a day of clear blue skies and winter crispness. I have yet to see Faugères in the snow, but I am told it happens – not every year, but not infrequently either.

So why write a book on Faugères? Because it is there. Because it is the nearest vineyard to my Languedoc home. Because I love the wines and the sheer variety of the wines within this small area. I tasted and drank my first Faugères on an early visit to the Languedoc in 1987, when Gilbert Alquier gave me a perfumed 1985 as well as his experimental *cuvée* of an oak-aged wine, and I immediately loved the spicy flavours of *fruits rouges* and *garrigues*. And I have never been able to resist them ever since.

Faugères is a compact vineyard compared to many of the other appellations of the Languedoc with, for red wine, the same five grape varieties, grown on similar soil. But none the less the variety is infinite, prompted by the human hand and the perceptible differences between the different villages. And the white wine, which accounts for a meagre 2 per cent of the appellation, amply demonstrates how the white wines of the Languedoc are developing and improving with every vintage, their wonderful herbal flavours conjuring up the scents of the herbs of the *garrigues*, fennel and bay and thyme. Pink Faugères, which accounts for just 18 per cent of the appellation, provides delicious refreshing drinking with acidity and delicate fruit. The wines of Faugères should always have a distinctive freshness which places them amongst the finest of the Languedoc.

Then there is also the village of Gabian, neighbouring the village of Faugères itself. This might have been part of the appellation of Faugères had the right decision been taken at the critical moment. Gabian has the schist of Faugères but it has other soils too, and its wine growers provide a fascinating picture of what happens to a village without a particular appellation. As you will see, the wine growers of Gabian encompass the innovative and inventive, the highly original, and also the traditional.

Since that first visit in 1987 I have returned regularly to the area, with increasing frequency over the last ten years, when Faugères became my nearest Languedoc vineyard. Then, over several months in 2014, and with subsequent visits in 2015 and 2016, I managed to visit every *vigneron* in the appellation as well as the cave cooperative, including four new growers who made their first wine in 2014. Some *vignerons* proved more elusive than others. So this book is the culmination of many highly enjoyable weeks of research, walking through vineyards, and talking and tasting in welcoming cellars.

Naturally things will not stand still. I know that there are other new wine growers and new wines from existing estates in the pipeline. A book about a wine appellation can only provide a snapshot at one particular moment, as I write this to conclude the introduction on a sunny spring day in early April 2016. With it I hope to offer a tribute to one of the most individual appellations of the Languedoc.

1

THE HISTORY OF FAUGÈRES – FROM THE GREEKS TO AN APPELLATION

There are various theories about the origin of the name Faugères. Some say that it comes from *fougères*, which means 'fern' in French, but there are no ferns amongst the vegetation of the *garrigues*. Claude Caumette, the local historian (of whom more later in the chapter), is firmly of the view that 'Faugères' means *forêt de hêtres*, a forest of beeches. Again, there are no beeches in Faugères today, but maybe there were in 1000 AD. As will be seen, the name of the wine comes from the reputation of the village for its *fine* or *eau de vie*. Although the broad brushstrokes of the viticultural history of the Languedoc have not made much impact on Faugères itself, it is worth considering the development of the region and situating Faugères in that context. However, it is impossible to emphasize sufficiently that Faugères has the history of a poor viticultural region and events often passed it by. Much of the development of the Languedoc focuses on the vineyards of the plains, rather than those of the hills in the hinterland.

THE GREEKS AND THE ROMANS

It all began with the Greeks. First they founded Marsilia, on the site of the modern city of Marseilles in the sixth century BC, and a few years later they settled along the coast around Agde. Excavations at Lattes outside Montpellier have uncovered a vast quantity of grape pips from the fifth century BC, indicating with certainty the presence of vineyards in the

Languedoc before the arrival of the Romans, who founded a colony at Narbonne in 118 BC. Viticulture flourished under the Romans. Domitian's edict of AD 92 ordering many existing vineyards to be pulled up – in an attempt to ensure that land suitable for the cultivation of wheat was retained for that purpose – had a temporary braking effect, but only until the repeal of the edict by Emperor Probus in AD 276. Ever since then viticulture has been a vital element of the agricultural activity and economy of the whole region in which Faugères has played its small part.

THE MIDDLE AGES AND THE CHURCH

During the Middle Ages, the increasingly powerful Catholic Church contributed considerably to the development of viticulture throughout the region. At one time there were as many as fifty Benedictine abbeys in Languedoc Roussillon, including St Guilhem-le-Désert and Lagrasse, as well as Cistercian abbeys such as Fontfroide and Valmagne. The production of wine was an essential part of monastic life for all of these. It was needed not only for the Eucharist but also for hospitality; the monasteries were the four-star hotels of the medieval traveller. The monastic houses played an important role in maintaining and expanding the viticultural traditions of the South throughout the Middle Ages, especially during the periods of social upheaval caused by the Albigensian Crusade and also the Hundred Years War, in which the region featured when England's Black Prince crossed the Orb valley and sacked Bédarieux.

As for Faugères itself, there were three religious sites, with vines, in the twelfth century, namely Sylva Plana or Sauvanès, Grézan and Haut Fabrègues. Faugères was on one of the many pilgrimage routes to Santiago de Compostella, coming south from Lodève via Joncels, Bédarieux to Faugères. The monastic grange of Sauvanès was founded in 1139, with its mother house being the Cistercian abbey of Sylvanès, further north, closer to Millau. Today the remaining building is overwhelmed by trees and vegetation; it was destroyed three times during various religious conflicts and on the last occasion was not rebuilt. The monks originally chose the spot for its access to water, making a dam in the little river Sauvanès to form a lake for carp, and this lake still exists. The remains of the abbey now belong to the Bâtiments de France and have never been deconsecrated. It is a peaceful spot, surrounded by vines belonging to the Abbaye de Sylva Plana estate.

At Grézan, where there had first been a Roman villa, there was a *commanderie* of the Knights Templar in the Middle Ages. Haut Fabrègues was also built in 1145 by the Templars, who were the great crusaders of the Middle Ages – and traces of a Roman vineyard have also been found at Fabrègues.

The village of Faugères itself had both Catholic churches and Protestant temples. During the Wars of Religion in the sixteenth century Faugères and Laurens were Protestant while neighbouring Autignac and Gabian were Catholic. The baron of Faugères, Charles de Narbonne, converted to Protestantism in 1562 and died in 1578, ensuring that Faugères was an important centre of Protestantism in the sixteenth century. It was fought over during the Wars of Religion, when the ramparts of the village were destroyed, but vestiges of the Protestant temples are still to be found if you walk round the village. Over the next century the revocation of the Edict of Nantes in 1685 caused numerous problems for the Protestants of the village.

Once the Languedoc was assimilated into France, wine from the region began to travel north and there are records of Languedoc wine being enjoyed at the Valois court of Charles V towards the end of the fourteenth century – but there is no specific mention of Faugères. None the less, the Massif Central represented a substantial barrier throughout the Middle Ages and transport difficulties would ensure that the wines of the south remained relatively unknown. The end of the Wars of Religion and the accession of Henri IV in 1589 brought a hope of prosperity. Vineyard plantings increased enormously in the first half of the seventeenth century as a result of the clearing of scrubland in the hills, while the plains remained indispensable for the production of wheat.

THE CANAL DU MIDI

The reputation of virtually every wine has depended upon ease of transport. Most great vineyards are close to river systems which were vital in those days of impassable roads before the development of the railways. The building of the Canal du Midi in the seventeenth century under the impetus of

Colbert, Minister of Finances under Louis XIV, had a dramatic impact on communications for the whole area, but not specifically for Faugères. The Canal du Midi opened in 1681 and represents a colossal feat of engineering; it is also appropriately called the Canal des Deux Mers because it links the Mediterranean with the Atlantic. However, the wine merchants of Bordeaux maintained their privileges, and during the eighteenth century only 5 per cent of the wines and *eaux de vie* of the Languedoc were exported along the Canal du Midi; Bordeaux did not want the Languedoc as competition. In 1742 a royal decree allowed the sales of wines from the Languedoc from the feast of St Martin on 11 November until 8 September of the following year, when any unsold wine would have to be returned to its source for distillation.

The terrible winter of 1708–9, when severe cold lasted from the middle of October until the end of the following February, caused untold damage to agriculture all over France but particularly in the northern part of the country. Many vineyards were devastated by frost and only those near the sea in the south, with their more equitable climate – particularly those of the Languedoc and also Provence – survived. None the less, temperatures in the Languedoc dropped to -20°C and there are anecdotes about beards freezing, so cold it was. However, the South did manage to benefit from the shortage of wine in the northern part of the country.

DOMAINE de St-MARTIN-D'AGEL - E. GRANAUD, Propriétaire

THE NINETEENTH CENTURY

It was not until the nineteenth century that the vineyards of the Languedoc experienced a time of real prosperity. The period of industrialization after Napoleon III's reign, which ended with the Franco-Prussian War in 1870, brought an immense demand for the wines of the Midi. With the Industrial Revolution came a new clientele, the factory workers and miners of the North, who wanted a cheap, energy-inducing drink, namely wine, at a time when water was usually unfit for human consumption. The coastal plains rather than the steeper hillsides inland were particularly suitable for the production of thin acidic wine that barely reached 7 or 8% abv. Today it would be considered quite undrinkable, but it is on this that the economic and agricultural success of the Midi was built. This was the period that saw the building of many fine châteaux, with immense cellars that catered for the production of enormous quantities of wine. A building such as the Château de Grézan outside Laurens on the edge of the appellation of Faugères may look from a distance like a medieval edifice, but in fact it dates from the nineteenth century; apparently it was built with the proceeds of a single harvest. It is but one of many so-called *châteaux pinardiers* (châteaux built from the profits of the wine trade, with *pinard* a derogatory term for wine) designed by the Bordelais architect, Louis-Michel Garosse, who apparently offered potential clients a catalogue of different buildings. The château in Autignac, which is now part of Domaine des Prés-Lasses, is another nineteenth-century construction.

The Languedoc, rather than Bordeaux or Burgundy, is where some of the greatest technical advances in winemaking took place during the nineteenth century. In a vineyard near Mauguio in the Hérault, Henri Bouschet created a new grape variety, Alicante Bouschet, by crossing Grenache Noir with a hybrid of Aramon and Teinturier du Cher. He lamented the demands of the market that chose wine by colour, irrespective of taste. Alicante Bouschet was to become one of the most widely planted varieties of the Midi in the years following the phylloxera crisis towards the end of the nineteenth century; these days it has well nigh disappeared, but you do occasionally find examples of old vines. I do not know of anyone in Faugères with it, but can recommend Arômes Sauvages, Pays de Cessenon from Château Viranel in St Chinian.

DOMAINE de St-MARTIN-D'AGEL - Les Vendanges

By the beginning of the nineteenth century the department of the Hérault, where Faugères is situated, was one of the most productive departments of France, after the Gironde, the Charente and Charente Inférieure (as the Charente Maritime was then called). At that time the viticultural fortunes of the Languedoc were based on *eau de vie*. In 1820, 60 per cent of the production of the Hérault was distilled and in 1854 Noël Salles set up the distillery in Autignac, which was to give the name of Faugères a wider recognition.

The nineteenth-century authorities wrote about the wines of the Languedoc with varying degrees of enthusiasm, sometimes singling out specific *crus*. A. Jullien, in *Topographie de Tous les Vignobles Connus*, noted that the red wines of the Languedoc generally had body and alcohol and that some were very good. He designated three categories, in addition to the *vins de chaudière* for distillation, and mentioned various villages by name, such as St Georges d'Orques, St Christol and St Drézery, but not Faugères. By 1862 Victor Rendu in *Ampélographie Française* was more precise. He too classified the wines of the Languedoc into three categories: the vines of the hills or the *garrigues*, which provided wines for export; the vines of the terraces where the soil consisted of pebbles mixed with iron, which gave wines suitable for commerce; and finally the vineyards of the plains planted with Aramon and Terret Bourret vines, which produced wines for distillation. Although Faugères is not on the plain, the reputation of the name is nonetheless based on *eau de vie*.

In the 1860s Jules Guyot undertook a very detailed report on the vineyards of France for Napoleon III. He enthused about the quality of the Mourvèdre grape, called Espar in the Midi, and regretted the development of what he called the 'common' grape varieties. In the Hérault he found wines for distillation, ordinary wines and great wines, as well as fortified wines and brandy. He mentioned that some eminent wine growers of the Hérault were experimenting with Pinots, Cabernet, Syrah, Cot, Sauvignon and Semillon as well as Spirans, Espar, Carignan, Grenache, Morastel and Clairette, which gave some very superior wines and drinks that were much in demand. There were apparently as many as 150 different grape varieties grown in the South. Sadly many of them disappeared in the aftermath of phylloxera.

Yields increased enormously in this period. In 1848 the Hérault overtook the Gironde as the department with the largest area of vines, and between 1861 and 1867 production in the Hérault rose from 9 to 14 million hectolitres. The all-time record-breaking harvest was 1869 when the Hérault produced a breathtaking 15,236,000 hectolitres of wine from 226,000 hectares of vines. That makes an average yield of almost 68 hectolitres per hectare; compare that with today's limit of 45 hectolitres per hectare for red and white Faugères, and 50 hectolitres per hectare for rosé.

DOMAINE de St-MARTIN-D'AGEL - E. GRA(?)AUL Propriétaire

The development of the railways in the second half of the nineteenth century coincided with the period of industrialization. This encouraged the growth of the Languedoc vineyards as the trains provided an easy means of transport to the capital and the industrial North. The Paris–Lyons–Marseilles railway opened in 1856, and links were also provided with Sète, Montpellier, Béziers and Narbonne.

But there were problems too. A severe attack of oidium or mildew in the 1850s led to a change in the composition of the vineyards, for Carignan and Aramon became the principal grape varieties when replanting took place. And then in 1863 the phylloxera louse was found in the village of Pujaut in the Gard, in the vineyards of a grower who had imported some American vines. The louse began its steady munch westwards and northwards, although it did not reach the Hérault until 1875 and the Aude in 1885. People hoped to escape its devastating effects but its progress was relentless. The area of vineyards in Hérault fell dramatically from 220,000 hectares in 1874 to 58,000 in 1883.

In his book *Images de Faugères* Claude Caumette paints a picture of the viticulture of Faugères before the arrival of phylloxera. At that time the wines of Faugères were amongst the best of the Biterrois, as the area around Béziers is called. The wine was left in barrel to age for two or three years, and with two or three years in bottle could compete with the best *crus*. The hillsides were planted with vines. There were Alicante, Morastel, Oeillade and Clairette, giving wines which would have had between 11 and 13% abv. Some of these are still grown: Alicante is a nineteenth-century crossing that is generally rather despised these days, and Clairette still features in the Languedoc vineyards and in one appellation, but is less popular than it was. One or two people, not in Faugères, are replanting Oeillade, which is closely related to Cinsaut, and Morastel is a synonym for the Spanish variety Graciano which, as far as I know, is now not grown anywhere in the Languedoc.

These grapes had a bouquet that made the wines highly sought after. The *négociants* of Béziers hurried to Faugères after the harvest to buy the wines of the best cellars. For smaller producers, cart drivers arrived from the mountains bringing their produce and always returned with their carts filled with wine, because it was the best and also because it was one of the last villages before the Cévennes, where there were no more vines. Claude Caumette observes: 'The wine today [that is to say

DOMAINE de St-MARTIN-D'AGEL - E. GRANAUD, Propriétaire   M. Pera, phto

before the Second World War] no longer has the same bouquet or the same degree. It is only an ordinary wine, even though it is better than the wines of the nearby plains.'

During the latter part of the nineteenth century enormous energy was devoted to finding a remedy for phylloxera. After various experiments it was eventually realized that the only viable solution was to graft European vines on to American rootstock. By 1879 there were already 450 hectares of grafted vines in the Languedoc. Vines adapt more easily to grafting on the more fertile and less chalky soil of the coastal plains, and as the vineyards of the Midi were replanted in the last years of the century, there was a definite shift away from the hillsides towards the coastal plains, leading to a neglect of many of the vineyards of quality, of the *coteaux* and terraces mentioned by the nineteenth-century authorities. That was to endure until almost the end of the twentieth century. By 1900 there were 200,000 hectares in the Hérault, with an average yield of 66 hectolitres per hectare. And the Midi had become a region of monoculture, where once vines had been grown alongside wheat and olive trees.

During the same period the vineyards of Algeria, then a French colony, were being developed with a phenomenal increase in production. The wines of Algeria soon became known as *vins de médicin* (wines that would improve the wines of the Midi), and the port of Sète developed a lively trade with the Algerian port of Oran across the Mediterranean.

The rich full-bodied wines of Algeria had the necessary low acidity and deep colour to complement the pale thin wines of the Midi. At this time Sète developed a flourishing trade in all manner of spurious wines. The process of fabrication was described in what seems to have been a bestseller of the day, a book by Joseph Audibert called *L'Art de faire le vin avec les raisins secs,* which first appeared in 1880 and sold out five editions, each of 1000 copies, in six months. Audibert explained how to make a wine from raisins soaked in *eau de vie* and hot water, recommending mixing this so-called wine with wine from the Languedoc. It is impossible to know just how much spurious wine was fabricated in this way, but there were wines on the market that had never been near a grape, coming from glycerine, sulphuric acid and some colouring matter, while the most common process was simply to use sugar and raisins.

THE TWENTIETH CENTURY

Beneath this apparent prosperity, however, lay economic and social problems. The Languedoc had become such an important source of supply that a bad harvest in the region automatically meant a wine deficit in the whole of France, while an abundant crop resulted in a surplus on the market. With the large vintages at the turn of the twentieth century, the price of wine fell, and in 1901 supply exceeded demand by about 10 million hectolitres. Prices collapsed and things came to a head in 1907. The viticultural community blindly refused to see that the root of the crisis lay in overproduction, but insisted that the fault lay with fraud of the type practised in Sète, and also with the incompetence of the French authorities.

There were widespread protests all over the Languedoc in 1907, headed by a humble wine grower, Marcelin Albert. His powerful rhetoric inspired his fellow *vignerons* with a series of demonstrations. Things came to a head in Narbonne, and the demonstrations were not in vain. A law passed in June of that year laid down some sensible measures, instituting a system of *déclaration de récolte* – a declaration of the harvest – alongside a declaration of stock, which together gave an idea of how much wine was available for sale during the following twelve months. These two measures remain in force today. Action

was also taken against fraud by imposing some control over the sugar producers and taxing sugar destined for the wine industry. August 1907 saw the creation of the Répression des Fraudes, and in September the legal definition of wine was agreed as coming 'exclusively from the alcoholic fermentation of fresh grapes or from the juice of fresh grapes'. This was certainly a step in the right direction, but the real problem remained: the overproduction of mediocre wine. It was a problem that was to remain with the Languedoc for most of the twentieth century.

The creation of *caves cooperatives* was put forward as a possible solution to the problem of overproduction. The first cooperative of the Languedoc was created in the village of Mudaison in the Hérault in 1901, followed by that of Maraussan, which took the stirring name of Les Vignerons Libres. Some 340 cooperatives were founded in Languedoc Roussillon alone between 1919 and 1939, and French wine consumption per capita increased from 103 litres in 1904 to 136 litres in 1926. The cooperative of Faugères was not to follow until 1959, relatively late in the scheme of things; Laurens came quite a bit earlier, in 1938, as did Autignac, in 1937. The cooperatives are now a declining force in French viticulture although still very much a presence, especially in Faugères, where Les Crus Faugères account for about half of the appellation.

TOWARDS AN APPELLATION

The first half of the twentieth century was a difficult time for the *vignerons* of the Midi and the 1930s were a time of severe economic depression. However, 1936 saw the creation of the first appellations including two in the Midi, namely Rivesaltes and Muscat de Frontignan, and so not for table wine but for *vin doux naturel:* sweet fortified wines. The region had to wait until 1948 for any table wine appellations, for red Fitou and white Clairette du Languedoc.

The French were beginning to drink less, but better, wine – and the demand for the wines of the Languedoc began to fall. There was a very hard winter in 1956, when many of the olive trees of the Midi were destroyed. Olives, however, were less significant in Faugères than in other areas, as apparently they do not like growing on schist.

Algeria was given its independence in 1963 and many *pieds noirs,* the French who had made their lives in North Africa, were obliged to leave the country. However, their expertise and considerable experience of winemaking in a warm climate helped the Languedoc enormously. André Saur, the grandfather of Cédric (La Grange de l'Aïn and Haut Fabrègues), is one such example, buying Château Haut Fabrègues on his return to France from Algeria in 1965.

Gradually there was a realization that the way forward was to concentrate on quality. It became essential to believe in the quality of the Midi. The first thoughts of an appellation, or more precisely a VDQS, occurred in 1939 when Roger Teissonnier, the mayor of Faugères, André Salles from the distillery, Marcel Taillefer and others formed a *Comité de défense de l'appellation Faugères* – but then the war intervened.

After the war the first *grande fête* of the appellation was organized in the summer of 1945, and presided over by André Salles, as it was again in 1946. The idea of the VDQS was taken up again. The name Faugères was chosen as it was already known worldwide, but for *eau de vie* rather than for wine. Françoise Ollier of Domaine Ollier-Taillefer explains that the distillery of Noël Salles had an *alembic à repasse* (a Cognac pot still that requires two distillations, rather than just one). It was the only *charentais* alembic in the whole of the Languedoc at the end of the nineteenth century, a time when many of the villages had their own distillery. Although the distillery subsequently went bankrupt, the reputation of the name had been sufficiently established by the worldwide sales of Fine de Faugères during the first half of the twentieth century (there are further details in Chapter 6).

The vineyards were first delimited in 1948 and the VDQS was created in 1955, with Carignan, Grenache Noir and Cinsaut the permitted grape varieties, and interestingly the minimum alcohol level was 11% abv, as opposed to 12% abv for the appellation. At that time the uncle of Jean-Claude Estève from Château des Adouzes, Pierre Bénézech, was mayor of Roquessels. He was subsequently the first president of the Faugères cooperative, and made the suggestion that the village of Gabian might also like to be included in the VDQS as parts of Gabian – specifically an area between Gabian and Faugères – have the same schist as Faugères. But the mayor of Gabian, who was also director of the village cooperative, along with the cooperative's administrative council, laughed at the idea. Bulk wine, wine *en vrac,* was selling well at the time, and they simply did not want the hassle and constraints of the VDQS. That was to prove a short-sighted decision, especially for the village cooperative which has now closed. It could have made a Faugères *cuvée*, while Gabian itself has a flourishing community of dynamic wine growers. In 1982, when the appellation itself was created, Gabian asked to be included – but this time it was the INAO, the organization that controls the appellations, that said 'non'.

MEMORIES

There are still *vignerons* who have memories of Faugères at that time. Jean-Louis Pujol of Château de Grézan is not alone in remembering horses in the vineyards. His father, as an *ouvrier viticole* working for other vineyard owners, had one of the first tractors in the mid-1950s, which made an enormous difference to the efficiency of vineyard work. According to Claude Caumette, the first people with tractors were laughed at. At that time the typical Languedoc house had a cellar and stable on the ground floor, with a large arched door. The family lived on the floor above and their wealth was measured by the number of horses they owned. You will still see houses like this in the villages of the Faugérois.

Michel Abbal of Domaine Valambelle was born in 1940 and remembers his first vintage in 1954, the year he left school, and the year before the creation of the VDQS. He talks about the quality advantage of Faugères, that it never gave the big yields of the plains; at one time that would have been seen as a disadvantage, but more recently it has proved a trump card for quality. According to Nathalie Caumette of Domaine de l'Ancienne Mercerie, nobody in Autignac would consider marrying anyone who came from north of the cross on the northern edge of the village, as above the cross the yields were much lower, just 40 hectolitres per hectare as opposed to 200. The wine may have been better, but the price was the same; you were paid for quantity, not quality. However, the fortunes of Autignac did not last; there are many once fine but now sadly dilapidated houses in the village.

The role of the *négociant* has become significantly less important. In the immediate post-war years until the late 1980s, when few independent producers bottled their own wine, the main source of distribution was the *négociant*. *Négociants* bought wine in bulk, *en vrac*, and blended it, and any individual quality was lost in their vats. With the widespread development of the *vignerons* bottling their own wine, the balance changed. Jean-Claude Estève observes that the *vrac* market was still working well in the mid-1980s, which is when he left the cooperative: 'Those days the *négociants* called us; nowadays it is up to us to call the *négociants* and they negotiate the price.' Inevitably the *vrac* market is shrinking, but for some wine growers it does provide some immediate bread and butter, and acts as a cushion for new wine growers who have yet to develop a market for their wine.

Alain Ollier reminisces; he says that he was originally a farmer from Lodève and became a *vigneron* when he married a *vigneron's* daughter in 1963. At that time all the wine was sold to the *négociants* and they did not know how to sell it themselves. Then, in 1975, a broker told him that he needed to bottle his wine in order to make more money from it; with the small yields of Faugères, it simply was not profitable to sell it *en vrac*. So the Olliers began to bottle their wine, bottling their first in 1976, but they needed to learn how to sell. Their early sales were often at Béziers market, and it took ten years for them to sell all their wine in bottle. It was hard at first, as the Hérault was simply not known, but now Faugères has a fine reputation – and Alain's children are building the future of the estate, returning to Fos after experiencing other horizons.

Alain also recalls changes in the vineyards. They worked with a horse until 1975. The vines were *en carré,* planted in a square grid, with 3600 vines to the hectare, *gobelet* (bush-pruned) vines with no wires, and then in the 1980s they began to train the vines on wires and the rows became narrower. He could restrain the vigour of a vine by its root system. The main change in the cellar was the move from concrete to stainless steel vats but, he says, there are still people who prefer to use concrete vats. Alain's daughter Françoise also talks eloquently about Faugères: 'There is a difference in atmosphere between the villages of the coastal plain and the *petits villages de schiste.* The plain is another world. We were *pauvres paysans,* and had *capitelles* rather than *châteaux pinardiers'* – with the exception of Grézan, but that is almost on the plain. In so many ways the history of the wine industry of the Languedoc simply passed Faugères by. The terrain was quite unsuited for the creation of large estates with extensive vineyards, making for two stories in the Languedoc: that of the plain and that of the hills. One was prosperous and the other struggled. It was the development of sales in bottle that was to change the fortunes of Faugères and many other hillside vineyards.

The post-war years saw a lot of social change in Faugères. Claude Caumette has been cast in the role of local historian. He has an old house in the heart of the village, where he has lived for the last sixty years, and where there are still old vats on the ground floor and a press that dates from 1933. At the time it was considered the very latest in modern technology, as just one man could operate it. The *foudres,* or large barrels, have long since gone. Both his grandfather and father were *vignerons,* but Claude worked for the post office. He remembers the harvests when he was a child: '*C'était la fête,* with family and friends helping out. You picked into wooden boxes, and then the grapes were pressed down with a large mallet to crush them, and put into a vat, and the juice was run off a few days later. The best wine came from the free-run juice; and the pressed juice was kept separately. The wine was filtered through bundles of vine cuttings.' The use of the Occitan language – the original language of the Languedoc – was forbidden in French schools in the 1880s, but Claude recalls that his father talked French at home and Occitan to his workers in the vineyard. And everyone had horses; there were as many as fifty or sixty horses in the village of Faugères in the 1940s. People who had just a few vines worked for a larger wine grower, and then borrowed the boss's horse on Sunday to till their own vineyard. There were demarcation lines between the sexes; the men pruned and tilled, while the women picked up the cuttings and made them into *fagots* or bundles which were then used for heating the houses. It was the women who cleaned round the trunks of the vines, making a hollow into which the manure from the horses was added.

Faugères was known for its quality, but was not yet sold in bottle. It had a reputation in the Aveyron. Petafy is the name of a hill above the village of Faugères and for people of the Aveyron, there was an expression *Passe au Petafy, pour avoir du bon vin* – in other words 'pass Petafy to get good wine', namely Faugères. The wine was made from Aramon, Carignan, Terret Noir and Morastel, and was described as *le gros rouge* for the *montagnards*, the mountain dwellers, of the Aveyron.

There were two *négociants* in the village of Faugères who disappeared when the cooperative was founded in 1959. The *négociants* mixed everything together, so that there was a considerable variation in quality. The best wines went to Bordeaux and the Terret Blanc to Champagne (on that observation, I could not possibly comment). At the beginning of the last century, there were three *négociants* in Laurens, conveniently situated near the railway station, but both they and the station have gone. Claude Caumette regrets that the creation of the cooperative meant the disappearance of the little private cellars, *les petites caves particulières*. He also remembers how each *viticulteur* brought wine to be distilled until the *droits du brouilleur du cru,* or individual distilling rights, were suppressed. Claude's father had his own still which he stopped using in 1958. It could have just been sealed, but the officials insisted on actually destroying it, but Claude still has an instrument for measuring the alcohol level.

Writers have tended to pass by Faugères; the Languedoc as a whole gets fairly short shrift from English writers in the late nineteenth and early twentieth centuries. Maurice Healy, writing in 1949 in *Stay Me with Flagons*, disparagingly claimed that the Midi did not produce any wines of distinction. Charles Berry, in 1935, advised readers to go to Bessan, Caux and Roujan for rosé, but again there was no mention of Faugères. Basil Woon, writing in 1972 in *The Big Little Wines of France*, says that he was unable to obtain particulars of Faugères: 'I understand it uses for its red wines a large proportion of Cinsaut and for its very

THE HISTORY OF FAUGÈRES 17

palatable white wine Clairette up to 80%.' In *Les Vins du Rhône et de la Méditerranée,* published in 1978, Faugères is finally mentioned as one of the wines that was making progress in the Languedoc. So the reputation of Faugères was beginning to improve.

Michel Louison, who was at Château des Estanilles, recalls that when he bought his first vineyards in 1975 they were planted with Carignan and some Aramon, and the wine was sold to the *négoce*. There was an old cellar filled with concrete vats, which he eventually demolished in 1987. From the start he bottled all his wine. He had an old basket press, and in 1977 rented some refrigeration equipment in the form of a *groupement de froid*. Although he became known as a Syrah enthusiast with Clos du Fou, he actually planted Mourvèdre in 1982, before he planted Syrah. That decision was the result of a trip to Bandol, the home of Mourvèdre, with Jean Vidal, the father of Bernard. He remembers Jean Vidal using carbonic maceration for his Carignan; that was what saved Carignan. The first white wine in Faugères was made from Servant, which is a table grape.

Jean-Claude Estève of Château des Adouzes talks about the creation of the appellation. He remembers a visit by a delegation from INAO in 1980, a group of eight gentlemen all dressed in suits and ties, totally unsuitable attire for examining vineyards. They declassified 20 hectares of flatter land and it took two years to convince the INAO that the land was suitable for part of the appellation because it was the same schist as the hillsides. The original zone of the appellation did not include Autignac though it did include the nearby village of Pézènes-les-Mines; but in 1982 the INAO determined that Pézènes was too cold and that Autignac did have some interesting schist. Claude Caumette remembers that there were vineyards on the plateau behind the windmills above the village of Faugères, but they were abandoned as the soil is limestone and not schist. Instead wooded areas of schist have been cleared and planted with vineyards.

Initially there were moves to create a broader appellation that recognized the *terroir* of the schist of Faugères and also included parts of St Chinian, but local politics came into play, and the result instead was the homogenous appellation of Faugères. The movers and shakers of the aspiring appellation were people like Marcel Taillefer in Fos, Jean Vidal in La Liquière, Raymond Roque in Caussiniojouls and Gilbert Alquier in Faugères. There was a realization that they needed a name to be able to sell their wine in bottle successfully. As Françoise Ollier expressed it so eloquently: 'These were people who worked for the common good of the area. Without them Faugères would not exist – we would be *vin de table*.' The appellation for red and also rosé was born in 1982, with the white appellation following in 2005.

2

WHAT IS FAUGÈRES?

Unlike some appellations of the Languedoc, Faugères is a remarkably compact and homogeneous area, covering seven villages and a couple of hamlets, namely Faugères itself, Cabrerolles and the hamlets of Lenthéric and La Liquière, Caussiniojouls, Laurens, Fos, Autignac and Roquessels. The soil is schist, the climate that of the Mediterranean and the grape varieties are those that you find elsewhere in the Languedoc. So what makes Faugères special and different from the neighbouring appellations? Essentially there are four main factors that determine the taste of a wine. Three are the grape varieties, the soil in which the grapes are grown and the weather to which the vines are subjected; these are the subject of this chapter. The fourth factor, the hand of the *vigneron* who makes the wine, is covered in detail in Chapter 5.

SOIL

Let's take soil first. There is no doubt that schist is the key characteristic of Faugères. In the Languedoc there is a band of schist that stretches from the north-eastern edge of the Minervois and through the northern half of St Chinian to encompass all of Faugères. It then peters out beyond Cabrières. But even in a small area, the schist is remarkably varied. You only have to visit the tasting *caveau* at the Château de Grézan to appreciate all the different types of schist, with a range of colours – grey, blue, yellow or ochre – all based on different soils and rocks, with schist *ardoisier* (slate) and its golden reflections in the sunlight, *gréseux* (sandstone), *argileux* (clay) or basalt. There is marble schist from around the quarry at Laurens, and all are on show at Grézan, alongside an appropriate bottle of wine. As Jean-Louis

Pujol, the owner of the Château, observes, 'on tient au schiste, comme aux prunelles des yeux', which translates more prosaically into English as 'we are as attached to schist as we are to the pupils of our eyes'.

So what is schist? It is often translated as 'shale' in English, but is also increasingly understood as schist. Schist is a metamorphic rock that was shaped by intensive heat and pressure from compressed clay, and that is hard and compact. The name comes originally from a Greek word that means 'split', making reference to the foliated nature of schist. You only need to drive through the vineyards of Faugères to see a bank of schist that illustrates this point. The layers between the schist are important as they are where the roots, water and organic matter filter through. Usually they are vertical or sloping layers, which allow for the roots of the vines to travel down deep. Apparently schist accounts for 10 per cent of the world's vineyards. It is one of the most distinctive of soils, and is generally considered to be one of the great vineyard soils.

The schist of Faugères, squeezed between the Pyrenees and the Massif Central, is 350 million years old, making it 100 million years older than the schist of neighbouring St Chinian. In Faugères the layer of schist is perforated by limestone, like a Roquefort cheese, and is quite different from that of St Chinian and Berlou, and more like that of Roquebrun. Schist is acid, but the pH is not too low. The soil is quite mixed: there is clay and sandstone as well as schist. The schist crumbles and the sandstone forms pebbles, so the soil is very stony and drains well.

Although they are adjacent, the schist of Cabrières is also quite different from that of Faugères, being more alkaline with an almost neutral pH. Nor is it in sheets like that of Faugères, but looks almost like weathered wood with holes, as it has been neutralized by the weather and is very friable. Apparently it more resembles the schist of the Moselle or of Priorat, rather than that of Faugères. Blame the extinct volcano, the Pic de Vissou, which dominates the skyline of Cabrières.

There are other vineyards in the south that are based on schist, such as Maury, one of the villages of Roussillon. The vineyards there are on an island of black schist in the middle of a sea of clay and limestone, some seventeen kilometres by three. The vineyards of nearby Banyuls are planted steep terraces of schist. Olivier Gil, one of the new vignerons of Faugères, has also worked at Domaine la Tour Vieille in Collioure and observes that the schist there is quite different. In Collioure the schist is red and not as degraded as in Faugères, so the soil is very shallow and you need to use dynamite to plant vines. In Faugères the schist is older blue schist and is more degraded so that it retains water better, resulting in more freshness in the wine. And, as it also retains heat, the grapes carry on ripening at night.

Schist is also the distinguishing feature of the vineyards of Priorat in northern Spain. Pierre Jacquet of Domaine Binet-Jacquet sees similarities with Priorat, not only from the point of view of soil, but also with regard to altitude and climate, the position of the sea and the use of some of the same grape varieties, notably Grenache Noir. In Portugal you find schist particularly in the dramatic vineyards of the Douro, and the Portuguese-French producers Roquette e Cazes even make a wine that is labelled Xisto, the Portuguese for schist. The Moselle is another vineyard area based on schist, again with fabulous scenery. The Valais in French-speaking Switzerland has schist, and in New Zealand Nick Mills at Rippon Vineyard, that most photogenic of all vineyards on the shores of Lake Wanaka in Central Otago, attributes the quality of his Pinot Noir to schist.

Ask the *vignerons* of Faugères about typicity, and what really determines the character and taste of their wines, and schist will feature in most of their responses, for it is schist that is the bedrock of Faugères and a key component in the flavour profile. Curiously, although schist is high in acid, and although Faugères has relatively high acidity for a wine from the Languedoc, that acidity does not come from the soil. The acidity level in the wine is linked to the nutrients in the soil, with a high level of potassium in the soil resulting in a wine with less acidity. Any wine grower worth their salt in Faugères will have an opinion about schist. Catherine Roque of Mas d'Alezon observes that schist is very fragile and more sensitive to drought than her vineyards of *argilo-calcaire*, limestone and clay, at Clovallon outside Bédarieux. She is convinced that schist has a fantastic and as yet untapped potential for white wine; Clairette on schist will be '*géant*', producing wonderful minerality. Simon Coulshaw of Domaine des Trinités is adamant that Faugères is about schist. 'Do not mess around with it and it will give you fruit, spice and freshness'. For Vincent Vallat of Château Sauvanès, schist makes for concentration in the wine, whereas limestone gives freshness. And for Brigitte Chevalier of Domaine de Cébène, schist canalizes the *côté virile* of Mourvèdre, a grape variety that she particularly likes – '*C'est formidable de travailler avec les schistes*'. 'It is wonderful to work with schist' – and when searching for her vineyards, she looked particularly for schist combined with altitude. There is no doubt that schist has many qualities for vineyard soil. It provides good drainage. It is poor soil, so the yields are low and the wines have fresh minerality and pepper, according to Arnaud Barthès of Château des Estanilles. And there were comments too about the colour. Red schist has iron and a lot of stones, whereas blue-grey schist is not as stony, owing to the effect of erosion. And some think that brown schist is better than grey schist.

GRAPE VARIETIES

Let's consider the red varieties first. The appellation regulations recognize three '*cépages principaux*', namely Grenache Noir, Mourvèdre and Syrah, while Carignan is considered to be a *cépage complémentaire* and Cinsaut a *cépage accessoire*. In this context, Lledoner Pelut, which is closely related to Grenache Noir, is included in the regulations for Grenache Noir. And the appellation regulations lay down very precisely the required percentages in the vineyard, but not necessarily in the wine. A red Faugères should contain at least two grape varieties, but I can think of at least one *vigneron* who gave me the blend of one of his wines as 50 per cent Syrah and … 50 per cent Syrah. So in the vineyard the three *cépages principaux* must amount to a minimum of 50 per cent, with no maximum percentage laid down, and within that 50 per cent there must be at least 20 per cent Grenache Noir, 15 per cent Syrah and 5 per cent Mourvèdre. Carignan, as a *cépage complémentaire*, must account for between 10 per cent and 40 per cent of the vineyard, and Cinsaut must be less than 20 per cent. But in the cellar, quite frankly, the wine growers can pretty much do what they like, and that is where the fun starts. There are as many views and opinions about grape varieties as there are *vignerons* in Faugères, and even with just five varieties, there is infinite scope and variation in the artist's blending palette.

When Faugères was recognized as a VDQS or Vin Délimité de Qualité Supérieure in 1955 the vineyards were mainly planted with Carignan and Cinsaut, as well as some Grenache Noir, and not to mention Aramon and Alicante Bouschet, which were not allowed in the VDQS. Although Aramon and Alicante Bouschet are now firmly excluded from the appellations of the Languedoc, you do still occasionally find odd pockets of them, such as the Aramon belonging to André Balliccioni in Autignac, and also to Clos Fantine in Lenthéric.

It could be argued that the original typicity of Faugères came from Carignan. The 1970s and 1980s saw a distinct shift, with the planting of more Grenache Noir and the introduction of Syrah and Mourvèdre as the three *cépages améliorateurs*. It is quite difficult to ascertain who actually planted the very first Syrah. Gilbert Alquier (Domaine Alquier) was certainly innovative, planting Syrah as early as 1963 and, when I met him in 1987 on my very first visit to Faugères, he said that his father had planted the very first *cépages améliorateurs* in the appellation, just after the Second World War, so that he had Grenache Noir which was then nearly forty years old. He also thought, then, that no more Carignan would be planted, so despised was the variety, and also Cinsaut. But these days the balance has shifted again, and there is a renewed appreciation of the quality of Carignan (and Cinsaut too), especially from old vines, and the realization that these grape varieties cope much better with heat and water stress than either Syrah or Mourvèdre. Centennial vines are not uncommon. As Didier Barral observes, the mistake of the Languedoc is to plant early ripening varieties, as their acidity is burnt in August; Carignan and Mourvèdre ripen much later and therefore retain their acidity. And Bernard Vidal from Château la Liquière explains, describing himself as *un grand amoureux du* Carignan, 'the quality of the *terroir* of Faugères was recognized, but we were told that the grape varieties were not suitable and that if we had more Grenache Noir and more Syrah, the quality would improve. But nobody thought to ask: can we improve Carignan? Instead we were advised to pull it up and plant Syrah and Mourvèdre. The INAO said we needed Mourvèdre and Syrah and we believed them, so Faugères started to resemble the other wines based on Syrah, like St Chinian and Pic St Loup. If only we had been encouraged to keep Carignan, Faugères would have had another identity.'

Carignan was criticized for its rusticity, but an improvement in its flavour has come with the development of better vineyard and cellar techniques, such as carbonic maceration. People are now replanting Carignan but face the problem that the vines take several years to come into their own, so they are really planting Carignan for their children, or even their grandchildren. In the vineyard Carignan is a late ripener, and a particular characteristic of Carignan is a tough skin, which means that rain is less of a problem than with other, softer-skinned, varieties. Those who like Carignan often think it deserves better than carbonic maceration and, with gentle handling, find that it gives body and structure and also ageing potential, and that the rustic fruit is softened by barrel ageing. Not everyone would have agreed fifteen years ago that Carignan could age. Boris Feigel of Domaine des Prés-Lasses, who has 8 hectares of Carignan that are between sixty and ninety years old, is very definite on the subject. 'Carignan may be more complicated than Syrah, but it retains acidity and really represents the *terroir*, and it is as good as Mourvèdre for structure.' Didier Barral of Domaine Léon Barral also enthuses about Carignan, observing that it performs well in Faugères. Pierre Jacquet talks about the grainy, *granuleux mais en finesse* tannins of Carignan, providing the base of the pyramid while the tannins of the other varieties complete the picture, so that each variety contributes something and no single variety dominates the wine. Catherine Roque, on the other hand, has a different view, preferring the vines to the wine.

In contrast with neighbouring St Chinian, in Faugères growers must have a small amount of Mourvèdre, and nobody is quite sure why. Maybe it enhances the ageing potential, or possibly the idea was to provide a tangible difference between Faugères and St Chinian. This meant that, when the appellation was created in 1982, there was a rush to plant Mourvèdre amongst the people who did not already have it, and that consequently quite a lot was planted on sites that are not really suitable for this temperamental variety. Mourvèdre is generally considered to be the fussiest of grape varieties. In Bandol, where it is at its most expressive, they say that it likes its head in the sun and its feet in the damp. Ideally it likes to see the sea, which is why it performs so well in Bandol. It is a late-ripening variety, even on good sites, and virtually always the last one to be picked. Catherine Roque observes that it only ripens one year in three in her coolest vineyards, and says she has learned to like Mourvèdre. Brigitte Chevalier of Domaine de Cébène is more emphatic – '*J'adore Mourvèdre*' – and it accounts for a high percentage of her Cuvée Felgaria. She finds that it has 'a unique aromatic range, with soft spices, that are not at all aggressive'.

Another Mourvèdre enthusiast is Christian Godefroid from Les Amants de la Vigneronne. Their vineyards comprise 30 per cent Mourvèdre and he does not think that anyone else has quite so much. For him it is Mourvèdre that gives character to his wines, and accounts for their typicity. Frederic Albaret from Domaine St Antonin also likes Mourvèdre, but he does note that it can be difficult to ripen and needs work in the vineyard; it gives *finesse* to a wine, but is not easy, because it is capricious and late. For Pierre Jacquet it is difficult to find the *finesse* of Mourvèdre: 'It develops shoulders!' Or, to put it another way, 'Mourvèdre is our Cabernet Sauvignon. It is the grape variety that gives structure and ageing potential.' Jean-Claude Estève of Domaine des Adouzes suggests that a *vendange verte* or green harvest helps ripen Mourvèdre, but adds that it must be planted in a good spot in the first place, preferably somewhere west facing, for it to ripen properly. According to Antoine Rigaud of Domaine Anglade, a good year for Mourvèdre is one that is not too hot, with regular rain. Mourvèdre likes to be *arrosé* – watered – as it enjoys any maritime influence and needs some water. In short, it can be the best and the worst variety. Jean-Michel Mégé from Domaine de la Reynardière argues against Mourvèdre: the soil is not suitable; it is often difficult to ripen and the yield is difficult to control. For him it is simply not a Languedoc *cépage*, and he would prefer it in a *vin de pays* rather than in the appellation. So it seems that Mourvèdre has a difficult reputation – but also that the people who like it, really like it.

Both Grenache Noir and Syrah are deemed to be more reliable than Mourvèdre. A lot of Grenache was planted in the 1960s, and then people discovered Syrah. And while Lledoner Pelut is a variant of Grenache Noir, it has one significant difference: it ripens much more slowly than Grenache Noir, as it has hairs on the underside of its leaves which enable it to cope with drought more easily; and consequently it is lower in alcohol than Grenache Noir. Grenache Noir can reach a heady 15% abv and is less structured, so that it provides richer fruit and body. However, it does not keep as well as Syrah. It is seen as a more fluid variety in the glass.

Gilbert Alquier was possibly the first to plant Syrah in 1963, with Bernard Vidal's father Jean following in about 1967–8. Talking of his father's pioneering work, Bernard describes him as someone who was incredibly dynamic, '*un sacré locomotive*'. Jean-Luc Saur from Château Haut Fabrègues was another pioneer, planting his first Syrah in 1970 because he thought it would enhance the ageing potential of his wines. And his son, Cédric Saur of Grange de l'Aïn, has some Syrah planted by Lucien Vidal, Bernard's uncle, in the early 1960s, which must rival Gilbert Alquier's vineyard for the oldest Syrah of the appellation. Now the enthusiasm for Syrah is widespread. For Luc Salvestre, director of the cooperative, Syrah is quite simply magnificent; for Philippe Borda at Domaine du Rouge Gorge, it is Syrah that makes Faugères, and half his vineyards are planted with Syrah because he finds it more stable and more reliable.

There are various expressions of Syrah. It can be more floral, more exuberant and more peppery. For Corine Andrieu of Clos Fantine, Syrah is the variety '*qui nous parle le plus*', so that their Cuvée Courtiol is usually predominantly Syrah. However it is not always so simple. Syrah is affected by drought and there is a view that it performs better on cooler, north-facing slopes. In the cellar it needs oxygen, as it can easily suffer from reduction. However, it is generally accepted that the structure of Syrah is easier to get right, whereas Carignan and Mourvèdre are much more complicated. Syrah may have been a relatively recent arrival in the vineyards of Faugères, but these days everyone has it. The general view is that it is reliable, compared to Mourvèdre or Carignan, but not always. Pierre Jacquet very thoughtfully sums up some of the differences: 'Carignan is fundamental to Faugères. Syrah is easier, but it can be a trap, a *piège*, when there is not enough acidity. Grenache is tricky and capricious. Mourvèdre is the worst, if the year does not suit it.'

And then there is Cinsaut, which amongst other things can provide a solution for lowering the alcohol level, as it is ripe at 12% abv. In Faugères it is used particularly for rosé. Mas Onésime has a rosé that is as much as 90 per cent Cinsaut from seventy-year-old vines, with a little Grenache Noir. But there is also a growing appreciation of its quality as a red wine. One new example, though not officially Faugères, is L'Etranger from Domaine des Trinités, with 90 per cent Cinsaut and some Syrah, and a modest 13.5% abv. The flavour is delicious, with ripe but refreshing cherry fruit. Le Producteur de Plaisir from Montgros is also largely Cinsaut, with some Grenache Noir and Syrah. Cinsaut is another relatively late ripener, and although it can cope with drought, it does appreciate a little water at the end of the growing season in order to ripen fully.

For the much more recent appellation of Faugères Blanc, two grape varieties are required, and the permitted varieties are Grenache Blanc, Marsanne, Roussanne and Rolle, which are considered *cépages principaux* and individually may not exceed 70 per cent of the blend. Clairette and Viognier are *cépages accessoires* and are limited to 10 per cent, either together or separately.

Marsanne and Roussanne have been successfully introduced to the Languedoc from the northern Rhône valley, where they perform particularly well in Hermitage Blanc. The first experimental plantings in Faugères were done at the beginning of the 1990s by people like Jean-Michel Alquier, Bernard Vidal, Michel Louison, Luc Ollier and Genevieve Libes who went on to persuade the INAO of the validity of white Faugères. Roussanne and Marsanne naturally complement each other, but Roussanne is generally considered to be more interesting, nicely filling out the palate, with a touch of white blossom. For Simon Coulshaw, who makes a pure Roussanne *vin de pays*, it is so much more than a simple blending wine, but has a real character all of its own. Françoise Ollier dismisses Marsanne as being too soft and uninteresting, while she finds Grenache Blanc too alcoholic.

Rolle (or Vermentino, for its Italian synonym is often used) is a grape variety that is found along the Mediterranean from the Languedoc through Provence to Tuscany, and taking in the islands of Sardinia and Corsica. Luc Ollier of Domaine Ollier-Taillefer was one of the first to plant it in 1991 – or rather he grafted cuttings obtained from the pioneering François Guy at Château de Coujan in St Chinian onto some forty-year-old Carignan Blanc. Generally Rolle adds a fresh, sappy note to white wine, with some natural freshness and herbal flavours.

Although Viognier is allowed in white Faugères, it does have a very distinctive character and as little as 5 per cent in a blend can quite dramatically change the style of a wine, and even overwhelm the flavour with rich peachy-textured notes. At Ollier-Taillefer they planted some in 1995, and pulled it up ten years later, as they found the flavours too soft. Those who have Viognier usually prefer to make it as a varietal *vin de pays*.

Clairette, on the other hand, is a traditional grape variety of the Languedoc, with the oldest white appellation, Clairette du Languedoc, created in 1948, bearing witness to this. Essentially Clairette is a grape variety that can be short on flavour, but it does perform well in the warm climate of the Midi. Catherine Roque is convinced that Clairette could produce wonderful results on schist. Curiously, although Grenache Blanc is allowed in white Faugères, Grenache Gris can only be used for *vin de pays;* possibly there was simply not enough planted at the time when the white appellation was being established for it to merit the attention of the INAO. One of the most diverse examples of white Faugères comes from La Grange de l'Aïn, which has seven different varieties, namely Grenache Blanc, Vermentino, Marsanne, Roussanne, Clairette, Viognier and Bourboulenc. The interest is in the blending and the result is intriguing.

As elsewhere in the Languedoc, people are taking a new look at some of the older varieties which were initially dismissed as worthless. There is a suggestion that Terret Blanc should be allowed in the appellation, and what about Macabeo and Carignan Blanc? Boris Feigel at Domaine des Prés-Lasses suggests that Carignan Blanc preserves acidity and also represents the *terroir.* Then there is Bourboulenc, which is characteristic of La Clape, but very little remains in the vineyards of Faugères. When he was at Château des Estanilles, Michel Louison experimented with Chenin Blanc but found it to be too heavy. Somebody else had the temerity to suggest Petit Manseng, but the INAO firmly stamped on that idea for being '*hors region*' and therefore completely unacceptable. Quite often a white will be *vin de pays* or Coteaux du Languedoc rather than Faugères as the wine is a single variety or includes a variety such as Carignan Blanc.

With the development of white wine in the Languedoc there is a general feeling that there is more to be learnt about the white varieties and even the *gris* varieties, those grapes that have a pale pink skin when ripe. Thierry Rodriguez of Mas Gabinèle considers Grenache Gris much more interesting than Grenache Blanc, saying that it is more complex with better acidity and better ageing potential. He is planning a small vineyard around his new cellar for *gris* varieties, 100 to 120 plants of each of varieties such as Pinot Gris, Picpoul Gris, Sauvignon Gris, Carignan, Muscat à petits grains, Gewurztraminer, Clairette and Ribeyrenc.

CLIMATE

The climate of Faugères is dominated by the mountains of the Espinouse, the foothills of the Cevennes, which form a backdrop to the vineyards and protect them from the prevailing north winds. There is a significant difference in temperature between the village of Faugères and the small town of Bédarieux, which is in the valley of the Orb on the other side of the hills. Within the appellation of Faugères there is again a big difference in altitude, and therefore also in temperature. The northern villages are Faugères itself, La Liquière, Roquessels, Fos and Caussiniojouls and Cabrerolles. There the nights are cooler in summer, and in the winter they may well even have snow in Faugères while there is none in Laurens. Happily spring frosts are very rarely a problem. In the northern part of the appellation the grapes tend to ripen later, by as much as seven to ten days, and consequently the wines are more *aerien*, fresher and long lasting.

In contrast, Laurens and Autignac are lower in altitude and therefore warmer, with more sheltered vineyards, and consequently the wines are riper and more opulent. In Autignac the vines are at an average of 140 metres, rising to 300 metres in Faugères, while the highest vines of the appellation are around 450 metres. Some disparage Autignac as '*Faugères de la plaine*' but, as will be seen, there are some fine wines from here. However, there is no doubt that the backdrop of hills helps to provide the conditions which make for an important element of freshness in the red wines, not to mention the significant potential for white wines.

It would be a very unusual year if there were insufficient sunshine and warmth to ripen the grapes. It is really rainfall that accounts for the key vintage variations, with the average annual rainfall totalling around 500 to 600 mm. The Mediterranean climate dictates warm, dry summers and mild, wet winters, implying that most of the rainfall occurs during the autumn, winter and spring, but that pattern is in fact far from regular. Ideally the water reserves are replenished during the winter, but the spring of 2013 was one of the driest since records began, while July 2013 was one of the wettest ever. The weather conditions during the 2014 harvest posed problems with heavy rainfall in the second half of September. Even if the summer is dry, ideally the vines would enjoy some rain around 14 July and 15 August, the two public holidays of the summer. But that is far from predictable, and seems to be becoming increasingly so. Jean-Michel Mégé at Domaine de la Reynardière observes that the weather between 15 August and 15 September is the most critical. A heavy rainstorm on 15 August is good, but the humidity must not continue. Drying north winds, the Tramontane, are essential after the storm, while the *vent marin* from the south brings humidity and – potentially – disease. Geneviève Libes of Domaine du Météore remarks that the disturbing effect of the equinox in late September is most worrying, especially if you are still harvesting.

I like to think of Faugères as a homogeneous whole with a more consistent identity than many of the other appellations of the Languedoc, but within the appellation there is nonetheless a mosaic of different grape varieties, villages, and *vignerons,* each with their own individual style, experience and philosophy.

3

VITICULTURE: FROM VINEYARD TO CELLAR

Work in the vineyards of Faugères has undergone similar developments as elsewhere in the Languedoc. What singles out Faugères from the other appellations is the high percentage of wine growers who work organically or even biodynamically, or, if neither of those, then they at least practice *lutte raisonnée*, which translates as sustainable viticulture. Generally there is a greater awareness of the importance of vineyard work. Most *vignerons* would agree that their work in the vineyard is the most important aspect of winemaking. If you produce good healthy grapes, you will make good wine, and if your grapes are healthy then the work in the cellar and the quality of the wine follows naturally.

So what impacts on quality in the vineyard? To me it seems that work in the vineyard is a series of details and when everything fits into place and the weather also plays its part, the result is a delicious liquid in the glass. What follows below are examples and observations from the various growers. Probably one notable change is quite simply a better understanding of vineyard work. Catherine Roque says that the *vignerons* are becoming real *viticulteurs* again and actually observing their vines; she thinks it took her ten years to get to know her own vines in Faugères properly.

THE DENSITY OF VINES

The average density of vines in the vineyard has increased with the aim of enhancing quality. In the 1970s, vineyards were usually planted with a maximum of 3000 vines per hectare to accommodate tractors and other machinery. The appellation, which was created in 1982, dictates a minimum of 4000 vines, with a maximum width of 2.5 metres but no minimum width, and within the row a minimum 80 centimetres, so that there is no maximum limit to the number of vines per hectare. However, many of the old *gobelet* vines are lower density, with plantings of 1.75 metres by 1.75 metres, which gives 3330 vines per hectare.

The accepted view these days is that 5000 vines per hectare makes for a greater concentration of flavour, whereas 7000 vines is seen as even better for flavour, but with a loss of yield. Narrow rows of vines can be problematic for vineyard machinery. The new plantings at Domaine Cottebrune are pretty classic, at 2 metres by 80 centimetres, making for 6250 vines per hectare. However, initially Pierre Gaillard was influenced by his experience of the Rhône Valley, and some of their earlier plantings had 9000 vines per hectare, spaced at 1.40 metres by 80 centimetres, which makes for a large *surface foliaire*, but also necessitates the use of a caterpillar tractor rather than a conventional one on the steep terrain. If there is a higher density, the vine roots will hold the soil better, making for fewer problems with erosion.

SURFACE FOLIAIRE OR RATIO OF LEAF TO FRUIT

It's also necessary to consider the leaf area in relation to the quantity of grapes. Perceived wisdom in the Languedoc holds that it takes a square metre of leaves to ripen a kilo of grapes. Most people consider that ideally the *surface foliaire* should be as large as possible, but neither should the vine be out of balance. However, at Cottebrune they aim initially for 2 square metres per kilo, and then leaf pluck on the side of the rising sun, which aerates the vines and helps against rot. Leaf plucking or *effeuillage* enables you to expose the grapes to sunlight and avoid shading, or you keep the leaves to protect the grapes against sunburn. For this reason *effeuillage* must be done according to the light orientation, so that it is less critical for rows going north–south as opposed to east–west.

PRUNING

Pruning is one of the key factors that determine the yield, regulating the crop and ensuring that the vines are in balance, producing neither too few nor too many grapes. If pruning is late and the spring is dry, the crop is likely to be small, and so pruning should ideally be finished by the middle of March, which is about the time the sap begins to rise in the vines. The appellation regulations dictate a maximum yield of 45 hectolitres per hectare for red and white wine, and 50 hectolitres per hectare for rosé, but in practice that is rarely obtained amongst the quality-conscious *vignerons*, who prune carefully and tightly, so that about 33 hectolitres per hectare is a more realistic average. Quite simply, Faugères is not an area of high volume; that is for the vineyards of the plain.

The traditional pruning method of the Languedoc was *gobelet*, the low stubby bush vines, which remains the favoured method for old Carignan and Cinsaut vines. There are distinct advantages to *gobelet* as a method of pruning. The two Laugé brothers at Mas des Capitelles talk of a *gobelet* vine making a parasol so that the heat, which is retained in the schist, is reflected back on to the vines. They also believe that there will be more problems with drought if the vines are *palissé*, trained on wires, as shading effect would be lost.

These days there have been modifications to accommodate increasing mechanization in the vineyards so that virtually all new plantings are on wires, with the *cordon de Royat* method of pruning, where one branch is trained along a supporting wire. *Guyot*, a not dissimilar method of cane pruning, is not allowed for red vines, as it is deemed to be too productive. At Cottebrune, with their links to Côte Rôtie, they have vines *en echalas*, individual vines on a supporting pole with three branches, and planted at 1.30 metres by 80 centimetres. Antoine Rigaud also has a vineyard just by his house on the outskirts of Caussiniojouls also planted *en echalas*; he refers to it as his 'garden'.

The spread of Syrah in the Languedoc necessitated the training of vines on wires, as Syrah has fragile branches compared to Carignan or Grenache Noir and needs support, especially in strong winds. *Palissé* vines also allow for better air circulation which helps combat disease, and another big advantage of a *palissage* is that you can pick with a mechanical harvester, which would be impossible with *gobelet* vines. Jean-Michel Alquier talks of the importance of the *palissage* for photosynthesis and effective ripening. He likes all his vines on wires, even Carignan. That way the branches spread out, in order to expose the grapes to light but not to direct sunshine.

FLOWERING

This is another critical moment for determining the size of the crop, but it is in the hands of the gods rather than the *vigneron*. Bad weather at flowering, with wind and rain, can result in a bad set. All three colours of Grenache are particularly susceptible to *coulure*, when the grapes do not set properly, and that was very noticeable in 2013, when yields of Grenache were dramatically reduced.

GREEN HARVESTING OR *VENDANGE VERTE*

This can be used as a last resort to regulate any excess crop. However, timing is critical. Too early and the exercise fails, for the vine simply produces even larger grapes in the remaining bunches; too late and it is pointless. The moment to really judge the potential crop is just before *véraison,* when the grapes begin to change colour. Others, though, firmly believe that if you prune properly in the first place, the vine will be in balance and there should be no need for a green harvest.

VINE AGE

The appellation regulations dictate a minimum age of three years for white varieties, and six for red wine. However, vine age can be a significant quality factor. Young vines tend to give more exuberant fruit in the first couple of vintages, and then the wines become more closed in flavour as the vines concentrate on developing their root systems. Then, when they reach fifteen years or so, the flavours of wine begin to develop greater depth and flavour, as though the vines have emerged from adolescence to adulthood. Older vines inevitably have a much more developed root system, which should enhance the flavour of the wine. And that means that grafting can be an effective way of changing the composition of a vineyard without losing the advantage of vine age, or indeed a substantial loss of crop. It is difficult to give a precise average age of the vines of Faugères, but thirty-five years is a considered figure. You can still find some very old Carignan or Grenache Noir. Venerable centenarian Carignan vines are not that unusual, whereas plantings of Mourvèdre and Syrah are much more recent, dating at the very earliest from the mid-1960s. Vineyards of Marsanne, Roussanne and Rolle will be even younger, with the first plantings in the 1990s. Ideally, when replanting a vineyard the soil should rest for at least four years; seven years is even better, but is not always commercially viable. After all, a vineyard is intended to last for fifty years, not just twenty.

ORGANIC VITICULTURE

At its simplest, organic viticulture is a return to what the grandparents of today's generation of *vignerons* practised before the introduction of chemical fertilizers, weedkillers and insecticides. Traditional viticulture would be a better way to describe it, especially as the French term '*biologique*' sounds more like warfare than farming to many English speakers. In a climate with generally warm sunshine and drying winds during the growing season, the growers of the Languedoc are fortunate compared with those in northern France. The prevailing winds provide a healthy environment in which grapes can grow without developing disease or rot. Gwenaël Thomas, who works with the oenologist Jean Natoli, observed that Faugères is perfect for organic viticulture. The soil is poor so there are fewer weeds and that makes the care of the soil easier. The vineyards are well exposed to sun and wind, which means less pressure from disease. Nor are the vines particularly vigorous, so there is not too much rot or mildew. And schist soil drains well. What more can anyone want?

One third of the vineyards of Faugères are now certified as organic, which includes about half the independent producers as well as four members of the cooperative, who have 60 hectares between them. Essentially, if you are registered organic, you cannot use any chemicals at all in your vineyards, except for mild doses of copper and sulphur. Nature et Progrès, which is one of the oldest organic organizations in Europe, accepts a three-year conversion period, as does Demeter for biodynamic viticulture, and there are several estates which are in the process of conversion. For example, Marie-Geneviève Boudal at Château Peyregrandes was encouraged by her son Hervé. Initially they selected two plots, a total of 2.5 hectares, and found that it was not difficult to adapt from *lutte raisonnée*; they already disliked using chemicals and are pleased with the results. Thierry Rodriguez of Mas Gabinèle talks of how it takes time to restore the balance in a vineyard after years of chemical treatments, commenting that he had bought vineyards which did not produce a weed for five years.

Domaine Raymond Roque was one of the first organic estates of the appellation in 1999. Marc Roque observes that his father's generation talked about *mauvaises herbes* or weeds, but says they are not *mauvais*, and that it is all a question of balance; the soil must be living and there must be insects in the vineyard. It is often a case of allowing the fauna to return to the vineyards; at Domaine de Causse Noir, Jérôme Py's wife has beehives in his vineyards. Ludovic Aventin talks about biodiversity and is producing honey, but he is not interested in olive trees, another potential crop, as they are not financially remunerative. Nathalie Caumette talks about making the soils live: how you must work them properly, limit pesticides and preserve the old *gobelet* vines; you need to obtain the most from your vines and your *terroir*. As an aside, she adds that climate change is a concern – you cannot move the vines north. Geneviève Libes believes that if you really care about your vineyards and your *terroir*, you should not be adding lots of chemicals; being organic is only logical.

Some wine growers, such as Frédéric Albaret at Domaine St Antonin, are organic, but prefer not to say so on the label. It then becomes a question of marketing. Frédéric is organic for three simple reasons: for the health of his employees, for the environment and for the wine itself. With organic viticulture, he says, you can be confident in your raw material and in how you are treating the environment. He finds that weaker, less disease-resistant vines tend to be those fed by chemicals, whereas vines that are 'auto-sufficient' are much more resistant to disease.

BIODYNAMIC VITICULTURE

Biodynamic viticulture is even more demanding than organic viticulture. Essentially it follows the biodynamic calendar, which is divided into root, leaf, flower and fruit days. Some are better for work in the vineyard and others for work in the cellar. However, Pierre Jacquet comments that 'if the weather is bad, we are farmers, *paysans*, first. We can choose the best moment, *les grands dates*, according to the calendar, but there is no point in being obstinate about it.'

There are several preparations that a biodynamic grower will use, with at least three homeopathic treatments during the year, sometimes necessitating the growing of various herbs for the biodynamic preparations or *tisanes*. When she was working for Domaine Brouca, Camille Chauvin talked about the biodynamic preparations: Preparation 500 was based on cow horns and done at the end of April for the soil; another preparation was silica, again for the soil, which entailed dynamizing cow manure and adding it to the soil after the harvest and then again in the spring.

Didier Barral, who is never one to mince his words, observes that if you were organic in the early days you were deemed to be an idiot, while these days, if you are not organic, you are considered *un con* – and he is scathing about people who are organic without any real conviction. He is undoubtedly one of the most articulate of the growers of Faugères. He believes that there is a definite correlation between the permeability of the soil and the freshness of the wine. The more the soil is worked, the more *les êtres vivants*, such as insects, plants, roots and worms, are killed; and if the grass was eliminated, the weeds would compete with the vines. He talks of Lafontaine's fable of *Le Laboureur et ses enfants*. *Labourer*, tilling the soil, was originally deemed to be positive; if you didn't *laboure*, you got grass and low yields. Nowadays people do not *laboure* but mow instead, which is a mistake as a plant that is cut grows more, so you obtain more grass and more roots. Didier then tried half and half, both mowing and tilling, but he was not sure what he was doing to the soil balance. Since 2006 he has used a rolafaca, as does Pierre Jacquet – this is a machine that flattens the grass, partially cutting it so it turns to mulch. It then composts, making for better drainage as well as retaining the micro-organisms and protecting the soil and allowing more nutrients into it. Didier also has cows in his vineyard, as well as a donkey and a mule, for their manure. He explains that cows favour earthworms; he originally had horses, but noticed that their dung did not encourage the worms, whereas cowpats do. Imagine a picturesque vineyard view, with cows as well as a donkey and a mule amongst the vines. Didier is very keen to break up the monoculture of the area, so he has planted olive, fruit and pistachio trees as well. He has also had sheep in his vineyard to eat all the grass. Cows, in contrast, can compact the soil, as their feet are small and their bodies heavy, whereas sheep have larger feet for their size, so the balance is better.

With organic viticulture you cannot, of course, use systemic treatments which the vine absorbs internally. The alternative of spraying sulphur, used against oidium, can be problematic with rain, but these days it is possible to obtain sulphur that will stick to the leaves. Copper is effective against mildew, but its use should be limited, especially as it leaves residues in the soil.

One disadvantage of organic viticulture is that it uses more fuel. Organic growers go into the vines with a tractor more often, and that too can compact the soil, hence the occasional use of a horse by some. Before the advent of the tractor in the 1950s everyone used horses; these days it is the more philosophical *vignerons* who occasionally employ a horse. Cédric Saur explains that the horse replaces the work done *à la pioche*, by hand, and with a horse you can get rid of grass close to the vine, but that could also be done with an *intercep*. Hiring a horse costs €65 an hour; it is not something that Cédric does every year.

LUTTE RAISONNÉE, OR SUSTAINABLE VITICULTURE

For some, *lutte raisonnée* is the stage before organic viticulture. The key to *lutte raisonnée* is observation, rather than action, with minimal chemical intervention and using organic products wherever possible. Weedkiller may be used, but for those converting to organic viticulture, the purchase of an *intercep* that will mechanically remove the weeds between the vines within the row is essential. Philippe Borda at Domaine Rouge Gorge prides himself on the cleanliness of his vines. It entails a lot of tilling, manual weed killing between the rows, and chemical weedkillers between the vines, which is normal for *lutte raisonnée*. Damien Guérande at Jeanjean's estate Domaine de Fenouillet (Jeanjean are one of the biggest players in the Languedoc, with estates in several areas: see page 122), talks about the problems of working on terraced vineyards: they practise *lutte raisonnée,* and it can be quite difficult on narrow terraces which are limiting for machinery like an *intercep.*

Terra Vitis is the organization that controls the practices for *lutte raisonnée.*

TILLING

To remove the weeds or not? Some people favour *enherbement,* growing grass between the vines, to give the vines some competition and thereby eliminate the weeds. Some do not like grass at all, as initially it competes with the vines – but it also maintains life in the soil, plus the appropriate level of nitrogen. The presence of grass also impacts on water stress, but it can help prevent erosion and also provide a better soil texture. Tilling can also cause water evaporation when water stress is a significant consideration. Didier Barral finds that his rolafaca helps retain humidity. Jean-Michel Alquier talks about experiments with *enherbement,* describing it as the reversal of the vegetative cycle. The grass grows from October to May and stops growing when the temperature reaches 20° to 24°C, and then reseeds itself the following year. Irrigation is not actually forbidden, but it requires specific installations and of course a source of water; given the limited rainfall in Faugères, there is simply not enough water available.

ACIDITY IN THE SOIL

The high level of acid in the schist of Faugères needs correcting with *chaux* or powdered calcium, which is essential for the balance in the wine. If the soil is too acidic, the vine cannot absorb nutrients, which impacts on the vigour of the vine and on its yields. Syrah in particular is susceptible to acidity in the soil, and acidity is linked to nutrition; more potassium in the soil means less acidity. Corine Andrieu comments how, in the last ten years, the pH of the soil has fallen at Clos Fantine because of their work in the vineyards. They have not used any fertilizers and the vines simply 'eat' the minerals.

DISEASES AND PROBLEMS IN THE VINEYARD

Vers de la grappe – larvae that attack vines – pose a problem, but there are things that you can do to reduce their effect. Cédric Saur wonders why some plots are affected by *vers de la grappe* and others are not. The worms like shiny surfaces, that is to say grapes rather than leaves, so 'you can discourage them by spraying something on to your grapes to make them look less shiny. Vines surrounded by woods tend not to get attacked by *vers de la grappe*.' Didier Barral favours planting hedges between his vineyards, as hedges help bats (the best predators of *vers de la grappe*) to navigate. Hedges have other advantages, acting as windbreaks and preventing erosion. *Vers de la grappe* can be treated with insecticides, both conventional and organic, and there is also a lot of interest in a treatment that has already been tried out in other regions, namely inducing sexual confusion with the use of pheromones. A small group of wine growers had already begun to work on this, covering about 100 hectares, but the *syndicat* has now taken it up as a collective project and the area being treated this way increased to 233 hectares in 2015. You need blocks of 5 to 10 hectares to make it really worthwhile and effective, so neighbours do need to agree. Meanwhile research is being carried out to find other effective solutions.

Flavescence dorée, which can be translated into English as grapevine yellows, is another potential problem. For the moment it is under control, but the vineyards are checked regularly, particularly before the harvest, and the only really effective treatment is to pull up the infected vines. The earlier an infected vine is spotted, the better it is, so that the infection is contained. There are conventional treatments which organic wine growers would prefer not to use.

Wild boars have a knack of finding ripe grapes with unerring accuracy, which can severely reduce the yield. Luc Salvestre, director of the cooperative, talks of how the *garrigues* are encroaching on the vineyards; once there used to be fields with animals grazing, but now the habitat has changed. Apparently the size of a litter of boars will depend on the availability of food, a natural regulation – so if there is more food available the litters are larger. Some believe that the hunters control them; others might disagree. Arielle Demets of Vignoble les Fusionels describes the wild boars as a scourge, while Catherine Roque talks of having to persuade the hunters to go up to her isolated vineyard in Soumartre, as they prefer to stay closer to Faugères. She is lucky to get a yield of 9 hectolitres per hectare there as it is surrounded by chestnut trees: 'Quite simply, it is nothing less than a supermarket for the wild boars!'

THE HARVEST

The critical decision is when to pick. As Gwenaël Thomas from Jean Natoli's *cabinet* puts it, 'you decide the picking time by tasting the grapes. You need to observe the changes in the vineyard and then begin to taste. Does the juice explode in the mouth or stay in the flesh of the grape? If you want to spit it out, the grape is not ripe and, if it is ripe, you can even crunch the pips. The alcohol level itself is not the most important thing.' Some people do wait longer to harvest, as they want higher alcohol levels and more extraction. With his Australian experience, Paul Gordon from Domaine la Sarabande observes that in other parts of the world, you need to add lots of tartaric acid if you wait until the grapes taste nice. Happily that is not the case in Faugères, and the natural acidity of the grapes plays an important role in enhancing the fruit characteristics of the wine.

A difficult vintage, as in 2013, requires a good team of pickers who know what they are doing. At Domaine Binet Jacquet they went through the vineyards twice, as the ripening was uneven. Normally small boxes holding 25 kilos are used so that the grapes are not crushed on the way to the cellar – though distances in Faugères are pretty short, so that should not pose a problem. However, the larger estates such as Domaine Rouge Gorge and the Château de Grézan favour mechanical harvesting, as do many of the cooperative members. That said, the cooperative members are paid a bonus for hand harvesting. Marc Roque is quite clear: he much prefers a mechanical harvester, saying *'Je suis mauvais patron.'* He does not want to have to handle a team of pickers, and mechanical harvesting also enables you to do what you want, when you want, giving you much greater flexibility and also speed, if necessary. Philippe Borda also favours mechanical harvesting, admitting that he likes to keep things simple, but for him the real excitement starts when the grapes arrive in the cellar – and that is the subject of the next chapter.

4

WINEMAKING: FROM FERMENTATION TANK TO BOTTLE – AND BEYOND

Wine growers have just one opportunity a year to make wine from their own grapes, though obviously apprentice winemakers could take themselves off to the other hemisphere and squeeze in another vintage, but the experience would be quite different from that with their own vines. Catherine Roque talks about the vintage: '*On se sent toute neuve* with each new harvest. You forget the experience of the previous years, and accept that each year is different. It's a good idea to remember the mistakes, so that you don't repeat them' – but in nearly thirty years as *vigneronne*, first at Domaine de Clovallon and then Mas d'Alezon, she says that she has never had an identical vintage. And I suspect that the other growers of Faugères would agree with her. The broad guidelines may be the same, but the details are always quite different.

Faugères has enjoyed or suffered the same fashions and learning curves as the rest of the Languedoc. There is nothing that singles out Faugères alone. The traditional cellars of the Languedoc with the enormous old oak *foudres* (barrels) have long gone. You can admire them at Domaine Rouge Gorge in St Geniès-de-Fontedit, but they are just for show. Key factors such as temperature control, insulation and cellar hygiene are taken for granted in a way that would have been unthinkable thirty years ago. The biggest changes in the cellar come from the use of oak, with a move away from excessive extractions towards elegance, and the realization that red Faugères is a wine that is age worthy. In addition, the development of white Faugères has brought other factors into play.

Cellar equipment has evolved; pneumatic presses are much gentler and can be finely programmed, while some *vignerons,* such as Pierre Jacquet, still favour a gentle basket press. So did Simon Coulshaw – until he spent a fortune on a new pneumatic press which gives particularly good results for white wine.

SELECTION OF GRAPES

With a better understanding of the characteristics of individual vineyards comes an appreciation of the need to select the most appropriate grapes for each *cuvée.* Plots with the best aspect, or grapes from older vines and lower yields, will be used for the *cuvées prestiges,* whereas those from younger vines and with maybe higher yields will go into more accessible wines. And the grapes will be vinified accordingly.

When the grapes arrive at the cellar, these days you may well see a sorting table to eliminate any rotten or damaged grapes, not to mention leaves and other debris. Alternatively the sorting is done in the vineyards with the pickers given strict instructions as to what they should leave on the vine or on the ground.

FERMENTATION

Essentially the fermentation process is very simple. The yeasts attack the sugar in the grapes to produce alcohol and carbon dioxide, but there are many things a wine grower can do to influence that process and the ultimate flavour of the wine in the glass. Maceration times, the length of time the juice stays in contact with the grape skins, are critical and there are as many thoughts about that as there are wine growers in Faugères. Here are some of their ideas on this, and on other issues around fermentation.

Maceration times

Generally, and happily, there has been a move away from very concentrated and over-extracted wines. The choices are *pigeages*, *remontages* and *délestages*, in any combination and maybe all three at some time during the fermentation. The length of time on the skins, the *cuvaison*, will have an impact, with the grapes from better vines, and wines intended for longer

*The technique of remontage, which helps add colour
and flavour to the wine*

ageing, enjoying a longer *cuvaison*, as long as three or four weeks, to give more concentration. Lighter wines will have a shorter maceration of maybe not even a week.

It is all about how to extract *matière*, body and flavour from the grapes, and most people carry out *remontages* (pumping over), *pigeages* (punching down) or *délestages*, (rack and return), whereby they run off the juice so that the cap sinks to the bottom of the vat and then add the juice back to the vat, so the cap gently rises up through the wine – not unlike the action of a coffee percolator. Gwenaël Thomas explains that growers need to adapt the method to the quality of their grapes, and work on the grapes more at the beginning of the fermentation when there is less alcohol. Extraction at the beginning of the fermentation entails more colour and some tannin but, as the alcohol increases, they need to move to a more gentle extraction with lighter *remontages*, rather than *délestages*, and some *pigeage*. *Pigeage* at the beginning can extract some green flavours, while *mouillage*, which entails removing a small quantity of wine to dampen the cap, like an infusion, can have the effect of melting the alcohol. Pierre Jacquet, for example, finds *remontages* too violent, whereas *pigeage* is more delicate and subtle.

Checking the temperature of the vat – a critical control in the process of winemaking

At Château de Ciffre, Miren de Lorgeril with her new winemaker, Bernard Durand, favours a *maceration à froid*, a cool stabilization before the fermentation, which allows the juice to infuse, with a gentle extraction, while the cap is submerged. Then they carry out *délestages* during the fermentation, and allow the malolactic fermentation to occur on the skins, which retains *gras* (fat, literally: a wine with some weight would be described in this way) and body in the wine. Then they do some *remontages à l'air*, which gives density to the wine.

Maxime Secher at Domaine Cottebrune also favours a pre-fermentation à froid at 7 to 8°C to obtain fresh fruit. Then he ferments at 25° to 30°C, rising to 30° to 35°C as the fermentation finishes, with a post-fermentation maceration for ten to fifteen days to round out the tannins and enhance the *souplesse*, so the wine spends an average of about a month on the skins. The *vin de presse* is kept separately, and the malolactic fermentation takes place in barrel.

Alexandre Fourque at Domaine de la Tour Penedesses also practises a pre-fermentation maceration for a week at 7°C, followed by *pigeages* and *remontages* during a three-week fermentation.

Frederic Albaret at Domaine St Antonin favours gentle extractions. He does not like hard tannins, so he wets the cap, doing a little *mouillage* over three or four weeks, without any *pigeages*, *remontages* or *délestages*. The carbon dioxide liberates *matière* in the *marc*, the grape skins, at around 20°C. If the fermentation is too cold, nothing moves and, if it is too hot, the aromas cook. He does not think you need to raise the temperature at the end of the fermentation; if it is cooler, it just takes longer. Others, such as Julien Seydoux at Château des Estanilles, would argue that heat at the end of the fermentation adds *gras* and weight.

Égrappage or not?

Once again there are several opinions as to whether to destem the grapes or not. Firstly, if picked by machine, the grapes are automatically destemmed or *égrappé*. It is only if they are hand picked that there is any choice in the matter. Cédric Saur finds that *non-égrappé* grapes enable a wine to age better, doubtless because the tannins from the stalks add something to the final wine. In contrast, Antoine Rigaud always destems, as otherwise he finds his wine too tannic. However, the stalks provide a useful filter for *remontages* and also perform a useful role as an antioxidant but, if the stalks are unripe, it is essential to destalk as the stalks can impart green flavours to the wine. Marc Roque observes that if you do not destalk you can obtain a rustic note, whereas Didier Barral finds the stems can give a slight bitterness which he likes, and he has not destemmed any of his red grapes for ten years. Camille Chauvin, who made the 2013 vintage at Domaine Frédéric Brouca before going on to Domaine de l'Horizon in Roussillon, mixed both whole bunches and destemmed grapes for her one harvest there, and she favoured a short maceration.

Yeast

One of the debates is about whether to use natural yeast or not. The Laugé brothers at Mas des Capitelles find cultured yeast to be more efficient even though they work organically, saying that natural yeast can tire and run out of energy before the fermentation has finished. The Australian winemaker Richard Osborne, who recently started working for Château Laurens, observes that cultured yeasts are an insurance. He does not yet know the condition of his cellar at Laurens – it had not been used for a number of years – and so he thinks it would be risky to rely on the natural flora of the cellar. Marc Roque uses cultured yeast, even though he is organic, believing that a traditional fermentation may not necessarily be the best option. Ludovic Aventin, on the other hand, wants to cultivate his own yeast, as he feels strongly that the yeast helps establish the identity of a wine, and for him a great wine is a wine with a real identity.

Carbonic maceration

This became a popular way of fermenting grapes, especially Carignan, in the 1980s, when wine growers were looking to soften some of the rough tannins of the Midi. The technique is to put whole bunches of grapes into a vat full of carbon dioxide; the fermentation starts inside the grapes themselves, which are then pressed in the normal way a few days later. In this case the pressed juice is considered to be finer than the free-run juice; normally it is the other way round. Today there is much less reliance on carbonic maceration, but some do still favour it. Domaine Cauvy is one such example. They worked with the Vignerons Val d'Orbieu group in the mid-1980s, with Marc Dubernet – one of the pioneers of carbonic maceration in the Languedoc – as their oenologist, and they continue to work with Marc's son, Mathieu. They find that carbonic maceration seems to make for lighter, more supple wines. In contrast, for Jean-Michel Mégé of Domaine de la Reynardière carbonic maceration can cause problems with *élevage* (literally the 'raising' of wine – best translated here as ageing), because the fruit fades quickly and he does not obtain sufficient tannins for the lengthy *élevage* that he prefers. Nathalie Caumette does not like carbonic maceration either. She is considering trying *vendange entière*, which is what Catherine Roque practises – she called it the traditional vinification of *les anciens*, and it entails putting whole bunches into the vat, without adding any additional carbon dioxide or, indeed, sulphur. Cellar hygiene must be meticulous. She presses the grapes after three weeks and puts the wine straight into wood until the following summer, when it is blended and then bottled. With whole bunches you obtain tannins from the stalks, and the stalks can also give some fresh peppery notes.

ÉLEVAGE

Oak - and its issues

Most entry-level wines are kept in vat – which may be stainless steel, fibreglass or concrete – until bottling, as these are wines for more immediate drinking and do not require any *élevage* in oak. However, most serious *cuvées* usually entail some *élevage* in oak, but again that depends very much on the wine grower's personal preference.

In the early 1990s, there was a concentration on over-extraction. People wanted to obtain the most from their grapes but, towards the end of the decade, there came a happy realization that less can be more, with a shift in the search for elegance and *finesse* and lower alcohol levels. Marc Roque admits that he no longer favours long macerations or big extractions. Likewise, Luc Salvestre, the director of Les Crus Faugères, talks about the fashion for wood at the end of the 1990s: the consumer wanted the taste of oak, but often the winemaking was not well executed, which resulted in coarse flavours. Fortunately things have evolved and *élevage* has become more refined, and flavours more complex. Essentially it is the *élevage* that makes the wine.

I asked Gwenaël Thomas if the wine growers of Faugères understood the use of oak for *élevage* any better. He isn't sure, saying that there are excesses, but not too many. 'Faugères uses both old and new wood; one is not necessarily better than the other. It all depends how the barrels are used and if there is a rational policy. You should not chop and change and you should replace your barrels gradually. A *parc de barriques* [barrel store] needs to be managed properly, with a regular cycle, which often entails replacing a third or a quarter of the barrels every year, with a three-to-four year rotation. Experimenting with different coopers, to see whose barrels suit your wine best, is a valid exercise, but again you must not change all your barrels at once. The nub of the problem is that there is no tradition or culture of *élevage* in the Languedoc. The wine growers are still learning about *élevage*, and of course they are experimenting. They may try larger barrels and they may then return to the smaller *barrique*, which is more practical to handle in the cellar. Everyone needs to find their own style.'

Needless to say there are nearly as many opinions as there are wine growers. Barrel size is one consideration: *barriques* or 500-litre *demi-muids*? Thierry Rodriguez of Mas Gabinèle does not think that there was much difference between the two, but others such as André Balliccioni (Domaine Balliccioni) see a growing preference for *demi-muids*, as the bigger ratio of wine to oak makes for a less obviously oaky impact on flavour. Geneviève Libes at Domaine du Météore is experimenting with larger oak, moving from *barriques* of 225 litres to barrels of 300, 450 and even 600 litres. Arnaud Barthès, the winemaker at Château des Estanilles, finds that smaller, 15- to 20-hectolitre *foudres* are suitable for Grenache Noir, which has less structure, whereas Syrah, which needs more oxygen, performs better with *demi-muids*, or even *barriques*. Frédéric Albaret has a selection, with 20-hectolitre *foudres* as well as *barriques* and 500-litre *demi-muids*. As he says, 'If you have a choice, you can play, but if you only have *barriques*, the wine tends to lose its freshness and fruit.' Christian Godefroid from Les Amants de la Vigneronne notices a lot of variation between the sizes, as the relationship of the wood to the wine is quite different. He has *barriques*, 600-litre *demi-muids* and 6-hectolitre *foudres*, and favours a longer *élevage* over two winters to soften the tannins.

The choice of cooper is another consideration. Christian Godefroid has experimented with different coopers and particularly favours the Austrian cooper Stockinger, who uses Austrian wood. He explained how he first came across Stockinger in Bandol, at Domaine Pibarnon and Domaine Tempier. The Austrian wood is very fine with less obvious oaky flavours, so that it softens the wine with a gentle oxygenation. They are small coopers but there is a big demand for their barrels, so orders have to be made in March for September, and the oak is as expensive as French oak – currently €700 for a *barrique*, €2400 for a *demi-muid* and €7000 for a 15-hectolitre *foudre*. *Ce n'est pas donné*, as they say in French, but some of the most quality-conscious wine growers of the Midi favour Stockinger. Christian Godefroid also uses a few François Frères barrels, and other names that are mentioned include Seguin Moreau, Saury, Taransaud and the local cooper Boutes in Narbonne. Medium is the preferred level of toasting.

Arielle Demets of Vignoble les Fusionels is not alone in saying that she does not want the wood to overwhelm the fruit. The *élevage* is more for micro-oxygenation than for the tannins. Pierre Jacquet experiments to lighten the oak component, often finding that the less wood, the better the wine. He feels oak is useful for its effect of micro-oxygenation, which polishes the tannins. And Julien Seydoux (Château des Estanilles) makes the interesting observation that schist is more sensitive to wood than limestone, contrasting Faugères with the wines of Pic St Loup.

Usually any oak is firmly French or – as noted above – maybe Austrian, but to my knowledge Jean-Claude Estève is the only wine grower to put his Syrah in American oak, remarking that the American wood adds an oaky flavour much more quickly and makes for supple, sweet vanilla notes in the wine.

Barrels, whatever the size, need to be looked after properly and that entails regular *ouillage* or topping up to ensure that any wine lost through evaporation, or indeed tasting, is replaced – otherwise the flavours will dry out. Bungs may be on the side or on top of the barrels, with an *ouillage* every couple of weeks, depending on the humidity level of the cellar.

Tronconique vats are another consideration. They are the slightly tapered large vats, which are usually made of oak, but can also be made of concrete or stainless steel. Pierre Jacquet likes them for vinifications, but finds them a touch rustic and lacking in finesse for *élevage*. He is also experimenting with a 700-litre barrel for *élevage*. He fermented a wine in it in order to season it, and is planning a two-year *élevage* in it, from which he expects interesting results.

All would agree that any oak should not overwhelm the fruit, but some people have a higher threshold for oak than others; you can still find over-oaked wines but they are probably less frequent now. Quite often not all of a *cuvée* necessarily goes into oak, which allows for much greater flexibility with blending.

Concrete eggs

These are yet another option, both for fermentation and *élevage*. One of the advantages of concrete eggs is that they encourage a natural movement of the wine, but, as Pierre Jacquet observes, you do get movement in barrels too. The eggs are also very expensive and take up a lot of space, which is a consideration in many cellars where space is a luxury.

Amphorae

No one in Faugères uses amphorae yet, but there is some interest. Philippe Borda admits to trying out an amphora as an experiment, which proved to be unsuccessful. Pierre Jacquet is curious as he thinks that porous terracotta would allow for oxygenation without the risk of imparting any taste of oak. There is a producer of amphorae in the Minervois, but I wonder where Pierre would fit an amphora in his already cramped cellar.

Questions of time

Another consideration is the length of *élevage*, which may be ten or twelve months, up to and including two winters, as favoured by Boris Feigel at Domaine des Prés-Lasses. Jean-Michel Mégé at Domaine de la Reynardière is unusual in favouring a long, three-year *élevage* in vat, which typifies his house style. He also has a *cuvée fût de chêne,* which is the same wine, but with three months in new oak after four years in vat. I have to admit that I did not find the oak very harmonious.

New cellars are being built, often with natural insulation, which will facilitate the ageing process. Domaine Ollier-Taillefer's new cellar has been built with *pierre de Gard,* which has natural insulating properties, and is partially buried into the hillside, as are the relatively new cellars of Domaine de Cébène and Vignoble les Fusionels. There is no doubt that there is a greater realization that careful *élevage* is an intrinsic part of the quality of Faugères and that Faugères does produce wines that benefit from bottle ageing to develop greater depth and complexity. Modern purpose-built cellars designed for contemporary equipment have other advantages. That of Vignoble les Fusionels operates by gravity, for example, so that any harsh pumping can be avoided.

OTHER ISSUES

Sulphur

Sulphur can solve a lot of problems. It is an antiseptic and an antioxidant, but is often treated as the universal remedy, without asking the question of why it should be so. Boris Feigel believes that every time you add sulphur, you lose something. These days there are alternatives to sulphur, such as inert gas, to prevent oxidation; there is no doubt that you can make stable wines without sulphur, but you need to know about microbiology. Although he favours minimal intervention, he admits to using a little sulphur at bottling, observing firmly that he is not in the natural wine market. Indeed he is not alone in wanting wines without defects that are complex and age worthy. Didier Barral says that if you use sulphur when you put the wine in vat, you kill your yeast, so it is best to try and avoid using sulphur until after the malolactic fermentation or even until bottling.

Alcohol

Alcohol level is an important aspect of any wine. There is no doubt that, with the greater awareness of phenolic ripeness, alcohol levels are higher than they were twenty or thirty years ago, possibly as a consequence of global warming. This is not the place to discuss the social implications of alcohol. What needs to be said is that for flavour alcohol is not the most important aspect of a wine. It stabilizes the wine and makes a slight contribution to flavour – alcohol gives *rondeur* and a hint of sweetness or richness. However, there are vinification techniques that lower the alcohol level, and also amendments can be made in blending, ensuring the alcohol is not too heavy. What needs to be avoided at all costs is that heavy alcoholic burn on the finish of a wine, which really does indicate that the alcohol level is too high. Balance is everything. The appellation dictates a minimum of 12% abv, but most wines are likely to be significantly higher – that is to say 13.5 to 14% abv on average. You will sometimes find wine at 15% abv, but that is not typical.

BLENDING, RACKING AND BOTTLING

Usually each variety is fermented separately and then the challenge is the blend. Most people, but not all, usually blend within a few months of bottling. For Miren de Lorgeril, blending is the key. She can play with the *assemblage*, and prefers to do it as late as possible, because that gives her greater control over the final taste of the wine. The blending or *assemblage* is the moment when the wine grower can really express his or her originality.

Racking or the removal of the lees is another consideration. Pierre Jacquet favours *laissez-faire*. 'The spring is when the wines wake up and eat their lees; the Burgundians say that when the lees have all gone, the wine is ready.' Boris Feigel leaves the wine on its fine lees during the winter and then blends in the spring, and he mentions, intriguingly, that the climatic conditions at blending can be critical for their effect on oxidation. There is no doubt that the taste of wine is affected by the barometer. The reductive character of Syrah can be problematic, and racking is one way of eliminating that.

Obviously a wine must be clear and bright when it is bottled but, depending on the *élevage*, there is perhaps less need for fining and filtering. Paul Gordon at Domaine de Sarabande does neither, but he does use a little sulphur at bottling, while Simon Coulshaw of Domaine des Trinités talks of the use of temperature replacing fining and clarification; he has two heat exchangers. Bottling must not be undertaken at too cool a temperature, as otherwise the wine might retain oxygen, which in turn has an impact on flavour and its longevity as oxygen dissolves in the wine; the ideal temperature for bottling is considered to be 16°C. Some people have their own bottling machine; others prefer to use a mobile bottler. Mobile bottlers consistently keep their equipment up to date, but have the disadvantage that they have to be booked a long time ahead.

Some wine growers are happy to discuss their methods; others are more reticent, saying 'It's a secret'. They may have learnt from a parent, following a natural instinct and talent, or increasingly these days they may have followed some formal training and even travelled further afield for experience in other parts of France or even in the New World. Marc Roque, whose experience is firmly anchored in Faugères, considers that the whole process should be as natural as possible; there is a palette of possibilities, but essentially he aims to avoid using sulphur and let Nature takes its course.

THE ROLE OF THE OENOLOGIST

In today's modern world, the oenologist has become very important: 'like a doctor', for Jean-Claude Estève. And most people, unless they have their own degree in oenology, need a consultant oenologist for their analyses as well as for some reassurance.

I talked to Gwenaël Thomas, the genial and thoughtful oenologist who works with Jean Natoli in his *cabinet*. He explained that most people employ oenologists primarily for their expertise in chemical analysis, but sometimes the former members of the cooperatives need more help. Then oenologists may perform a teaching role, providing a kind of apprenticeship; sometimes the oenologists may need to stimulate the wine growers' ambition. When they meet a potential client for the first time, they need to find out what kind of wines he (or she, but it is often he) makes, and understand their vision and their range of wines, and also their state of mind. What are the vineyards like? Are there commercial problems or technical problems? There is a lot at stake.

'Oenologists help the wine grower to develop a reassuring routine, so he can make wines which express themselves in their simplest form. They look for charm, wines that give pleasure, and not necessarily serious wines. There is a variable reaction to the observation "Your wines are not *rigolo*" – are not fun! If you are helping a wine grower to start from scratch, you cannot foresee the *cuvées* in advance. You need to taste everything, so that you know the potential palette of aromas and flavours and can put them together.' Gwenaël talks of a unity of place, time and action; the commercial aspect is equally important. He observes that wine growers should not just make the wines they like, but also wines that sell. 'With an established wine grower, you sometimes need to rebuild the cards, and question existing ideas and provoke new ideas. But an oenologist should never dictate a style of wine to the wine grower.' I could quite see why Jean-Claude Estève likened an oenologist to a doctor. Gwenaël asserts: 'It is the *vigneron* who makes the wine. We avoid mistakes and suggest new ideas, and question accepted practices. We work as a team; the oenologist must not put himself forward; it is a work of collaboration.' Others, however, admit that an oenologist is useful for the overview he or she has of the vintage, as they will work with several wine growers. An oenologist also has a wider view when blending, which needs to happen in a neutral environment – in an oenologist's laboratory rather than in a wine grower's cellar.

For growers without their own vinification cellar, of whom there are a handful, there is Vino-Tec in Autignac, which is run by Fabien Pujol, whose family own Château de Grézan. Jacques Clamouse makes his wine there, renting cellar space, vats and equipment, and he finds that it works very efficiently for him as he does not have the resources nor the inclination to build his own cellar.

ROSÉ

Most people, but not everyone, make a little rosé, for it has been part of the appellation since the beginning in 1982. The grape varieties are the same as for the red wine, with a possible preference for a higher percentage of Cinsaut in the blend, as well as some Grenache Noir and Syrah. However, Bernard Vidal suggests that Mourvèdre improves the quality of rosé. There is no doubt that the best rosés are made from grapes which are grown specifically for a rosé and, therefore, harvested earlier than for red wine so they retain more acidity.

The colour of a rosé is a significant quality factor, meaning that rosé is almost more complicated to make than either red or white wine. The critical decision is the length of time the juice spends in contact with the skins: too long and it looks like a light red wine, too short a time and it simply looks anaemic. Consequently the main decision is the choice of method for removing the juice from the skins, *saigné* or *pressurage direct*, bleeding or running juice off the tank, or pressing, or indeed a blend of both. There are advantages and disadvantages to either choice. Simon Coulshaw finds pressing too aggressive and prefers to leave the grapes for two to three hours in vat, considering this a more delicate way to extract juice. Syrah, however, needs to be pressed immediately as it produces a lot of colour, whereas Luc Ollier finds that you can leave Grenache Noir and Cinsaut for as long as ten to fifteen hours. He prefers a slightly higher fermentation temperature of 15° to 16°C, whereas 12° to 14°C can give a taste of what the French so eloquently call *bonbons anglais* or boiled sweets, with notes of amylic acid. The yeast strain can also be responsible for *bonbons anglais*. Thierry Rodriguez puts a quarter of his *cuvée* in wood with some *bâtonnage* or lees stirring to add richness and weight. Marie-Geneviève Boudal at Domaine des Peyregrandes also ages a small part of her second rosé in wood for four months, as a contrast to her first label, resulting in a deeper colour and more weight, and making a *rosé de repas*. Inverso Rosé from Château des Estanilles is given eight months *élevage*, which again makes for a richer, more mouth-filling wine.

WHITE WINE

White wine is becoming more important in Faugères since the recognition of the appellation for white wine in 2005, even if Faugères Blanc accounts for just 2 per cent of the appellation. For the moment only about fourteen estates produce a white appellation Faugères, while some others make a *vin de pays* or two, usually from vineyards outside the appellation. Some of those prefer a simple classic white wine vinification with fermentation in vat at a cool temperature. The malolactic fermentation is often blocked for white wine, with the aim of retaining freshness. Others aim for something more characterful. Cédric Saur at La Grange de l'Aïn produces an intriguing blend of seven grape varieties, all vinified in wood without any temperature control, and with regular *bâtonnage* which gives some weight and salinity to the wine. Damien Guérande, the winemaker at Jeanjean's Domaine de Fenouillet, talks about working with the lees. He wants to gain in volume, but not lose aroma, and thinks six weeks of *bâtonnage* is long enough. A white wine such as Inverso from Château des Estanilles is vinified in *demi-muids* and given some *bâtonnage* until October, and then again when the weather has warmed up in March. Boris Feigel uses *barriques* for part of the blend of his white wine, picking the grapes when they are fully ripe and fermenting them at a relatively high temperature, or at least not at a particularly low temperature. He states that he wants white wines with character which can age, and barrel-ageing undoubtedly makes for longer-living white wine, and also rosé.

NATURAL WINEMAKING

Another aspect of winemaking in Faugères which is gaining in importance, or possibly in media attention, is natural winemaking. The key exponents of this are Didier Barral, Corine Andrieu and Cédric Saur, who would describe himself as biodynamic in the cellar. For instance, Cédric bottles during a north wind, which he says is less disturbing for the wine, as the temperature is lower and the pressure higher than during the *vent marin*.

So how do you define natural winemaking? I would suggest winemaking with minimum intervention, using natural yeast, no chemicals in the cellar and simply allowing nature to take its course. The most contentious aspect of natural winemaking, with its very laudable criteria, is whether or not to use sulphur. Sulphur has been used as a disinfectant in the cellar since Roman times and it is highly effective in restraining any vinous deviations, but it can mask flavours. There is a commendable trend of limiting its use, and sulphur levels have been effectively reduced as cellar hygiene has improved. The purists of the natural wine movement use no sulphur at all, which can result in some curious tastes and aromas. The best of these wines are undoubtedly delicious, but others are distinctly unsuccessful with off flavours, not to mention notes of excessive volatile acidity, so more conventional winemakers favour a little sulphur at bottling for the sake of stability and, from the consumer's point of view, there is much to support that argument. However, for Didier Barral, the great asset of *vin nature* is its digestibility, which in part originates from a lack of sulphur. And for Corine Andrieu at Clos Fantine there is no doubt that the essential characteristic of *vin nature* is no sulphur dioxide – and of course she uses natural yeast.

Cédric Saur talks about the microbiological profile of a wine. Yeasts are sensitive to sulphur and to alcohol, and can produce a notion of acetate but it is not volatile. If sulphur is added, it will kill the yeast, and here he draws a comparison between pasteurized and non-pasteurized cheese. If you carafe the wine, any volatile notes disappear and the fruit emerges with vibrant freshness. He said that there are two ways of working: very reductively, allowing no contact with air, or oxidatively, which Cédric prefers. He describes himself as *nature restraint,* and Clos Fantine as purists, *des pures;* Jérôme Py calls them *pures et dures.* Gwenaël Thomas, on the other hand, expresses the oenologist's view. He observes that acetate does diminish, but that it can linger – and in any case, wine is not natural but made by man, the noble craftsman, practising *le noblesse artisan.*

Corine Andrieu of Clos Fantine talks about the evolution of her winemaking. Since 2011 she has simply put the grapes with their stalks in the vat and then does not touch them. She used to do *délestages* but does so no longer, as she finds that no *délestages* reduces any volatile acidity because there is no war between the different yeasts – she suggests that a fermenting vat has several colonies of yeast and believes that you should not mix them up. She used to look for robust wines, wanting to extract everything from the grapes, but now she looks for the *côté fruit* and *la force du terroir*. She follows her instincts; she is seeking purity and admits to learning from her mistakes. She keeps her wine in a closed environment and does not rack it, so that the carbon dioxide gas remains to protect it. On the subject of sulphur, she observes that it can be mistaken for minerality with its drying effect on taste buds and saliva; her point of departure is indigenous wild yeast, which express *terroir*. Her first vintage using natural yeast was in 2000, and she says that she saw a great difference between it and her previous four vintages made with cultured yeast. She follows the biodynamic calendar in the cellar.

PUSHING THE BOUNDARIES

Jérôme Rateau of Château Haut Lignières talks about his recent wine, Empreinte Carbone. It was originally initiated in 2011 by a *stagiaire*, a trainee, who was particularly interested in experimenting with natural wine. He was allowed to make three barrels: two went to the distillery but one was delicious, and so Jérôme was sufficiently interested to carry on with the experiment in 2012. The wine comes from a 22-are plot of Syrah (an 'are' is equivalent to 100 square metres); he uses a tractor for ploughing, but otherwise everything is done by hand. The wine is made in a barrel, with *pigeage* by hand. Jérôme talks of the feel of the grapes: of how you can feel when the fermentation is stopping as the cap begins to fall, and you know if the *pigeage* is being done properly. His yeasts are indigenous and the *élevage* for the 2011 lasted twenty-two months. The 2012 was still in barrel in May 2014, but I was lucky enough to taste it, and also the 2013. The flavours were rich and intense, with a fine tannin balance and a fresh finish. And the two barrels of 2013 were quite distinct, one more perfumed and the other more restrained. That is the charm of a micro-vinification.

At Domaine de Fenouillet Jeanjean are also pushing the boundaries in an attempt to see just what their vineyards can produce when treated with particular care and attention. They refer to '*les jardins de schist*'. I tasted the 2010 vintage, from which just 1500 bottles had been made. The colour is deep, the nose powerful and the palate rich and concentrated, but with an elegant finish. The grapes were hand-harvested in small boxes, cooled for twenty-four hours down to 8°C, and then sorted by hand and destalked. They were vinified in

Pigeage, where the grape skins are pumped down

500-litre barrels as well as a 30-hectolitre *tronconique* vat. Syrah was the principal grape variety used. The 2011 is more restrained, with more oak, more acidity and more tannin, and they feel it was more homogenous than the 2010. In early 2016 the first vintage of Le Père la Minute was released, a culmination of several years of research and experimentation.

Simon Coulshaw's Cuvée 42 represents his venture into biodynamic viticulture and natural winemaking. It comes from three separate 1-hectare vineyards planted with Grenache Noir, Syrah and Mourvèdre, which are hand picked and co-fermented. No sulphur is used during the winemaking and the *élevage* is in 500-litre barrels for eighteen months. There are just 2000 bottles of the 2009 vintage. It is a hefty 15.1% abv and almost Amarone-like in its intensity. Simon has also produced a 2010, but as yet no more.

Jean-Louis Pujol at the Château de Grézan also talks about going to the limit for his *cuvée* Les Schistes Dorés and fermenting in *demi-muids*, which entails taking off the tops of the barrels and doing a manual *pigeage*, taking time to extract the flavours, so that the soft Grenache Noir skins almost dissolve. In contrast to Grenache Noir, Carignan and Mourvèdre have much tougher skins. Then everything is pressed, and the barrels, with their tops replaced, are refilled for the *élevage*, which lasts two years. The wine is rich and concentrated.

'Orange wine' is the current term used to describe a white wine that is vinified like a red wine, destalked and fermented on its skins at a high temperature, followed by a long slow pressing. Didier Barral, who is the main exponent of orange wine in Faugères, talks of three or four days. In contrast, Catherine Roque's Cabretta undergoes no skin contact, nor are the grapes destalked. She picks them and presses them, and the juice goes into *barriques* for the malolactic fermentation, without the addition of any sulphur.

Maybe some of these innovative wines are perhaps a little extreme. None the less, Catherine Roque sees a general trend in the new generation of younger wine growers towards less wood and lower alcohol, while for me a large part of the appeal of Faugères is its elegance and underlying freshness. The next chapter will tell you in more detail exactly who does what.

5

WHO'S WHO BY VILLAGE

FAUGÈRES

Faugères gives its name to the appellation and boasts the largest number of wine estates. As mentioned in the introduction, it is well worth exploring its narrow streets, with the vestiges of Protestant temples as well as the Catholic parish church.

Les Crus Faugères

Mas Olivier, Faugères 34600
Tel: 04 67 95 08 80
contact@lescrusfaugeres.com
www.lescrusfaugeres.com

The cooperative in Faugères was founded in 1959, which makes it one of the newest and last cooperatives of the Languedoc. At that time Faugères was already recognized as a VDQS. These days it has 110 members from all over the appellation, as it has absorbed the now defunct cooperatives of Autignac and Laurens. In 2000 that of Autignac was taken over by the Laurens cooperative, which then made some bad commercial decisions, so Faugères took control of Laurens in 2010. Altogether the cooperative is responsible for some 1200 hectares, of which 1000 are Faugères, in other words half the appellation. The average size of a vineyard holding is 13 to 14 hectares, from which a family can earn a comfortable living; the largest is 50 hectares and the smallest about 2 hectares.

Luc Salvestre came to the cooperative as its director fresh from oenology studies at Montpelier in 1996 and has seen some significant

Luc Salvestre, director of the cooperative les Crus Faugères for many years

changes over the years. These days the *vrac négociant* business is much less important. They now sell 85 per cent of their production in bottle or bag-in-box, some 4 million bottles a year, and their biggest export market is China. Luc spends five to six weeks of the year there, and says that the Chinese are most interested in the more expensive wines, for the gift market. As director of Les Crus Faugères, Luc is responsible for the ultimate taste of the wines. And what does he look for? He wants wines that represent the typicity of Faugères and express its *terroir*. The vineyards are classified, with criteria based on viticultural practices as well as *terroir* and aspect, so that the best are used for the smaller, more select *cuvées*.

Mas Olivier is the cooperative's principal brand, accounting for a million bottles a year, which makes it the biggest brand of the Languedoc. It is a classic Faugères blend of 40 per cent Grenache Noir, 20 per cent Syrah, 30 per cent Carignan and 10 per cent Mourvèdre, of which 60 per cent has been aged in barrels.

The cooperative has encouraged the replanting of Grenache Noir and Syrah to replace Carignan and Cinsaut, resulting in different viticulture practices with vines trained on wires. They consider the surface area of the leaves, preferring a north–south aspect and there is more detailed work in the vineyard. Bonuses are paid for hand picking.

In 2013 they produced their first organic wines. These are made at Mas Olivier, the large vinification plant just outside the village of Faugères, while the cellars of Laurens are used for the conventional wines. Luc explains that they currently have four members who work organically, with a total of 60 hectares converted to organic viticulture, making a red and a rosé under the Mas Olivier label. I was able to compare the two wines in both colours. The organic rosé is a blend of Grenache Noir and Cinsaut with some Syrah, all pressed, making for ripe strawberries and very good balancing acidity. The non-organic rosé has less Syrah and seems less expressive, with less acidity, even though the two wines were made in exactly the same way. The organic red wine does not spend any time in wood and so has some fresh peppery fruit, while the non-organic wine is more tannic with a note of vanilla. Both are easy to drink, which is the primary aim.

You can taste an extensive range of the cooperative's wine in their tasting *caveau* on the main road near the village of Faugères. The name of the *caveau*, 'Les Crus Faugères', is misleading, for it implies lots of different Faugères from different growers, whereas in fact the wines come from just one source: the cooperative. Mas Olivier white is a blend of Roussanne, Marsanne and Grenache Blanc, and is delicate and fresh. Rosé des Schistes, presented in an outsize perfume bottle, has more depth than Mas Olivier. Of the red wines, I like Parfum des Schistes best. It is a blend of 50 per cent Syrah, 30 per cent Grenache Noir and 20 per cent Carignan, entailing a selection of several vineyards, with some warm peppery fruit and more depth than Mas Olivier. For my taste buds, Les Tourelles, their *haut de gamme*, is a little too solid and oaky. I left with a feeling that, while the wines were sound, they did not excite. Price is to their advantage, but none the less they could do better.

Les Amants de la Vigneronne

1207 route de Pézenas, Faugères 34600
Tel : 04 67 95 78 49
lesamantsdelavigneronne@yahoo.fr
www.lavigneronne.com/les_sites/amants

If you are looking for a particular bottle and have neither time nor inclination to visit the wine grower in question, the chances are that you will find it at Les Amants de la Vigneronne on the outskirts of the village of Faugères.

Christian and Régine Godefroid are initially shy, but warm to their subject and you get a sense of great affection for each other – and an enormous, but restrained, enthusiasm for the wines of Faugères. This Belgian couple bought a rundown property in 2000, and spent three years reconverting it into *chambres d'hôte*. Then, in 2004, they opened a shop and tasting *caveau* with thirty-three independent wine growers, and these days they work with forty *vignerons*.

Their enthusiasm for Faugères led them to buy 1.5 hectares of vineyards in 2004 and to make their first wine in 2005. Since then the estate has gradually grown. They began with Syrah, Grenache Noir and Mourvèdre, as well as 50 ares of Grenache Blanc, and now have 8 hectares, including a substantial holding of Mourvèdre, as well as Syrah and Grenache Noir, and a little Carignan, but no Cinsaut. Christian is not very keen on either Carignan or Cinsaut, but some Roussanne has been added to the Grenache Blanc. The early vintages were made in the rather cramped cellar of the *chambres d'hôte*, but now they have a large new cellar at the entrance to the village opposite Mas des Capitelles, while the original old vaulted cellar is used for tastings and storage. Christian admits ruefully that the first purchase of vines was '*pour le plaisir*' and he had certainly not initially intended to develop his vineyards.

Their welcoming shop features wines whose names play on the theme of *les amants*, the lovers. First I tasted La Rouge aux Lèvres, or lipstick. This has spent eighteen months in old wood. Christian is adamant that he wants to emphasize the fruit, and not the wood, and that he wants a wine that is *gourmand* and for immediate appeal. There he has certainly succeeded. In the 2012 vintage, Grenache Noir is the dominant variety with some Syrah and Mourvèdre, and the wine is rich and supple, combining the spice of the Syrah and the fruit of the Grenache Noir. Percentages change with the vintage, so that for the 2011 vintage two-thirds Grenache Noir was blended with one-third Syrah. Again there is spicy black fruit with good balancing tannins.

De Chair et de Sang ('of flesh and blood') has Mourvèdre as the dominant variety. It is aged in oak, both *barriques* and *foudres*, with some new oak for the Mourvèdre. Christian observes that the new cellar has given them more space for *élevage*, so he has been able to try out larger 600-litre barrels plus *foudres* of 6 hectolitres. He notices a lot of variation between the different sizes. Here it is the Mourvèdre that gives the character to the wine, with some ripe fruit, firm tannins and a peppery streak.

When I ask about his typicity, Christian immediately replies, 'Mourvèdre'. No one else has quite so much, up to 30 per cent, in their vineyards, so there are not many Faugères with Mourvèdre as the principal variety. Unlike most of the other growers, he has very little Carignan, and he never does carbonic maceration. He wants wines that are *soyeux*, or silky; the tannins should not be aggressive, so he favours an eighteen-month *élevage* over two winters to soften the tannins.

Dans la Peau (to have someone 'dans la peau' means you are crazy about them) is 80 per cent Syrah with some Grenache Noir and Mourvèdre. The flavours are firm and intense, with rich fruit, benefitting from an *élevage* in new oak. Christian has experimented with numerous coopers and favours Stockinger, the Austrian cooper who uses Austrian wood, which Christian rates very highly as the flavours are less obviously oaky and the oxygenation softens the wine. Dans la Peau enjoys a maceration of at least three if not five weeks with a lot of *pigeage*, but not much *remontage*.

J'ai Soif de Toi, meaning I need you or I love you, is the white wine of the estate, with very Burgundian winemaking methods, fermentation in barrel and *élevage* on the lees. Christian wants his white wine to be fresh, and so he usually picks at the end of August, observing that he is the first to pick his whites, and the last to pick his Mourvèdre. The flavours are quite intriguing: the 2012 has lemony freshness, but is still a bit adolescent, while the 2011 is richer and heavier.

The tasting finished with what Christian calls *un petit joker*, namely a blend of everything, in the proportion to the number of bottles of each *cuvée*, so 45 per cent Syrah, 40 per cent Mourvèdre and 15 per cent Grenache Noir, an experiment of 1000 bottles for fun. It is rich, soft and spicy, with supple tannins but no oak.

Finally, and not content with only wine, the Godefroids also have 250 olive trees – Lucques for eating and Aglandau and Bouteillan for oil, pressed at the oil mill in either Gabian or Murviel-lès-Béziers.

Mas d'Alezon

1 route de Pézenas, Faugères 34600
Tel: 04 67 95 19 72
mas@alezon.fr
www.alezon.fr

I first met Catherine Roque when I was researching *The Wines of the South of France*, just as she was beginning to explore the possibilities of a vineyard in Faugères, discovering the excitement of schist. At the end of the last century she was making some of the Languedoc's most successful Pinot Noir, as well a host of other lovely wines, in the cool vineyards of the Orb valley at Domaine de Clovallon outside Bédarieux. Things have moved on and in 2014 her daughter Alix made the wine at Domaine de Clovallon, while

Catherine Roque of Mas d'Alezon, one of the leading biodynamic wine makers of the appellation

Catherine concentrated on her Faugères at Mas d'Alezon. At this point I should declare an interest; Catherine has become a good friend over the years and I may well be biased when I say that her wines are amongst some of my Faugères favourites.

Catherine recently moved from her old house, the Presbytère, by the church in Faugères, across the road to a house next to the *mairie* in the village, where she has her cellar *sur place*, as well as a tasting caveau. Her old cellar in the village was sold to Olivier Gil of Mas Lou for his first vintage in 2014.

Catherine discovered Faugères in 1997. She had heard that *un vieux monsieur* who sold wine *en vrac* to the *négoce* was retiring, and thus she came to buy 7 hectares at Montfalette outside the village of Soumartre. There were two plots. Montfalette itself she kept because there was Syrah and some 60-year-old Grenache Noir, but Cabretta she pulled up. It has subsequently been replanted with Clairette and Roussanne. Catherine was not able to make Faugères immediately as she had no Mourvèdre, so she sold her first two vintages to the *négoce* while she got to know her vineyards. She admits it was quite a big learning curve. At Clovallon she could invent everything, while in Faugères she had to adapt to the appellation: quite a different challenge. Clovallon is limestone and north-facing; Faugères is schist and south-facing. In 1999 she bottled her first wine and initially it was Coteaux du Languedoc; in 2003 (by which time she had acquired some Mourvèdre) she made her first Faugères; and 2007 saw her first vintage of Presbytère. She now has three plots of vines, in three different zones: Caussiniojouls, Soumartre and Faugères itself, including some very old Carignan. However, she is not at all enthusiastic about Carignan: '*J'ai du mal avec Carignan.* Maybe I don't know it well enough. It can be very linear. It's the alcohol that saves Carignan, at 14 to 15% abv and that's the opposite to what I like. It's not my – *tasse de thé.*' On the other hand Mourvèdre is much better: 'People were wrong when they said it would not ripen.' She has just taken over some Lledoner Pelut, 40-year-old vines *en gobelet,* from which she expects good things. Grenache Noir can be quite alcoholic, whereas Lledoner Pelut, as a variant of Grenache Noir, copes better with the drought. It has hairs on the underside of its leaves which help, and it ripens much more slowly than Grenache Noir. So Catherine's Faugères has evolved into two *cuvées*: Montfalette which is Mourvèdre and Syrah, with Grenache

Noir providing the link between two characterful grape varieties, and Presbytère which is mainly Grenache Noir with some Mourvèdre.

Catherine has progressed over the last twenty years from *lutte raisonée* to organic and now biodynamic viticulture; she uses no sulphur dioxide in the cellar, so hygiene must be meticulous. Nothing is destemmed as she favours a traditional vinification *des anciens*, in an open vat. The grapes are pressed after three weeks. She seeks lower alcohol levels. She observes that Pinot Noir has made her more exacting; she likes complexity. She is particularly enthusiastic about white wine from schist: 'Clairette *en schiste est géant.*' She would love to do more white wine, and suggests that Faugères Blanc should include Clairette and Carignan Blanc. The potential is enormous. As for *élevage*, Catherine favours larger barrels rather than small *barriques,* and is adamant that vine age is a quality factor. In 2014 she made rosé for the first time, from a new plot that includes some Cinsaut. When asked about typicity she talks about the wines she likes: '*aerien, profondeur*, you can drink them young or old. Faugères is not immediately generous; there is a certain austerity that gradually reveals its character.'

Domaine Frédéric Alquier

6 route de Pézènes-les-Mines, Faugères 34600
04 67 95 15 21

Gilbert Alquier, one of the great pioneers of Faugères, sadly died too young, in 1989. He had four children, including two sons – Frédéric and Jean-Michel – who took over the family vineyards and then, in 1996, decided to divide their inheritance into two estates.

Since we spoke, Frédéric has sadly succumbed to cancer. Frédéric had vineyards in three plots, the furthest only 3 kilometres from his cellar in the village of Faugères. There are differences between the three: the schist varies and the altitude is different. When I asked about the typicity of Faugères, Frédéric talked about the *terroir*, the climate and the *côté garrigue*. The vineyards have some 80-year-old Grenache Noir and Carignan, and he practiced *lutte raisonnée* in them, and when I asked about his winemaking methods, he was reticent: they were a secret. He had learned from his father and from experience.

The estate has a hectare of white varieties, for a Faugères Blanc from Roussanne and Marsanne, fermented and aged in vat for bottling the following spring. Frédéric picked the grapes really ripe so the colour was quite golden and the wine was rich and textured, with a slightly honeyed note that develops with age. However, Frédéric thought it was best drunk young.

He also made two red wines, a Tradition with a high percentage of Syrah, with some Grenache Noir, Carignan and Mourvèdre, which was aged in vat after a classic vinification. Red fruit and leather were the descriptions that came to mind. The second red, Eugénie, came from 2 hectares of Syrah and was named after his daughter. This red was given between one and two years of oak ageing in *barriques* and larger barrels, depending on the vintage. It was quite solid and leathery with some ripe fruit, and the essential *côté garrigue* of Faugères.

In the cellar was one of the very earliest bottles of Gilbert Alquier, a 1967 rosé; Faugères was not yet an appellation and the wine is labelled Coteaux du Languedoc, Faugères, VDQS. It made a venerable tribute to Gilbert Alquier.

Frédéric's last vintage was 2014; the grapes were picked in 2015 (by someone else). His daughter is training to be a chemist; his son Timothée had been showing more interest in wine, but the future of the estate is currently uncertain.

Domaine Jean-Michel Alquier

4 route de Pézènes-les-Mines, Faugères 34600
Tel : 04 67 23 07 89
jmalquier@jmalquier.com
www.jmalquier.com

There have been Alquiers in Faugères since 1870; Jean-Michel and his late brother Frédéric are the fifth generation. I was lucky enough to meet their father, Gilbert, back in 1987, just a couple of years before he died. He told me how his own father had planted the first Grenache Noir vines in Faugères just after the Second World War and that he had planted Syrah at the beginning of the 1960s and Mourvèdre in about 1970. Gilbert was also one of the first to age some of his wine in *barriques*, in order to make a Cuvée Prestige from his better grapes. I tasted the 1985 vintage in the spring of 1987, which had spent ten months in new *barriques* of Tronçais oak. It was quite revolutionary at the time.

Things have moved on. The two brothers worked together until their mother retired in 1996 and then decided to go their separate ways. It is now Jean-Michel Alquier who is generally considered to have taken his father's place, making some of the most stylish of Faugères. He has a large house on the edge of the village, with an elegant brass plaque telling you the opening times of the bureau, but no indication of a name to reassure you that you are at the correct front door: '*Je suis anti-marketing*', he says. Altogether he has 11 hectares of neatly trimmed vineyards, including just a single one of white, all within the *commune* of Faugères itself, on south-facing slopes. Jean-Michel works organically, but does not make a point of it: 'If you were truly organic, you would only travel by bicycle,' he remarks. In some plots the weeding is done by hand, as the terrain is so stony that a tractor would be impossible, while in other plots he keeps grass between the rows of vines. There is a ruined house hidden in the trees, with an old dovecot; Jean-Michel would love to restore it, and no Faugères vineyard is without a *capitelle*. Partridges scuttle in the vineyards, but Jean-Michel asserts that he is not a hunter, unlike so many of the local wine-growing community. In the spring, the scent of *garrigues* is intoxicating, with wild mint, fennel, thyme, rosemary and cistus.

Jean-Michel talks about his winemaking. The range has evolved over the years, and so has his approach. He observes that his tastes have changed; he no longer uses as much oak as he used to, finding now that oak can be too heavy. He does not use any oak at all for his white wines, because without the barrel effect they have more minerality and vivacity. His white Faugères, Des Vignes au Puits, is a blend of 50 per cent Marsanne with 20 per cent Grenache Blanc and 30 per cent Roussanne – from vines that are indeed by a well (*puit*). There are flavours of fennel balanced with firm acidity and a mineral note, amply illustrating Faugères' potential for white as well as red wine. Jean-Michel also has just fifteen rows of Sauvignon, planted for the simple reason that he and his wife like it. He enthuses about a New Zealand Sauvignon that he had drunk in Thailand and now makes an elegantly understated interpretation of that variety.

Next come the red wines, the range evolving from year to year. Les Premières, a blend of Syrah, Grenache Noir and Mourvèdre, is nicely redolent of rich tapenade. It spends sixteen months in wood. Maison Jaune, made only in the years of good Grenache, is a blend of about 70 per cent Grenache Noir, with 20 per cent Syrah and a little Mourvèdre; the three varieties are blended after the malolactic fermentation and age together in barrel for about eighteen months. Les Bastides is made with grapes from the higher vineyards, including the oldest Syrah vines which account for 70 per cent of the blend, as well as some old Grenache Noir and just a drop of Mourvèdre, with eighteen months' *élevage*. The wine is denser and richer with more concentration. Jean-Michel loves Syrah; for him it is the finest grape variety of the appellation.

On my last visit I tasted a new wine, Les Grands Bastides d'Alquier, made for the first time in 2010 from Syrah and a little Grenache Noir. Jean-Michel had left the grapes to hang on the vines for two weeks longer than usual, then 60 per cent of the wine was put into new wood and spent two years in barrels. It was aerated four times, by literally emptying the barrel, washing it and then putting the wine back into the same barrel without using a pump. Nor was it fined or filtered. It was bottled in December 2012 and Jean-Michel will sell it when he judges it to be ready.

How would Jean-Michel describe the typicity of Faugères? He explains that the soils of Faugères are lightly acidic, so that you can have really ripe grapes while retaining freshness in the wine, while the schist gives a slightly animal note, adding something a little wild to the blend. Above all, Faugères is an association of elegance and power, he says. He talks of the need to improve each year, to work on the raw material and not to deviate from your aims. And then he admits that he would have liked to have been a musician, but that he came to love wine later. 'The life of a wine grower is a noble one'; he likes the feel of the soil. He has no regrets and is philosophical as to whether his children will show any inclination to follow in his footsteps.

Domaine Binet-Jacquet

11 rue du Ponget,
Faugères 34600
Tel: 06 21 14 82 07
domaine@binet-jacquet.com
www.binet-jacquet.com

Pierre Jacquet has a discreet cellar door right in the heart of the village of Faugères. The Binet part of the estate is Olivier Binet, who lives in Switzerland and comes to Faugères at key moments in the viticultural year, such as for the *assemblage*. It is Pierre who does the work *sur place*, and for him wine is a second career after working in international business.

Pierre explains that the partners have 19 hectares and make just red wine, which he believes is complicated enough, without white and rosé. They bought bare land, planted their first vines in 2001 and made their first wine in 2005 *chez* Didier Barral in Lenthéric, before acquiring their own small cellar in 2006. Also in 2006, they bought 2 hectares of old Carignan; this is the only vineyard that they bought, rather than planted or replanted. Their vines are in the villages of Lenthéric and Cabrerolles, with about seventeen different plots altogether. Pierre particularly appreciates the schist of Faugères, and points out that each *cépage* has its own particular *univers à lui,* considering aspect, slope and micro-climate.

Pierre looks for finesse and elegance, and wants natural acidity which will emphasize the minerality of the wines. It all depends on the *travail du sol.* He uses no chemical products and minimal sulphur, merely as a disinfectant. Yeasts naturally produce a little sulphur and that is a good thing, he says – otherwise the end result would be vinegar. He also uses a little sulphur at bottling. He is biodynamic and registered with Demeter, which is very strict; the Demeter dose of copper for oidium is half that of the usual dose for organic viticulture, for example. There is a *tronconique* vat which they use for fermentations, but not for *élevage,* as it can give rather rustic results; *élevage* is better in *barriques.* They also ferment in some open barrels, as well as in cement and fibreglass vats. Essentially Pierre aims to do as little as possible to the wine.

At a cellar tasting a Cinsaut was fresh and perfumed; Carignan had some rustic berry fruit with more structure; Syrah was fresh and peppery, while Grenache was riper and more perfumed. Mourvèdre was sturdier with some black fruit. It was fascinating to taste the characteristics of the individual varieties before they were blended.

The 2012 Reserve from vat, with a majority of Grenache Noir with some Syrah, Carignan and Mourvèdre, has restrained fruit on the nose, with red cherries on the palate and a lovely long finish; it promises well. The amount of oak ageing has evolved; initially all the wine was aged in barrel, and for twelve months, but for the 2012 only 40 per cent was aged in wood, though for two years: 'Oak is for micro-oxygenation and the less wood, the better it is.' The Grand Réserve is based on

Sampling wine from the vat

Mourvèdre, while the Tradition is aged only in vat, and is a blend of Carignan, Syrah, Grenache Noir and Cinsaut. I enjoyed a glass of the 2011 Tradition later at the Dame Jane restaurant in the village; it was fresh and perfumed, with a mineral streak and an elegant finish.

Pierre says that he looks for *finesse*, by which he means balance, for minerality and *terroir*, and for elegance, which apparently is not the same as *finesse*. And that is certainly what he achieves.

Calmel & Joseph

www.calmel-joseph.com

Négociants play a much less significant role in the Languedoc than they used to, but you do still find *négociant* labels for Faugères, and it is an important item in Calmel & Joseph's portfolio. They are quite unlike the usual *négociant* as they work in a quite different way; I would call them a *négociant* for the modern world. For a start they are not interested in volume, and they have very close relationships with their suppliers. I met Laurent Calmel to talk about his work at the Distillerie in Pézenas (incidentally, it is not a distillery, but a hotel). Understandably Laurent would not reveal who he works with in Faugères, but he was very happy to tell me exactly how he works.

Although Laurent grew up in Cassis, his grandparents had vineyards in the Hérault, at Puisserguier. He studied oenology and then worked in Washington State, in Moldova and as a flying winemaker in Chile and Argentina as well as in various cooperatives of the Languedoc. After a hectic ten years or so he took a step back to think about what he really wanted to do, which was not necessarily to have his own vineyards, but to participate in the winemaking. He was captivated by the richness and variety of the *terroirs* of the Languedoc, feeling that they were often overlooked. He had also met Jérôme Joseph, who had the necessary commercial experience, so their roles are now neatly defined. Laurent works with two or three people in each appellation, always the same people each year, as he believes in the importance of long-term relationships. At the beginning he selects the vineyards that will provide his grapes; he says he works like an independent wine grower, like a *cave particulière*, but with the flexibility of a *négociant*. However, he wants to make a wine that is absolutely representative of that appellation: 'A *vigneron* is tied to his appellation and his own vineyards; a *négociant* can make changes more easily.'

Their first vintage was 1998 and appropriately their first wine came from Faugères, just 3000 bottles from a producer near Lenthéric. The obvious question was why they chose Faugères for their first wine. In reply Laurent enthuses about the personality of Faugères; he loves the character of the *garrigues,* of the holm oak and the strawberry tree. 'The wine always smells of the *garrigues,* with spices, herbs and juniper. You always obtain good pH levels in Faugères with good acidity and a good balance. The soil is not rich, so the vines are never vigorous. There are few bad vineyards in Faugères.' He still works with their original producer, whose grapes give him the *garrigues* character he wants, and *viandé* (meaty) notes, sometimes a bit too much, so he tones them down with the grapes of a second producer in Autignac, with more Grenache Noir and riper, fuller flavours. Thus the 2012 that I tasted was 50 per cent Syrah, 30 per cent Grenache Noir and 20 per cent Carignan, with a touch of Mourvèdre, given an *élevage* in vat. The *garrigues* were present, with some leathery notes and an underlying freshness. Laurent explains that he did not want an expensive wine, but an affordable and representative example of the appellation.

In talking about winemaking, Laurent observes that he had learned to work with modern technology in Australia and New Zealand, and he realizes that the more you learn, the less you know; you need to accompany the wine, not lead it. Consequently his winemaking has become much less interventionist over the years. He uses natural yeast, a light *pigeage*, a long maceration, minimum filtration, and just watches everything very carefully. His wine is very likely to be quite different from the wine grower's own wine; in the vineyard the growers follow a *cahier de charge* that does not allow for weedkiller and favours minimal cultivation.

The range from Calmel & Joseph has gradually evolved and now includes varietal wines as well as convincing examples of most of the appellations of the Languedoc, and also Roussillon. Each appellation's wines have distinctive labels illustrating a piece of cellar equipment. For Faugères there is a hammer for a barrel; it is indeed nicely representative of the appellation.

Mas des Capitelles

1707 route de Pézenas, Faugères 34600
Tel: 04 67 23 10 20
mas.des.capitelles@laposte.net
www.masdescapitelles.com

Cédric and Brice Laugé are brothers, and you sense that they work well together, complementing each other's skills. Their father, Jean, was a cooperative member, but when Cédric completed his studies he decided the time was ripe to set up his own estate, and his brother joined him. They have 24 hectares in some thirty plots all over the *commune* of Faugères, including a 3-hectare plot just outside their cellar on the approach to the village. Those vines are 50 years old, while the oldest are centenarian. The name of their estate is appropriate, as they have more than their fair share of *capitelles*, with four altogether scattered around their vineyards, though none is in the immediate vicinity of their cellar.

They only have red varieties, as they are not interested in white wine because it is not important commercially; different equipment is also needed, so they prefer to concentrate on red wine. They do everything themselves, apart from some extra help at the harvest. They began the conversion to organic viticulture in 2008 and were certified in 2011; it was not a difficult transition. Nothing changed in the cellar. They never filter, use minimal sulphur and prefer cultured yeast, as they believe it is more efficient than natural yeast, which can tire and not finish the fermentation.

The disadvantage of cellar visits in January – when I was there for a tasting – is that they can be a chilly experience, not just for the taster but also for the wine. The entry-level red, La Catiède, which is the Occitan name of the *lieu-dit* of the vineyard, is based on Carignan, with Grenache Noir, Mourvèdre and some Syrah, which spend twelve months in vat. The grapes are destalked and they ferment each variety separately in stainless steel vats. They have the advantage of a recently built cellar, streamlined and with sufficient space.

Vieilles Vignes includes 25 per cent of very old Carignan, as well as 50 per cent Mourvèdre, part of which is aged in wood to soften it as it can be too powerful, and the balance is Syrah. There is a touch of oak and a pleasantly rustic note from the Carignan, which was vinified traditionally. For young Carignan vines, they prefer carbonic maceration, and they want to extract as much as possible from the grapes to ensure a wine with ageing potential.

Loris is named after Cédric's son and spends thirty months in older wood. The blend is 80 per cent Carignan, from the 50-year-old vines by the cellar, with 20 per cent Mourvèdre. The *cuvaison* lasts four to six weeks, so that the flavour is dense and solid with oak dominating the fruit in the young wine.

Collection is made only in the best years, and for the first time in 2007, from Mourvèdre with just a hint of Syrah. This 2007 Collection No. 1 spent two and a half years in wood, followed by a year in vat. Cédric observes that Syrah is always good, but Carignan and Mourvèdre are trickier. It is oaky, with solid chocolate notes on the palate. Collection No. 2 was made from Syrah, with some Carignan and Mourvèdre in 2011. Collection No. 3 will be from the 2015 vintage, predominantly Mourvèdre, and is maturing in the cellar as I write. When asked about typicity, they exude total confidence: 'We make the wine that we like to drink'.

Domaine de Cébène

Route de Caussiniojouls,
Faugères 34600
Tel : 06 74 96 42 67
bchevalier@cebene.fr
www.cebene.fr

Brigitte Chevalier arrived in the Languedoc in 2004 and made her first Faugères in 2008. She comes from Bordeaux where she worked for a couple of *négociants,* but she really wanted to make her own wine. The variety of the *terroir* and the choice of grape varieties attracted her to the Languedoc: 'Here you have a wonderful impression of liberty, compared to Bordeaux where you are weighed down by tradition.' Cébène takes its name from the goddess of the Cévennes, the mountains that form a backdrop to the vineyards of Faugères.

For her earlier vintages, Brigitte worked in a tiny cellar on the edge of the village of Caussiniojouls, where she had cement vats and an old basket press, and worked by gravity. When we met, Brigitte announced that she

Brigitte Chevalier – a bordelaise who prefers to make wine in the Languedoc at Domaine de Cébène

would be leaving her small cellar very shortly and, as this would be the very last tasting there, she proposed opening a whole range of wines – in fact, most of the wines she had ever made in this simple set-up. In early September, just in time for the 2014 harvest, she moved into a new cellar outside the village of Faugères. It is neat, functional and buried in the schist, with views across the valley to the village and the Pic de Tantajo.

Brigitte has some wonderful vineyards. She has always looked for cooler sites in Faugères, so that her grapes have a long slow ripening time, and her estate now consists of 11 hectares in two large plots, divided into smaller vineyards, around her new cellar. She also makes a Pays d'Oc, Ex Arena, from her very first vineyard in the village of Corneillan, outside the appellation of Faugères, from 85 per cent Grenache Noir, with some Mourvèdre. Brigitte adores Mourvèdre. Ex Arena has the lovely, rich, cherry fruit of expressive Grenache Noir, tempered by Mourvèdre, with an elegant streak of tannin. Each label has a description that relates in some way to the characteristics of the wine, so for Ex Arena it is '*la mémoire vers la mer*', a reference to the fact that Mourvèdre enjoys cooling sea breezes.

Altogether Brigitte makes three Faugères. First is Belle Lurette, a name that comes from the expression '*il y avait une belle lurette,*' or 'once upon a time', for this is mainly old Carignan, seventy to a hundred years old, with a little Grenache Noir and Mourvèdre. And the description is '*la longue histoire des hommes*' or 'the long history of Man'. Les Bancèls, '*les balcons de schiste*', is mainly Syrah, with some Grenache Noir and Mourvèdre and a little Carignan, and no oak ageing, while Felgaria, '*les caprices de la terre*', is predominantly Mourvèdre with some Syrah. All three are labelled 'Grand Terroir de Schiste'.

This tasting showed above all how well Faugères will age. The 2009 Bancèls is elegantly evolved with peppery spice, while the 2008 is more supple with some lovely fruit. Felgaria 2012 has some lovely perfumed fruit, while the 2009 is ripe and fleshy with liquorice and an elegant finish. The 2008 is very intriguing; it almost tasted not unlike old Burgundy from Pinot Noir.

When asked about typicity, Brigitte says she looks for elegant drinkability. She likes what she calls the *côté digeste*, the digestibility of Faugères: *douceur,* or sweetness, and *finesse*, with elegant tannins. Mourvèdre is her favourite variety because it has an original aromatic range, with sweet spices, and is not aggressive. She observes that schist concentrates the virile character of Mourvèdre and enthuses about her enjoyment of working with schist. When she was looking for her vineyards, she sought out schist above all else, as well as altitude and north-facing vines. And you sense, tasting with Brigitte, that she is a very meticulous, observant, not to mention talented wine grower. She now has, she says, a much better understanding of her vines, and I think her wines have evolved beautifully in less than ten years. She will go far.

Château Haut Lignières

Le Bel Air, Faugères 34600
Tel: 04 67 95 38 27
hautlignieres@yahoo.fr
www.chateau-hautlignieres.com

The estate of Haut Lignières was initially created by a Swiss woman, Elke Kreutzfeldt, who sold an insurance business and bought vineyards in Faugères when her daughter married a local wine grower's son. Her first vintage was in 1995, and the first two vintages were made at the nearby Château de Grézan, until she bought her own cellar at the top of the village of Faugères, on the main road by the petrol station. Subsequently she acquired a second cellar, at the bottom of the village. Then, after a spell of ill-health, she decided to sell, and in 2007 Jérôme Rateau bought the property with its two cellars and 12 hectares of vines.

Jérôme Rateau comes from Normandy, from the Perche, and had no connections with wine at all other than a grandfather who had a small plot of vines in Champagne and a father who loved wine. He remembers helping with his grandfather's harvest as a small boy, but certainly had no ambitions to make wine himself. Initially he had planned a career in sport, but was forced to rethink this following an injury. He also enjoyed science, particularly biology, and that led to a degree in oenology at Bordeaux. His first job was to work for a large Bordeaux estate which produced 10,000 hectolitres a year. He learned a lot there – 'mainly what not to do', he says – and then worked as a consultant oenologist. He is quite entertaining about this, especially about how people respond to an oenologist's advice and whether they take it or not; apparently growers often employ an oenologist when what they really want is to know what their neighbours are up to.

But Jérôme realized that what he really wanted to do was to make his own wine. He wrote a business plan and enlisted support from his parents; after a lot of looking, initially in Bordeaux and then beyond, he eventually came to Faugères where he bought Haut Lignières in time to help with the 2007 harvest. He was taken by the *terroir*, the slopes of Faugères and the schist soil.

The estate consists of 12 hectares in Cabrerolles in one large block, planted with the usual five varieties of the Languedoc, and Jérôme has also rented another 3 hectares. The name of the *lieu dit* of his plot is Bas Lignières, so for the original Swiss owner the name Haut Lignières was a natural corollary. Jérôme has planted just 36 ares of white varieties – Roussanne, Grenache Blanc and Vermentino – but has yet to produce any white wine. The vines are taking their time to get established.

Jérôme has a tasting caveau at the top of the main street in Faugères. The rosé is a blend, mainly of Cinsaut with Grenache Noir and a little Syrah, all free-run juice. The juice gets darker depending on how long it spends on the skins. If you are running off juice, using the *saigné* method to concentrate your red wine, you should never run off more than 20 per cent of the vat, but for a vat intended to be nothing but rosé, 50 per cent is acceptable, and the Cinsaut is picked earlier than it would be for red wine. The nose is very fresh, and the wine very refreshing, with good acidity, some minerality and a dry finish. Jérôme observes that 'It is very easy to make a rosé that smells of raspberries and *bonbons anglais*. It is all to do with the volatile esters, and depends on the cultured yeasts and the fermentation temperature. That sort of rosé doesn't usually have any staying power.'

He makes four different *cuvées* of red Faugères. Faugères le 1er is the most representative. It is a blend of all five varieties of the appellation, about 20 per cent of each. It is usually blended in March and bottled in July after a simple vinification and an *élevage* in vat. It has lovely supple ripe fruit with a lightly tannic streak. 'This is what Faugères *gives* me', Jérôme says, 'but with the other *cuvées* I try to see what I can *make* from Faugères'.

Next comes Romy, which in 2011 was a blend of 50 per cent Grenache Noir and 35 per cent Mourvèdre with 15 per cent Carignan. The Carignan was aged in barrel for ten months, with the rest in vat. In contrast, for 2012 the blend is one-third Syrah to two-thirds Grenache, with no Carignan and all aged in vat; in 2012 the Mourvèdre was disappointing. Jérôme is guided by the character of the vintage, while retaining the style of the wine. That is the advantage of having all five grape varieties to play with. The 2012 is very expressive of Grenache Noir and more *gourmand* and concentrated than the 2011. Jérôme wants a wine that is rounded, silky and elegant. The oak gives an extra touch of spice and is beautifully integrated.

Faugères, Carmine Butis is mainly Syrah, with some Grenache Noir and a little Mourvèdre. Two-thirds of the wine is aged in *barriques* for about fifteen months. Jérôme has lots of *barriques* of individual grape varieties and then blends after the first racking, keeping the blended wine in barrel for a further twelve months or so. There is a vanilla touch on the nose, with a sturdier, denser, more youthful palate and a rich finish.

Jérôme used to make a Grand Réserve, but that has now been replaced by a new wine, Empreinte Carbone. In 2011 Jérôme had a *stagiaire* who was particularly interested in natural wine, so the *stagiaire* was allowed to experiment – the result was one barrel that was brilliant, and two that were sent to the distillery. Thus 280 bottles were bottled under the name of Empreinte Carbone, a pure Syrah, and the result of meticulous attention to a 22-ares plot of vines. Jérôme has pursued the experiment further and made both a 2012 and a 2013. However, he is quite dispassionate about natural wine, observing the problem of uncertainty with them; they are simply not reliable, and also people are tolerant of their defects because they are natural. He does not fine any of his wine, and he only filters Faugères le 1ᵉʳ and his rosé, as they are bottled earlier. Nor is he organic. He may use a small amount of a systemic product, which would reduce the amount of copper and sulphur he might otherwise use, and in any case he only treats when absolutely necessary.

In the future Jérôme has no ambitions to grow much bigger, he says; maybe 20 hectares at the most. He speculates that it might be more efficient to have fewer vineyards, so that they could receive even better attention. He is also planning to make a white wine to complete his range. For me, he is a fine example of the new generation of outsiders who are contributing to the success of Faugères.

Mas Lou

4 rue du Portail d'Amant, Faugères 34600
Tel : 06 77 81 06 44
contact@mas-lou.com
www.mas-lou.com

Olivier Gil and Adèle Arnaud have bought Catherine Roque's old cellar in the heart of the village of Faugères. Olivier comes from a family of *vignerons*; his father has 16 hectares in Tourbes, which Oliver is now running. Most, but not all, of the grapes go to the Montagnac cooperative, which has taken over the Tourbes cooperative. Olivier studied oenology at Montpellier where he met Adèle, who does not come from a winemaking family, though she describes her parents as '*grands amateurs*' or great wine enthusiasts. Studies then took them to Dijon and to Toulouse; they worked in South America, and in Collioure, which gave them a different experience of schist, and then they knew that they wanted to go it alone. Pierre Alibert from Domaine Ste Cécile, an estate which sold mainly bulk wine, was retiring and so they took over his vines in Fos on 1 January 2014 and have called their new estate 'Mas Lou'. There are 8.3 hectares, in seven plots, with the usual five varieties. The vines are in good condition, with some newly planted vines, some 45-year-old Mourvèdre, some old Grenache Noir, and some 100-year-old Carignan. Olivier says that he has had to buy a tractor suitable for hillsides as his father's vineyards in Tourbes are all on the plain.

As they had no Faugères for me to taste at our initial meeting, they brought a bottle of their very first wine, from 10 ares of Viognier among Olivier's father's vines. It had a touch of oak and some delicate peachy fruit. They used traditional Burgundian methods, with a gentle pressing, some *bâtonnage* and some barrel ageing; I thought it a great start. We then met again a few months later, the day before they were due to bottle their first Faugères, so I was able to taste vat samples of a rosé and the three reds.

The names of the various *cuvées* relate to their stay in South America. The rosé, Selva, for the Amazonian forest, is a blend of 80 per cent Mourvèdre with some Grenache Noir, with some fresh acidity and red fruit. The first red, Angaco, is a blend of old Carignan with some Grenache Noir and a smaller amount of Lledoner Pelut, with some ripe cherry liqueur fruit and fresh acidity and balancing tannins, with an appealing drinkability. Aksou is a blend of 60 per cent Syrah with Grenache Noir, of which almost half is aged in wood, giving some peppery fruit and nicely integrated oak. Tio, of which there are just three barrels, is a pure Syrah from one plot in Fos on a steep slope at 320 metres; it was redolent of black fruit and pepper. Olivier says that he was looking for elegance and concentration, and for supple tannins, and that is certainly what he has achieved. He sees himself as a traditionalist and wants wines that represent the appellation, staying within the classic Faugères framework of *finesse* and *fraicheur*. He has made a great start.

Domaine de la Tour Penedesses

2 rue Droite, Faugères 34600
Tel: 04 67 95 17 21
latourpenedesses@yahoo.fr
www.domainedelatourpenedesses.com

Alexandre Fourque has had a varied career. He was brought up in the Var and studied landscape gardening in Montpellier and worked in Cassis. Then he turned to viti-oenology studies, first in Beaune and then in Champagne, after which he worked at Clos Pegase and Domaine Chandon in California, and also in Oregon and at the cooperative in St Tropez. He finally landed up in the Languedoc, buying Coteaux du Languedoc vineyards in 1999, and Faugères in 2004. He has a large cellar just outside the village of Gabian, but Faugères has to be vinified within the appellation – so for that he has a small and rather cramped but atmospheric old cellar off the main street in the heart of the village, with a tasting *caveau* in what was once the old grocer's shop. There is some old equipment at the back, a plough and an old *pulverisateur*. Alexandre and his girlfriend Gaëlle have renovated the old house behind their cellar, turning it into a gîte, and decorating it with some attractive old wine artefacts and photos.

The name of the estate comes from a vineyard near Gabian, Clos Penedesses, with 75-year old Grenache Noir. Altogether Alexandre has 40 hectares, 15 of which are Faugères, and all are cultivated organically. He has created his estate from scratch, with no family help. Faugères was originally full of family dynasties, but things are changing with the newcomers; none the less, he says, life is not easy if you are not a *fils de vigneron*. In addition it is a tough job – not just the vineyards and the wine, but also marketing, planning investments, paperwork, administration, public relations; the list is endless. He wanted an estate with variety, and enjoys the diversity of the soils of the Languedoc.

Tasting with him entails an eclectic range of different flavours. Alexandre made his first Faugères Blanc in 2013. It comes mainly from Vermentino with some Marsanne and Roussanne, and a little Viognier. Part of it is fermented in oak with some *bâtonnage*. Alexandre has Corsican links and adores Vermentino, as it is the principal grape variety of the best Corsican whites. He is planting more Vermentino because he finds Marsanne and Roussanne can be complicated if there is a lack of water.

As for red Faugères, he makes two different *cuvées*. La Montagne Noire is 60 per cent Syrah, with old Carignan plus a little Grenache Noir and Mourvèdre. For the Syrah, the vinification begins in vat and is finished in 500-litre barrels. The result is sweet and ripe. The Cuvée les Raisins de la Colère (or the grapes of wrath) seems to reflect Alexandre's state of mind, as he feels that the village is sometimes not necessarily very helpful to outsiders. The wine is predominantly Syrah with 20 per cent Mourvèdre, coming from vineyards at 450 metres, fermented in new oak after a pre-fermentation maceration. I found it ripe and dense, with a strong impact of oak.

AUTIGNAC

Autignac is one of the larger villages of the appellation and repays a leisurely visit. There are some substantial houses, the vestiges of a wealthier period. Some have been restored, but others are sadly shuttered.

Domaine de l'Ancienne Mercerie

6 rue de l'Egalité, Autignac 34480
Tel: 04 67 90 27 02
ancienne.mercerie@free.fr
www.anciennemercerie.fr

Nathalie and François Caumette from Domaine de l'Ancienne Mercerie live and work in a house on the edge of the village of Autignac which was indeed once the old village haberdashers, hence the name of the estate and the theme of the names of their two *cuvées*.

The family history is probably not dissimilar to many others. François's grandfather was brought up in the Aveyron, but came south and bought vines. He joined the village cooperative, partly because he had no experience of winemaking and partly because he firmly believed in the socialist philosophy of the cooperative movement. He bought the only vines he could afford on the poor land of the hillsides, and always dreamed of having higher yielding and more remunerative vines on the plain. It was hard work. Yields from the hillsides of schist were low and yet all the cooperative members were paid the same for their grapes by weight, irrespective of quality and provenance. François's father did not stay on the land; he was an anaesthetist. When the grandfather died in 1986 they could not sell the hillside vines; some were pulled up and some were kept, since by then François was studying agriculture at Montpellier and specializing in viticulture. He and Nathalie met in Montpellier; she had come from Paris to study there. They quickly realized that keeping their vines with the cooperative, in this case the one in Laurens, was not a viable economic option, especially as the cooperative was on the verge of bankruptcy; the only thing to do was to make their own wine. They took over the existing vineyards in 1996 and bought more; it has taken them ten years to establish an estate of 17 hectares in Autignac

Nathalie Caumette, of Domaine de l'Ancienne Mercerie and the energetic president of the growers' syndicat

and Laurens, including 2 hectares of appellation Languedoc. The 2000 was their first vintage. François and Nathalie speak of how they had learned *sur place*. The vineyards are cultivated organically; the cellar at the back of the house is very simple and functional with stainless steel vats and some cement vats, as well as barriques and *demi muids*.

They make two *cuvées* of Faugères: les Petites Mains, and Couture. Les Petites Mains includes about 50 per cent Carignan, which gives it a *sympathique* note of rusticity and it is aged in vat, while Couture is at least 40 per cent Carignan, including their best plots of Carignan, with equal parts of Syrah and Grenache Noir. Couture is aged in lightly toasted *demi-muids* from the Bordeaux cooper Darnajoux. François likes Carignan, which makes up 40 per cent of their vineyards, while Nathalie is more enthusiastic about Grenache Noir, enjoying the way that '*il pinotte*' becomes Pinot Noir-like with age. Carignan is a very rigid variety, while Grenache is more fluid. Nathalie enthuses about the *esprit d'assemblage* that is essential with Faugères, 'and that you have to look after your soil, and work it well and preserve the old vines'.

They also make a Languedoc, Au Bonheur des Dames, a blend of equal parts of Mourvèdre and Grenache Noir from vineyards south of Autignac, outside the appellation. And, in 2014, they made their first white wine, a blend of Roussanne and Grenache Blanc. They had pulled up their Grenache Gris as it was not in the *cahier de charge* – 'what a mistake that was.'

Nathalie is currently president of the Faugères wine growers' syndicat. Her most recent achievement is the acceptance of Faugères as a *cru du* Languedoc, thereby enhancing its status in the hierarchy of the Languedoc.

Domaine Balliccioni

1 Chemin de Ronde, Autignac 34480
Tel: 06 11 12 02 41
ballivin@sfr.fr

Véronique and André Balliccioni have their cellar in the middle of Autignac, and offered me a friendly welcome. André originally hails from Corsica, from the town of Bastia, and arrived in the Languedoc when he was twelve. Subsequently he married Véronique, who was born and bred in Autignac. André has run a small PR business but had always wanted to make wine, which he did for the first time in 1998. However, he really considers 2001 to be his first proper vintage. He has learned from colleagues and worked three vintages at Domaine Laquirou in la Clape. Altogether they now have 9 hectares of Faugères as well as 3 hectares of Côtes de Thongue, which were reclassified from Coteaux de Murviel in 2013. André observes that the Coteaux de Murviel would probably disappear before too long.

André reminisces about the cellar, remembering how it had an earthen floor when he first arrived. It is part of a typical Languedoc house, which originally had the cellar and stable on the ground floor; the people lived above, and a hundred years ago wealth was measured by the number of horses you owned. The small vinification cellar is now crammed full of stainless steel tanks; for *élevage* André prefers 500-litre barrels.

André does not make any white Faugères because he does not have the correct grape varieties, so instead we started tasting with an IGP (Indication Géographique Protégée) Chardonnay; this is light and fresh. André is also wondering about Terret Blanc, as he likes the idea of preserving the old varieties.

Next came a rosé from Grenache Noir, which was *saigné*, and from Cinsaut, which was pressed. A cool fermentation made for a light fresh wine. Then we tasted a pure Aramon, a grape variety that has been much decried and despised in the past, but I enjoyed this. It can be quite *vif* or lively when young, but it has some light berry fruit with an appealing touch of rusticity. Cuvée Jules, named after André's father, is a blend of 80 per cent Aramon with 10 per cent each of Carignan and Syrah. It is richer and fleshier than the pure Aramon, with more weight, some ripe berry fruit and a tannic streak. André has just 50 ares of 100-year-old Aramon vines.

Léon, named in honour of Véronique's grandfather, is an IGP or *vin de pays* because, although it is made from Carignan, Grenache, Mourvèdre and Cinsaut, the vineyards lie outside the appellation of Faugères.

The Faugères Tradition is a blend of Syrah, Grenache, Cinsaut and Carignan, aged in vat. I like this a lot, with its rich spicy fruit and supple tannins. André explains that he looks for *rondeur, chaleur* and *puissance* with *douceur*, tasting terms which sound so much more poetic than the English 'rounded, warmth and power with some sweetness'. That is just what he achieved in 2012. However, I prefer his 2011, with the same blend, but with more prunes, liquorice and even a touch of leather, plus a silky finish.

Orchis is 30 per cent Mourvèdre, aged in wood, blended with 70 per cent Grenache Noir aged in tank, and named after a purple orchid found in the hills above Porto on Corsica, which is the colour of the wine. The Corsican theme appears again in the name Kalliste, which is how the Greeks described Corsica when they arrived there, meaning *la plus belle*, the most beautiful. The wine is mainly Syrah and Carignan, and sometimes includes Grenache Noir, aged in 500-litre barrels for about fourteen months. It is exuberant, with plenty of potential, and with ripe chocolate fruit on the palate. A great finale.

Domaine Clamouse

Impasse des Oliviers, Magalas 34480
Tel : 04 67 36 00 41
domaine.clamouse@orange.fr
www.domaine-clamouse.fr

For Jacques Clamouse, the first vintage in 2010 was the fulfilment of a lifelong ambition. Members of his family have been wine growers for eight generations in Faugères and nearby Pouzolles, but his parents wanted him to do something else, so he worked for Renault in Paris and Lyon, but was always passionate about vines and wine. He retired in 2000 and came south. Two hectares of abandoned family vines in the village of Laurens remained; the rest had been sold. He replanted with Grenache Noir, Syrah and Mourvèdre, and bought some Carignan, explaining that if you have not declared a harvest for eight years, you lose any planting rights, and to obtain planting rights, you need to be a wine grower. It is a chicken and egg situation, what Jacques describes as a *parcours de combatant*, fighting bureaucracy. His main objective is to make good wine in a small quantity.

Sadly his children are not interested in their father's vineyard – 'they think I am mad' – otherwise he would have developed more vineyards. He has also suffered a very severe bout of illness, after which wine proved to be a great way to help him regain his health. So he now produces 7000 bottles of red and 2000 bottles of rosé, using the Vino-Tec facilities at Autignac. His vineyards are run by the Château de Grézan, so they are worked sustainably; Jacques had been in the process of converting to organic viticulture when he was taken ill. Everything else he does himself: 'Wine growing is a noble profession, and it is complicated.' He is very proud of what he has achieved, and rightly so. His rosé is fresh and crisp, while his red Faugères is predominantly Syrah with some Mourvèdre, Grenache Noir and Carignan. It spends twelve months in a stainless steel vat and has perfumed fruit and spice, with supple tannins. I admire his courage and determination.

Château de Ciffre

c/o Château de Pennautier, Pennautier 11610
Tel: 04 68 72 65 29
contact@lorgeril.com
www.lorgeril.com

This is the one estate that crosses the boundary between St Chinian and Faugères with adjoining vineyards in both appellations; you can look out on a slope of vines and see the clear fault line which separates the two. Miren and Nicolas de Lorgeril, who own Château Pennautier in Cabardès, bought Moulin de Ciffre (now called Château de Ciffre) in 2007 after the previous owner, Jacques Lésineau, had died in a car accident. Initially they only thought to buy the vineyards, but they fell in love with the place, which is in a beautifully isolated and peaceful spot along a dirt track outside the village of Autignac. It is a historic wine estate – it has links with the Roman villa of nearby Château de Coujan – and has a water mill as well as a windmill, to which a previous owner added a house in the 1970s. A magnificent old pine tree shades the terrace.

The vineyards are in a cool valley, with the Pic de la Coquillade visible in the distance. The 15 hectares of Faugères are on schist, whereas those of St Chinian are on clay and limestone. The climate is the same; both appellations are predominantly Grenache Noir and Syrah, with vines of a similar age, but the soil is different and the wines do indeed taste different.

Miren de Lorgeril describes the estate as a sleeping beauty. They have a classic Languedoc cellar with large cement vats and some *barriques*, but the vineyards need attention. They need to *retravailler les sols*, improve the soil and replace some vines. The style of the wine is also in the process of transformation. The previous winemaker favoured a long *élevage* in oak, whereas Bernard Durand exercises a more restrained hand with barrels. Patrick Léon, who used to work at Château Mouton-

Rothschild, advises, and also helps to encourage the more subtle use of oak with more balanced wines.

I was treated to a series of mini-vertical tastings, of their Cuvées Terroirs d'Altitude for both St Chinian and Faugères, and then les Pins St Chinian and le Causse Faugères. In each instance the 2010 made by the previous incumbent is solidly oaky, whereas the 2011, which Bernard blended, shows a much more subtle expression of the *terroir*. The 2012s are still fairly adolescent, while the 2013s are definitely still in their nappies, but promise well. Bernard feels that oak works better on Faugères than on St Chinian, as Faugères has more body and the flavours are nicely integrated. As for the house style, they look for freshness and balance, and seek to express each *terroir*.

Domaine des Prés-Lasses

26 avenue de la Liberté, Autignac 34480
Tel: 06 03 40 27 75
boris.feigel@pres-lasses.com
www.pres-lasses.com

Denis Feigal was an oenologist in Alsace, working for the cooperative of Kientzheim, and then decided, with a friend, to create a wine estate. Buying vines in Alsace was not an option: they were either too expensive or not for sale. So they turned to the Languedoc and spent four years looking, focusing on Faugères and also Montpeyroux. Why the Languedoc? Because they liked the taste and vineyard land was affordable. The first 9 hectares were bought in 1999, with Prés-Lasses the name of the very first plot they purchased, and they now have a total of 30 hectares in the villages of Lenthéric, Autignac and Laurens, including 8 hectares of old Carignan that are between 60 and 90 years old. They have also bought the Château d'Autignac, which is one of the so-called *châteaux pinardiers*. It was built in 1860 from the proceeds of wine, and is now being completely restored for *chambres d'hôte* as well as a barrel cellar. The vinification cellar is across the courtyard.

Meanwhile Denis's son Boris had begun his interest in wine as a teenager. He first studied economics at university and then did a BTS *alternée*, which combines both studies and work experience with the latter, in his case, at Zind Humbrecht in Alsace. Now he runs Domaine des Prés-Lasses, and has been making the wine since 2005, although his father still retains a very active interest in the estate.

Initially there were just two Faugères. Chemin de Ronde includes all five grape varieties, and the name recalls the fact that the village of Autignac is one of the *circulade* villages of the Languedoc. The wine spends two winters in vat and is nicely spicy with some structure. Le Castel Viel is mainly Carignan with some Grenache Noir and Syrah and a little Mourvèdre, aged in old wood. Boris explained that his father loves old wines, especially old Burgundy, and considers that Carignan gives structure to the wine which allows for ageing potential. Next they added Amour Faugères, which is mainly Grenache Noir and kept in vat (their old cellars were in the rue de l'Amour, hence the name). The Grenache Noir makes for some ripe fruit, while the addition of some Cinsaut helps lower the alcoholic degree, as Cinsaut is ripe at 12% abv.

Boria (meaning a little *borie* or *capitelle)* is 90 per cent Syrah, aged for eighteen months in oak, some new and some barrels of one and two fills. It is ripe and oaky, and quite intense. Boris admits that he would not choose to make this style of Faugères, but his father's associate particularly likes Syrah; however, it is not made every year. Generally Boris likes a long ageing for his Faugères, over two winters. He uses natural yeast and favours minimum intervention, stating that each time you add sulphur, you lose something. He will, however, add a little sulphur at bottling.

Our tasting finished with their white wine, a blend of 70 per cent Carignan Blanc with Grenache Blanc. Boris wants a white wine with character that will age, so just 20 per cent of it is fermented and aged in barrel, which makes for a wine that is quite honeyed and ripe with a firm streak of acidity and a fresh finish. Boris considers that the Carignan Blanc preserves acidity and represents the *terroir.*

Boris also talks about his projects and about his vineyards. They are organic, with older bush vines. He tends to leave the grass and tills the soil, but not too often, and would like to plant some Mourvèdre and also some Grenache Gris. He is impatient to see the end of the building work in the *château* because he will then have a barrel cellar, which will enable him to age his wines for longer. I look forward to seeing the Château d'Autignac restored to its full splendour.

Domaine de la Reynardière

7 cours Jean-Moulin, St Geniès-de-Fontedit 34480
Tel: 04 67 36 25 75
domaine.reynardiere@orange.fr
www.reynardiere.fr

Jean-Michel Mégé has his cellars in St Geniès-de-Fontedit. He has 65 hectares of vines altogether, including 12 hectares of Faugères, with the majority
of his vineyards in the Côtes de Thongue. Faugères must be vinified within
the appellation, so he has a cellar in Autignac for that, while the cellars in St
Geniès are used for white and pink Côtes de Thongue. It all goes back to his
grandparents, he explains: his grandfather had vines at St Geniès, and his
great uncle had vines and a cellar at Autignac. Domaine de la Reynardière
was created in 1986 initially for *vin de pays* and then, in 1990, Jean-Michel
joined up with his cousins. They now produce both Faugères and Côtes de
Thongue, with 1990 their first vintage of Faugères in bottle.

I limited myself to tasting just the Faugères. His rosé, a blend of
Syrah and Grenache Noir, is quite light and crisp. We moved on to the
red Faugères, as he does not make any white Faugères. Unusually in
January 2014, he was selling 2007 Faugères as his current vintage. He
is very insistent that older wines represent the house style of the estate,
and they are very popular in China. His wine spends three years in vat,
and it did seem to me that it had aged gracefully, with notes of *sous bois*
and leather, but was there enough fruit?

The Cuvée Prestige comes from Syrah planted in the 1970s as well as
very old Carignan planted in the late 1940s; the latter has a high mortality
rate, making the vineyard difficult to manage. The 2008 has a little more
concentration and curiously did not taste six years old. The *cuvée fût de
chêne* is the same blend as the Prestige, but spends three months in new
wood after four years in vat. I found the nose rather oaky. Jean-Michel
says that an *élevage* in wood and then in vat did not work for him; I was
not sure the oak added anything, but he has clients who like it.

We finished with his Grand Terroir de Schiste, from his oldest vines:
Carignan planted in 1946, and Syrah and Grenache Noir from the
1970s. The wine spends four months in *barriques* after five months in
vat, with a three-week maceration for a classic fermentation. Although
the grapes are hand picked and not destalked, Jean-Michel does not do
a carbonic maceration, as he finds that can create problems, with the

fruit fading too quickly during the *élevage*. So, if you are looking for mature wines, Domaine de la Reynardière is the place to visit.

Domaine du Rouge Gorge

Route de St Geniès Magalas 34480
Tel: 04 67 36 22 86
sceaborda@orange.fr
www.borda-vins.com

The Borda family have two wine estates, Domaine du Rouge Gorge for Faugères and Domaine des Affaniès for *vins de pays*, making a total of 128 hectares, of which 44 hectares are Faugères. Although their Faugères is made in Autignac, they prefer to receive their visitors in St Geniès-de-Fontedit. I could quite see why Philippe Borda wanted to show off their wonderful collection of wine artefacts. There are old pumps, run on petrol or electricity, not to mention manual ones, and in the cellar there is an old alembic plus numerous old copper taps for vats, pristine and shining.

Philippe explains that his father Alain began in 1968 with just 5 hectares and bottled his first wine in 1982, with the creation of the appellation of Faugères. The name of the estate recalls a robin that would come to eat the crumbs when his mother shook the tablecloth outside after lunch, and a robin (or even two) features on all their labels.

Philippe took over a majority share in the estate ten years ago, and these days he makes three qualities of Faugères. There is a simple rosé which is light and fresh, and a rounded fruity red. Initially there was just the one red, but then they developed Privilege, with two robins on the label as it was the creation of father and son; Syrah dominates, with some Grenache Noir and Carignan, with older vines and some ageing in barrel. Then Philippe developed Le Souhait de Mon Père, which is more serious with a longer *cuvaison* and from older vines (asked if this did indeed correspond to his father's wishes, he observed that his father had not been very communicative on the subject). And as for his house style, Philippe replies: 'Easy to drink and a good price/quality relationship.' He is also very proud that his vineyards are the cleanest of the appellation: they till between the rows and use chemical weed killer between the vines. However, it is really the winemaking and the commerce that he prefers. His work starts when the grapes arrive in the cellar and, he says, stops when the taxes are paid.

Domaine St Martin d'Agel

Magalas 34480
Tel : 06 80 75 59 28
lugagne.delpon@wanadoo.fr

This is an extensive property with vineyards mainly on the flat land between Magalas and Laurens, an area which is not part of the appellation of Faugères, though in fact it is only 500 metres from the appellation boundary. Consequently the cellar there is used for *vins de pays* and appellation Languedoc, while the Faugères of St Martin d'Agel are made in a cellar in Autignac that the Lugagne-Delpon family once owned but now rent – it was sold to provide a dowry for a daughter who was going to be a nun. Altogether the estate consists of 11 hectares of Faugères, 11 hectares appellation Languedoc and 11 hectares for Pays d'Oc.

Céline Lugagne-Delpon and her brother are working with Pierre Roque to develop the wines of St Martin d'Agel. Their first Faugères vintage was 2008. These vineyards are in a large valley close to Laurens, and they have various projects to develop a tasting *caveau* at St Martin d'Agel, having just reunited the two halves of the property which was split by inheritance three generations ago. They concentrate on red Faugères, with no white wine and not even a rosé. Vat samples of 2013 have some appealing fresh perfumed fruit with some weight.

Auprès de la Vigne recalls the Georges Brassens song 'Auprès de mon arbre', while Le Pèlerin refers to the nearby route to Santiago de Compostella, with a wayside chapel. The final *cuvée* is La Chapelle, with an emphasis on Mourvèdre. Céline considers Mourvèdre to be a speciality of the estate. She is ambitious and has given Pierre Roque *carte blanche*. I learnt a new French expression there: '*on ne veut pas moutonner!*' implying that they were not going to hang about or waste time.

CABREROLLES, LENTHÉRIC AND LA LIQUIÈRE

The village of Cabrerolles includes the two hamlets of Lenthéric and La Liquière. It is one of the more northern villages of Faugères, lying at the foot of the Pic de la Coquillade. The path up to the top of the Pic starts in the centre of the village and takes you past the picturesque ruins of the medieval castle.

Domaine du Météore

Route d'Aigues-Vives
Cabrerolles 34480
Tel: 04 67 90 21 12
domainedumeteore@wanadoo.fr

Rather wonderfully, Domaine du Météore does indeed take its name from a meteor crater outside the village of Cabrerolles. The crater is a gaping hole in the earth's surface, some 60 metres deep and 200 metres in circumference, with 70 ares of vines at the bottom.

Geneviève Libes is the fifth generation of wine growers at Cabrerolles. Her great-grandmother grew Carignan and Aramon between the two world wars, and had vines at the bottom of the crater without knowing that was what it was – some visiting geologists in 1950 enlightened the family. It is an easy walk from the village and worth the detour to peer into the deep crater. However, it was Geneviève's father who really created the estate. The family had never been cooperative members, preferring to sell *en vrac* to the *négoce*, but her father began bottling in 1978. Geneviève took over the estate when her father died in 1983 and has gradually developed the vineyards, buying and replanting. Now they also make some St Chinian, as her husband's family have vines in St Nazaire which they took over in 2008.

Altogether they have 23 hectares, including 5 hectares of St Chinian, which they are allowed to vinify in their cellars in Cabrerolles as the two appellations adjoin each other. Their vineyards in St Chinian are also on schist, but the schist there is different, as Geneviève explains. It is grey *ardoisier* schist and more friable, whereas the schist of Cabrerolles is *gréseux*, brown in colour, and makes for more velvety wine.

All their *cuvées* are named after constellations. White Les Léonides is a blend of equal parts of Marsanne and Roussanne with 20 per cent Rolle, given some skin contact and some *bâtonnage* in vat. It is rounded and herbal with a certain weight on the palate and a firm finish. Léonides Rosé is a blend of Syrah, Grenache and Cinsaut, with fresh acidity and some cherry fruit, while Léonides Rouge, from equal parts of Grenache Noir, Syrah, Mourvèdre and 70-year-old Carignan, has a stony minerality. Geneviève and I compared it with their St Chinian, Clos de Bijou, which is mainly Syrah, with some Carignan and Grenache Noir. Unlike Faugères, there is no obligation to have Mourvèdre in St Chinian; the regulations say either Syrah or Mourvèdre. It is an intriguing comparison; Geneviève thinks the Faugères is more 'charmeur', and I think the St Chinian is fresher – but it is also a year younger, so I did not come to any great conclusions.

Orionides spends twelve months in wood, some *barriques* and some 300- and 400-litre barrels, and they are also buying some 600-litre barrels as well as experimenting with larger containers. Perséides, from 50 per cent Syrah and 50 per cent Mourvèdre, with a longer maceration on the skins and eighteen-month ageing in mainly new oak barrels, is altogether more serious, with restrained oak, a firm streak of tannin and some peppery sour cherry fruit, with a mineral finish.

Les Lyrides, which was made for the first time in 2006, is 80 per cent Syrah with 20 per cent Mourvèdre. It is not made every year as the Syrah has to be exceptional. After twenty-two months in new oak it is firm and peppery, with elegant concentration.

Geneviève talks about converting to organic viticulture. They already practise *lutte raisonnée*, but the key change was the purchase of an *intercep*, which weeds mechanically between the vines within the row. Then everything fell into place, though nothing changed in the cellar. I asked Geneviève about the typicity of the estate, to which she replies 'vins de garde'. She looks for *fraicheur* and *rondeur* with *finesse*. And I think that is what she has achieved.

Mas Nicolas

Chemin du Coudougno, Cabrerolles 34480
Tel : 06 87 49 81 28
contact@vin-masnicolas-34.com
www.vin-masnicolas-34.com

Nicolas Maury is one of the four new young wine growers who made their first Faugères in 2014. His father, Philippe, is currently president of the cooperative, as was his grandfather, so viticulture is in his genes. However, he is the first member of his family to make his own wine. He has rented 4.5 hectares from his father, plots that could be released from the contract with the cooperative. Nicolas learned his viticulture from his father, but realized he really wanted to make his own wine and that simply to continue as a cooperative member would not be very interesting or rewarding.

Nicolas is busy fine-tuning the small cellar on the family estate of Coudougno, on the road to Aigues-Vives from Lenthéric. It was previously a tractor shed with an earthen floor; horizontal tanks, which are almost square in shape, making for a good extraction of colour, have been installed, and Nicolas is preparing a small barrel cellar. As 'Coudougno' is used as the name of one of the cooperative's *cuvées*, Nicolas has decided on 'Mas Nicolas' for the name of his wines.

Asked about subsidies for a young *vigneron*, Nicolas explains that you have to have a minimum of 10 hectares in order to qualify, a viable vineyard holding and cellar, with your own tractor and so on. He feels that this is much too big for a beginner. And when I quizzed him about whether his father had given up the best plots, he pertinently says that they do not actually know how their wine would taste, as all the grapes go into the cooperative vat. He has vines at Caussiniojouls: some Carignan, Grenache Noir, Syrah, Cinsaut and just ten rows of Mourvèdre, and also some Viognier. He had made just 8 hectolitres of the Viognier so we tasted a wine that had barely finished fermenting; it promised well.

A second visit the following spring gave me the opportunity to taste his red wines, which were still in vat or barrel. A red from vat is a blend of 40 per cent each of Grenache Noir and Carignan with some Syrah, which has fresh cherry fruit and a streak of tannin. The wine from the 100-year-old Carignan was in barrel and shows good fruit with some sturdy tannins, while a Syrah has some peppery notes and the spice of the *garrigues*. Nicolas's label is illustrated with a quince flower as '*coudou*' in Occitan is a quince, and '*coudougno*' means a place where quinces grow. And Nicolas remarks 'I have everything to discover.' It will be a great adventure and he is not afraid; he has a lot of support from his family.

Domaine Raymond Roque

Place du Château, Cabrerolles 34480
Tel : 04 67 90 24 74
roqueraymond@wanadoo.fr

The Roque family have been making wine in Cabrerolles for at least five generations, since 1874 or maybe earlier. These days, as Marc Roque observes, 'we don't know how to do anything else'. You sense a quiet contentment with his lot, as well as a modest pride. It was his father, Raymond, who first put his wine in bottle back in 1975. They still have one of the original bottles with a delightfully old-fashioned label.

Marc has an old cellar at the top of the village of Cabrerolles, where he receives clients, below the ruins of the eleventh-century château. It has a wonderful vaulted ceiling and you need to avoid banging your head on salted hams hanging from it. The estate now comprises 30 hectares, all at Cabrerolles and all organic since 1999. Marc was amongst the first organic wine growers in Faugères, but he has reservations about the term, preferring to see it as a return to traditional cultivation. As for the winemaking, he aims to be as natural and as traditional as possible, avoiding the use of sulphur. He says that he vinifies '*au feeling*' and admits he had given up on studies and learned from experience. His vineyards are predominantly Grenache Noir and Carignan, and he particularly likes both Carignan and Cinsaut, but has nothing against Syrah: 'There are no bad grape varieties, only bad *vignerons*.' It is up to the wine grower to make the best of each variety.

His Tradition is predominantly Grenache Noir, with a short maceration, making for some rich cherry fruit. Grand Réserve is based on Carignan with more structured fruit and nicely rustic tannins. Marc does not favour long macerations or big extractions. Le Palais des Papes is a blend of Grenache Noir and Carignan with twelve months' *élevage* in barrel, with nicely integrated oak. And in 2013 he made Nature, without any sulphur at all. The wine has a wonderful freshness, and Marc observes that the acidity of the vintage compensated for the lack of sulphur; normally he would put ice cubes in his sun hat during the harvest in an attempt to keep cool, but they'd not been needed that year. He actually prefers a mechanical harvester, declaring '*je suis mauvais patron*': managing people is not for him. And then he adds that he is '*fainéant*', or lazy, jokingly adding 'I am not from the south for nothing'. Yet this relaxed attitude belies some shrewd observation and careful winemaking.

Vignoble les Fusionels

Route d'Aigues-Vives, Cabrerolles 34480
Tel : 06 07 03 56 16
arielledemets@outlook.fr
www.vignobleslesfusionels.com

I first came across les Fusionels at the Faugères *fête* in 2009 and was immediately struck by the quality. The name of the estate is inspired by the fusion of France and Australia, of the Old World and the New World. Nowadays it is more firmly Old World and describes itself as a fusion of *savoir faire* and imagination. Arielle Demets comes from Champagne, where her family have vineyards, and she studied in Adelaide, where she met Jem Harris. They decided to make wine together, but Champagne was not an option; Arielle's brother would eventually take over the family vines there and, in any case, Jem simply could not cope with the climate, so they looked in the Languedoc. They started their search outside Perpignan and gradually moved north to reach Faugères and fell in love with it. Arielle admits that she knew nothing about the Midi or Faugères before coming here, but they looked for vineyards with a very clear idea of what they wanted: vines at a higher altitude in view of global warming, and schist. They found vineyards in good condition with vines, on average, between 30 and 40 years old around Cabrerolles. The 2007 was their first vintage.

Things have moved on and Jem is now making wine in Limoux, while Arielle has settled into life in Faugères, with 10 hectares of vines and a modern cellar on a hillside outside Cabrerolles, which she shares with Olivier Villanova from Mas Onésime. The 2013 was her first solo vintage, but she had advice from a local oenologist, François Pennequin, and Pierre Roque helped her blend the 2012s. The cellar works by gravity with natural insulation and is very practical in its layout. A single plot goes into a single vat. Arielle favours *pigeage* as she does not want to extract too much tannin; above all she wants fruit. When asked about typicity, she talks about the altitude of her vines: at 350 to 370 metres in Cabrerolles there is more foliage and vegetation, as the climate is cooler, making for lighter wines. Arielle observes that Syrah suffers from drought in Faugères, whereas Cinsaut, Carignan and Grenache Noir fare much better.

Arielle makes a little rosé, but the emphasis is on red wine. Le Rêve is mainly Syrah, usually about 50 to 60 per cent, with 30 per cent Grenache Noir and a little Carignan, which gives some structure. Half the wine is aged in wood. A 2013 barrel sample is fresh and peppery, and the 2011 is rounded and perfumed with a supple tannic streak. In 2013 she tried out some carbonic maceration on her Syrah and Grenache Noir, just to see. And the 2012 Le Rêve is more solid and leathery, and less perfumed.

Intempus is approximately 30 per cent each of Syrah and Grenache Noir, with 20 per cent each of Mourvèdre and Carignan, which are given twelve to eighteen months' *élevage* in oak. Arielle uses *barriques*, but more for micro-oxygenation than for the *côté tannique*. She does not want the oak to overwhelm the wine. Intempus was richer than Le Rêve, with some silky tannins, combining structure with elegance.

Back in 2010 she made the first vintage of Renaissance, 80 per cent from 40-year-old Mourvèdre vines and 20 per cent Grenache Noir, all aged in *demi-muids* for eighteen months. The wine is blended before it goes into wood, and in the 2010 the oak is still quite obvious, partly on account of the new barrels. None the less there is an underlying elegance, which is the hallmark of the estate – appropriately, since Arielle said that her aim is *finesse*.

Domaine Léon Barral

Lenthéric, 34480
Tel: 04 67 90 29 13

Of all the Faugères wine growers, Didier Barral from the Domaine named for his father is one of the most opinionated. He has very firm ideas about the cultivation of his vines, declaring that – as previously noted – when he first started practising organic viticulture, you were considered an idiot, but these days, if you are *not* organic, you are considered an idiot. And he is scathing about people who are organic without having any sincere conviction.

Didier took the family vineyards out of the cooperative in 1993, which was his first vintage. He has 30 hectares of vines, ranging in age from vines planted in 1899 to some only two years old, and he has also planted 500 olive trees, as well as pistachio and fruit trees, to break away from monoculture. He has strong views about the care of the vineyards:

if you till the ground, you kill living things, insects, plant roots, earthworms; if you don't till, you mow, but that is a mistake too because a plant which is cut will grow more strongly. So since 2006 he has used a rolafaca, a Brazilian machine which flattens the grass, partially cutting it, so that it turns into mulch and compost. Didier can also enthuse about cowpats: they encourage the development of earthworms, and for that reason a herd of cows is to be found in his vineyard. It is an idyllic spot in spring sunshine, in a cool valley with a stream. Didier can also enthuse about hedges helping the bats, the best predators of *vers de la grappe*, to navigate. In short, he has some thought-provoking ideas about viticulture and does not fear to challenge accepted practices.

We tasted samples of the previous couple of vintages from vat and barrel, starting off with a white wine or, rather more accurately an orange wine, from Terret Blanc and Terret Gris fermented on their skins and then partially aged in wood. It is still very adolescent with some cidery notes and some residual sugar. I have always found Didier's white wine quite difficult on the various occasions I have tasted it.

As for reds, Didier makes three, with two named vineyards, Jadis and Valinière. We compared the Syrah component for both. For Jadis it is Syrah from a south-facing slope, and for Valiniere a north facing slope. The wine from the north-facing slope is lighter and fresher, as you might expect. But Didier is adamant about looking for freshness, observing that the mistake of the Languedoc is to plant earlier-ripening varieties, which means that the acidity is burnt in the heat of August. Carignan and Mourvèdre ripen later, and therefore retain their acidity. 'We've forgotten about acidity in the south', he states. In the cellar he uses an old but efficient basket press and he has not destalked his grapes for ten years.

A Cinsaut is redolent of ripe cherries with a fresh finish and some furry tannins from the stalks; a Carignan has an attractive rustic note with a fresh finish, and then came a blend of Carignan with a little Cinsaut. Another sample of Carignan has some acetate on the nose – 'Most people wouldn't give that to a journalist,' Didier quips, gleefully. Didier says that the acetate nose is not volatility but was produced by the yeast, and would need a year to disappear. He explains that if you use sulphur, which he does not, those yeasts would be killed. A final sample, of Grenache Noir, is deliciously fresh with cherry perfume.

Château des Estanilles

Lenthéric 34480
Tel : 04 67 90 29 25
contact@chateau-estanilles.com
www.chateau-estanilles.com

In the hamlet of Lenthéric, Château des Estanilles was created by Michel Louison, who arrived in Faugères from Geneva in the 1970s. He had worked as an electrician and then turned to wine. The name is a combination of two plots, Fontanilles and Estagnoles. I first met Michel in the late 1990s, when he still retained the challenging attitude of an outsider, in particular criticising the INAO: 'They prevent us from making progress.' He had predicted that in 2000 the best Faugères would be white, but the INAO was rather slower to allow an appellation for white Faugères. Michel was also particularly enthusiastic about Syrah and planted an exceptionally steep vineyard just outside the village, le Clos du Fou: 'The madman, that's me, for that is what people called me when I planted the vines here.'

Michel has now moved on to make wine in Limoux, selling Château des Estanilles to Julien Seydoux in 2009, who worked that harvest with him. Julien's family had made their money in cinema and in football; Julien grew up in Paris and later worked in finance in San Diego, but wanted to do something that allowed for passion and enthusiasm. His options were photography, cars or wine. Finally he opted for wine in the Midi. Why Faugères? Because it is a small appellation with a specific *terroir* and with ageing potential, he says, and has the possibility to develop, providing a challenge. There is nothing left to prove in Bordeaux or Burgundy. And why Estanilles? 'For its reputation, the quality of the vines, with an efficient cellar and the beauty of the site.'

For the day-to-day winemaking, Julien has employed the talented Arnaud Barthès, who I first met at Domaine Cottebrune, when he was running that estate for Pierre Gaillard. Arnaud showed me round. Michel Louison had built a state of the art winery in 1999 – I had seen it as a building site – and Julien Seydoux has implemented some renovation, adding more vats and a bottling line.

Altogether there are 26 hectares currently in production, with twenty different plots altogether, including a 1.5-hectare plot on the plateau of Fontanilles, while the furthest vineyard is a plot of Mourvèdre at La

Liquière. They harvest in small 25-kilo boxes and use a sorting table. The cellars are spotless. They use 15- or 20-hectolitre *foudres* for ageing their Mourvèdre, while the Syrah goes into *demi-muids* as it needs more oxygen. Part of the barrel cellar exposes a dramatic wall of schist.

L'Impertinent is their entry-level range, three wines without any barrel ageing. The white is a blend of Marsanne, Roussanne and Viognier, with a blocked malolactic fermentation to keep the flavours fresh and floral. L'Impertinent rosé is a blend of Grenache Noir and Cinsaut with a little Mourvèdre, from pressed grapes, making quite a vinous wine. And the L'Impertinent rouge includes all five varieties of the appellation, but mainly Syrah, making for some fresh spice.

Next level up is Inverso. The white is a blend of Marsanne and Roussanne, aged in *demi-muids* with regular *bâtonnage* until the weather cools at the end of October, and then starting again in March. The oak is quite obvious in the young wine, with some underlying acidity and minerality. It should age well. Pink Inverso is pure Mourvèdre, with eight months' *élevage* in *demi-muids* making for an original rosé with some weight, which is very much a food rosé, while red Inverso is 50 per cent Mourvèdre, with Grenache Noir and Syrah, aged in *foudres*, with some satisfying fruit, peppery flavours and quite firm tannins.

In addition they continue to make Le Clos du Fou, a pure Syrah given twelve months ageing in *barriques* and *demi-muids*. As a young wine it is firm and tannic, with fruit and power, and a beautifully balanced palate, with ageing potential. Raison d'Etre is a selection of the best barrels, from 50 per cent Syrah, blended with equal parts of Grenache Noir and Mourvèdre. In the spring of 2014, the 2011 was a lovely glass of wine, with rounded red fruit and well integrated tannins, with subtle nuances of flavour and a long finish.

Clos Fantine

Lenthéric 34480
Tel: 04 67 90 20 89
corine.andrieu@laposte.com

Clos Fantine is in a peaceful spot just outside the village of Lenthéric. The estate is owned by three siblings, Carole, Corine and Olivier Andrieu. The two sisters explain the division of labour: Corine makes the wine because she studied oenology at Montpellier; Carole does the paperwork, having gone to business school; and Olivier looks after the vines. But they all help with pruning and do not need to employ any extra people.

Carole explains that their grandmother was born there and inherited 3 hectares. Their father, Jacques, worked in Paris and then came back to the land and invested in his *patrimoine* by developing the estate. He was a member of the Autignac cooperative. He first converted the vineyards to organic viticulture and his children have taken this even further, becoming ardent supporters of natural wine. They now have 28 hectares, planted with Carignan, Grenache Noir, Mourvèdre, Cinsaut and a little Syrah, as well as some Aramon and Terret Blanc. They built a simple cellar in 2000, three years after their father's death. Their vines, all *gobelet* or bush vines, are all within about 7 kilometres of the cellar, in several plots, with different characteristics. They vinify by *cépage*, rather than by plot and then the wines are blended a few months later. They use no wood at all.

There are two *cuvées* of Faugères: their Faugères Tradition is a blend of Carignan with some Grenache Noir and Mourvèdre. Corine describes how the winemaking has changed. Since 2011 they have taken to putting the fruit into the vat with the stalks and just leaving it to ferment. They used to do *délestages,* but no longer; they just leave it. She explains that a fermenting vat has several different colonies of yeast, and by not mixing them up you stop them from fighting each other, so that you get less volatile acidity. They used to look for more robust wines, attempting to extract as much as possible from the grapes, but now with *sagesse* (wisdom or experience), they are looking for the *côté fruit* and the *force du terroir.* They blend at the last minute after about six months ageing in vat, and they play Gregorian chants in their cellar, saying that without music the wine is *très nerveux*, or agitated.

Their second Faugères is Cuvée Courtiol, which for the 2012 vintage was mainly Syrah. In the past it has been Mourvèdre, but Corine feels that Syrah is the variety that is the most expressive of the appellation or 'qui nous parle le plus', but it does depend on the vintage. In 2012 there was no water stress and the Syrah was quite uniform.

Their white wine, Valcabrières, a Vin de France, comes from 80- to 90-year-old Terret Blanc vines. Some of the grapes are pressed and sometimes they ferment whole bunches. The result is a wine that is quite orange, amber golden in colour, with a firm dry nose, and on the palate a certain leesy, stony note with some acidity and a touch of bitterness.

As well as Faugères, they make a couple of red Vins de France. The newest, Arc en Ciel, a blend of Syrah, Carignan and Mourvèdre, could be Faugères, but they do not make enough of it to justify the *cotisation*, or dues payable to the *syndicat*. Corine says that they had quite often experienced problems at the *labelle* or qualifying tastings for the appellation where their wines were criticized for being *atypique*, and not conforming to Faugères. I would venture to suggest that they *are* original; you may not like them, but they have a wonderful expression of flavour.

The second Vin de France, La Lanterne Rouge, is half Aramon and half Cinsaut. The Cinsaut is destemmed and, when fermentation starts, they add whole bunches of Aramon and press it all a couple of days later. It is aged in vat, to keep the fruit and the salinity. The resulting wine was very intriguing, quite tannic with some berry fruit and a certain rustic note.

Undoubtedly the wines at Clos Fantine are some of the most original of the appellation and, talking with Corine, you sense that she is a thoughtful winemaker, constantly searching to improve her winemaking, pushing back the boundaries and exploring the possibilities. Nothing will stand still at Clos Fantine.

La Grange de l'Aïn and Château Haut Fabrègues

La Grange d'Aïn, Fontanilles, Lenthéric 34480
Tel: 06 12 01 31 02
Château Haut Fabrègues, Lenthéric 34480
Tel: 04 67 90 28 67
cedricsaur@hotmail.com
hautfabregues@gmail.com

I had met Cédric Saur's father, Jean-Luc, in 1987, when I was writing the book which first took me to the Languedoc, *French Country Wines*. At the time Jean-Luc was one of the pioneers of the region, working hard to push the quality boundaries. These days he has retired and it is Cédric who makes the wines at both his own estate, La Grange d'Aïn, and at Château Haut Fabrègues.

La Grange d'Aïn is in a beautiful isolated place outside the hamlet of Lenthéric, reached at the end of a narrow dirt track. Cédric explains that there were two properties: Fontanilles, which means 'little spring' in Occitan and La Grange d'Aïn – he preferred the second name as it is more unusual. 'Aïn' means 'spring' or 'the eye of the spring' in both Arabic and Hebrew and appropriately there is a fountain in the garden, which he uses on his label.

Cédric tells how he had created his own estate, first buying some vines and then more coming from his parents. He now he has 11.5 hectares, all close together on the plateau of Lenthéric. After studying in Montpellier, he worked at a research centre in Bordeaux and then came back to Faugères in 1998 to work with his parents before starting out on his own in 2003.

He is passionately committed to organic viticulture, which he has practised since the beginning. His father never used weedkiller and was already working in *lutte raisonnée*. Cédric is gently moving toward natural winemaking, but the label does not say so; he would consider himself to be '*nature restraint*' or a restrained natural winemaker. He talks of the need for different thought processes – 'You need to anticipate and avoid the problem' – saying that the standard treatments are more certain, but less interesting. He is not biodynamic in his vineyards, as there are some preparations that he does not use which are imposed by biodynamic viticulture, but he is biodynamic in the cellar.

We had a comprehensive tasting of Grange d'Aïn, beginning with his white wine, an eclectic blend of 30 per cent Grenache Blanc and Vermentino with 30 per cent of Marsanne and Roussanne, and with the balance made up of Clairette, Viognier and Bourboulenc. All the grapes are fermented in oak, with some *bâtonnage*, and no temperature control. It is golden in colour, with a rich textured palate, dry honey, good acidity and an intriguing finish that leaves you wanting more.

Next we tasted vintages of his Faugères, Le Penchant du Cerisier, a blend of 80 per cent Carignan with 20 per cent Grenache Noir. The Carignan enjoys a classic vinification rather than a carbonic maceration and the wine spends eighteen months in *tronconique* vats, which fills it out, giving notes of cherry stones. The 2010 has what I call a natural note on the finish and the 2006 is quite solid and rounded, with good structure and acidity, while 2005 has some Mediterranean spice with less acidity. Essentially Cédric aims for very ripe grapes and then does as little as possible. He believes there are two ways of working – very reductively or oxidatively, and he prefers the oxidative route.

His 2003 Le Cèdre is the opposite to Le Penchant du Cerisier: 80 per cent Grenache Noir to 20 per cent Carignan, with the same vinification, and a shorter *élevage*. Cédric sees 2003, his first vintage, as a very good year, especially for Carignan. There is some ripe liqueur cherry fruit, so that the wine is quite like Châteauneuf-du-Pape in character.

Château Haut Fabrègues, the other property, is just outside Lenthéric. The first château was built in 1145 by the Knights Templar. Cédric's grandfather, André, bought the property with 30 hectares of vines all in one block in 1965, and his father Jean-Luc started putting the wine in bottle in 1978. But viticulture here goes back much further. There are traces of a Roman vineyard, which disappeared, and then vines were planted again for the religious community. The present day château is nineteenth century, a *folie languedocienne*, or folly, which belonged to an important Lyonnaise family. 'Fabrègues' derives from '*fabrique*' and 'Haut' is because the property is above Lenthéric, and at a higher altitude than the vines of La Grange d'Aïn. The harvest starts three or four days later. The soil is mainly schist *gréseux*.

Here Cédric employs a different philosophy, making *vins d'assemblage*, with a blend of grape varieties and vineyards. The plots for each wine are not the same each year, and there is a precise range of Tradition, Sélection, Prestige and Cuvée Gaëlle, and also a rosé, which Cédric describes as a *rosé de soif*, one to quench your thirst. It is crisp and fresh. Tradition is made from 20 per cent of each of the five grape varieties of the appellation. It is rounded and leathery, making for easy drinking. Sélection is Syrah and Grenache Noir, from older vines, with a longer *élevage* in vat, while Prestige is Syrah and Mourvèdre, with eighteen months in barrel. It is firm and leathery, with a sturdy finish. Cuvée Gaëlle is a blend of 80 per cent Syrah with some Grenache Noir, made for the first time in 1998, when Cédric joined his parents, and subsequently only made in the best years. The grapes are not destalked and it is given a sixty-five-day maceration before spending two years in barrel. It is still dense and sturdy, while the 1999, which was destalked, is more elegantly mature, with very good fruit. It is a delicious glass of wine, amply illustrating the ageing potential of Faugères.

Haut Fabrègues has a wonderful large vaulted cellar. The walls are built of stones of schist *gréseux*, while the arches are schist *ardoisier*, making a striking contrast. Our tasting finished with an intriguing pure Syrah, Mimosas, harvested at the end of October and given a very long, as much as four year, *élevage* in barrel. 'Some years it works and some years not,' observes Cédric, who is pushing the boundaries to the limit here. There were some barrel samples of white wines, with some fresh herbal notes, and we finished tasting with a sniff of smoky Fine de Faugères.

Domaine Montgros and Mas Angel

Domaine Montgros
Fontanilles, Lenthéric 34480
Tel: 06 85 32 65 97
www.montgros.fr

Mas d'Angel
ludovicaventin@free.fr
www.faugeres-masangel.fr

Ludovic Aventin is responsible for two estates, Mas Angel and Domaine Montgros, with neighbouring vineyards. Mas Angel, with 8 hectares, is funded by a group of 120 *amateurs de vin*. For Montgros the link is rugby, with an association of 130 rugby players who own 6.7 hectares between Cabrerolles and Caussiniojouls. The cellar for both is at the end of the chemin des Fontanilles outside the hamlet of Lenthéric.

Ludovic is a man who exudes energy and ideas, and you sense that he gets things done. He is enthusiastic about his work: 'C'est un vrai *métier*', a real profession to create vineyards. He has set up a *societé civil immobilier*, a property company, to buy vines and the associates have each bought a share in the property. He talks of an annual general meeting lasting five minutes, followed by lots of celebrations. But he is also anxious to give young people work opportunities, and he is highly motivated with a strong work ethic and sense of civic responsibility, so that some profits go to the Centre d'Aide pour le Travail and to needy children in hospital.

Originally Ludovic ran a wine shop in Rouen, but what he really wanted to do was to make wine. And why Faugères? It was all to do with a chance encounter with Angel Salvi, an elderly *viticulteur*, who was retiring and wanted to sell his vines. Angel now has a share in the estate, and the top *cuvée* is named Marius, after his father, who fled Mussolini to settle in Béziers. Montgros is a *lieu-dit*, but the name also has strong associations for rugby enthusiasts: '*les gros*' are the forwards and that '*allez mon gros*' is a common rugby term of encouragement.

Ludovic talks about his winemaking; he has help here from Mathieu Dubernet. Everything is hand picked and sorted, and no sulphur is added until the malolactic fermentation. Ludovic explains that he would like to cultivate his own yeast as he considers natural yeast to be part of the identity of a *grand vin*. I tried two barrel samples, one 80 per cent Syrah with 20 per cent Grenache Noir and the other with the opposite proportions. Not surprisingly, the oak was quite obvious with some firm tannins, but also rich fruit and perfume and body.

Mas Angel comprises four red wines. First is Elegance, based on Cinsaut with some Carignan and Grenache Noir and a splash of Syrah. The vines are, on average, sixty years old and the wine has fruit and substance. Harmonie is a blend of Grenache Noir and Carignan with some Cinsaut and Syrah, and includes a small proportion of carbonic maceration. The idea is that it should be like Elegance, but with more substance, and also with that slightly rustic note of Carignan. Prestige had sold out, so I was unable to taste it. The very first vintage of Marius was 2009. It comes from Carignan, with some Syrah and Grenache Noir, and is still rich and chocolaty with a firm streak of tannin.

The range of Montgros consists of three wines. Le Producteur de Plaisir is based on Cinsaut with some Grenache Noir and Syrah, and spends ten months in vat. The 2012 vintage is redolent of fresh cherry fruit. It is given a short maceration as Ludovic does not want too much extraction and consequently it is slightly lighter than the Elegance of Mas Angel. His aim is a red wine for easy drinking and that is just what he has achieved – deliciously so. Première Ligue, another reference to rugby, is a blend of 80 per cent Grenache Noir with 20 per cent Syrah, of which 40 per cent is given twelve months ageing in barrel. The 2012 still retained strong notes of vanilla when it was eighteen months old, but there was plenty of ripe fruit underneath the oak, with a satisfying streak of tannin. The top wine, Elite, also includes a high proportion of oak-aged wine, so that it is intense and chocolaty on both nose and palate (and it subsequently proved to be delicious with a succulent piece of beef).

Ludovic sees 2014 as the first real vintage, so the potential is considerable. He has also just acquired 2.5 hectares of white varieties at Cabrerolles – Roussanne, Marsanne and Grenache Blanc – and was planning to make a barrique of each to see what they are like. There is no doubt that these are two estates to watch.

Domaine St Antonin

Lenthéric 34480
Tel : 04 67 90 13 24
stantonin@wanadoo.fr
www.domainesaintantonin.fr

Frédéric Albaret is a thoughtful and observant winemaker, with the objectivity that comes from being an outsider; nor is he afraid to voice an opinion. His parents were townsfolk, but he studied agriculture and oenology. He always knew he would be a farmer, and possibly a grape grower, but not necessarily a winemaker. However, he has also always loved wine and says there is not much else to grow in the Midi, apart from vines. He arrived in Faugères and bought his first vines in 1995, 12 hectares, which he has gradually expanded to 25 hectares, with quite a lot of Carignan. He likes Mourvèdre, preferring it to Syrah, but 'it can be difficult to get fully ripe – you need to work in the vineyard'. In 2001 he built a smart new cellar outside the village of Lenthéric. He works organically, though the label does not say so because he thinks that would make it a marketing issue. On the other hand he believes that the environment lends itself to organic viticulture; vines fed on chemicals are less resistant to disease. In the cellar he minimizes the use of sulphur during the actual winemaking, but adds some for the *élevage* and bottling: 'Sulphur can dislocate the aromas during vinification. It is a question of confidence in your raw materials.'

There is no white wine, and the entry-level pink and red Les Jardins were sold out, so first we tasted Lou Cazalet, a *lieu dit*, and a blend of Grenache Noir, Carignan and Mourvèdre aged in vat, and Syrah aged in *foudres*. It is very spicy with notes of the *garrigues*, with some leather and red fruit, and silky tannins. Frédéric looks for *fraicheur*, silkiness and length, and these are certainly found in this wine. He sees the wines of Lenthéric as having *finesse* and length, and as being less powerful than those of Laurens.

Magnon, another *lieu-dit*, is a blend of Syrah, Grenache Noir and Mourvèdre, given two years *élevage*, with one 20-hectolitre *foudre* and the rest in 500-litre barrels. Frédéric is moving gradually towards more *foudres*, considering that *barriques* can result in a loss of fruit and freshness. He favours a gentle extraction, just wetting the cap – a *mouillage* – over three or four weeks, rather than any more violent *pigeage* or *remontage*, so that Magnon was more concentrated, with some well integrated oak and some liquorice fruit. A lovely glass of wine.

Château La Liquière

La Liquière 34480
Tel: 04 67 90 29 20
info@chateaulaliquiere.com
www.chateaulaliquiere.com

This is one of the old-established estates of Faugères. I first met Bernard Vidal when I was writing *French Country Wines* in the late 1980s, and then our paths crossed again for *The Wines of the South of France*. Bernard planted his own vineyards in the 1970s and then subsequently took over his father Jean's estate. These days it is his two children, Sophie and François, who shoulder most of the responsibilities, but it has to be said that Bernard does not strike me as somebody who would ever completely retire. Sophie admits that her father is always there when they need him, and her mother is still very much involved in the administrative side of things. The Vidals were amongst the pioneers of Faugères. Their first sales in bottle go back to the late 1960s and they were amongst the first to plant Syrah, while their oldest Mourvèdre vines date from 1980. Bernard was revolutionary in installing cooling equipment and carrying out some of the first vinifications by carbonic maceration.

From a wonderful viewpoint at about 400 metres, in the middle of their vines, you can see Caussiniojouls, Laurens and Autignac, and on a clear day you can make out a silvery strip of sea. Bernard had planted some vines here in the 1970s, and there is a small *mazet* that the family are restoring. There is another vineyard, also planted in 1970s, that follows the contours of the hillside, thus avoiding erosion; it covers about 100 hectares. This was the initiative of the mayor of Cabrerolles, who wanted to invest in quality and also wanted to help five or six young wine growers to set themselves up, people who otherwise would have had problems in starting out because they did not have access to family land. Various local bodies, as well as the Ministry of Agriculture, helped with the finance and the young wine growers received a loan for thirty years, repayable at the rate of just 1 per cent.

Bernard talks about the effect of altitude on the quality of Faugères, how higher altitude suits white grapes and also Syrah, whereas Carrigan performs better at lower altitudes. Since 2012 the estate has been registered as organic, although the family has been practising organic viticulture for much longer. Altogether they have 60 hectares of vines, in the villages of La Liquière, Caussiniojouls and Cabrerolles, in some seventy-five plots. White grape varieties represent 10 hectares, with Roussanne, Grenache Blanc, Vermentino, Clairette, Terret Blanc, Bourboulenc, Muscat and Marsanne. The red varieties are the usual five classics of the Languedoc.

There is a welcoming tasting *caveau* in the centre of the hamlet of La Liquière. Their vinification cellar is in Lenthéric, as the Vidal family come from there, but Bernard married a Mlle Gaillard from La Liquière. François talks about his wines and it is immediately apparent that he and Sophie know how to progress and develop the estate.

Les Amandiers is their entry-level wine, for red and pink Faugères, and white Coteaux du Languedoc. The latter is not Faugères as it includes some Terret Blanc, which is not allowed in the appellation. More serious is Cistus Faugères Blanc, in which Roussanne is the dominant variety, with some Grenache Blanc, Vermentino and Bourboulenc. They put the earlier picked Roussanne into vat and the second picking, about 20 per cent, into barrels, so that it spends six months on its lees to develop more body and weight. François feels very strongly that white wines from the Languedoc can age, and I certainly expect this one to develop with some bottle age. The latest addition to their white repertoire is Nos Racines Blanches, made for the first time in 2013. It, too, is Pays de l'Herault rather than Faugères because it includes Terret Blanc, Carignan Blanc, Grenache Blanc, Clairette and Bourboulenc, most of which are not allowed in the appellation. They are fermented in *demi-muids* and given a short *élevage* in barrel, making for a very satisfying texture and mouth feel.

Cuvée Vieilles Vignes is a red Faugères, from Carignan and Grenache Noir vines that are over 50 years old. This *cuvée classique* of the estate has existed since they first began bottling their wine, at a time when they had very little Syrah and Mourvèdre. It spends twelve months in vat – they have tried an *élevage* in barrel, but did not like it, finding that Grenache Noir did not work in wood. All the grapes are destalked and the vinification is traditional, despite them being amongst the pioneers of carbonic maceration. Bernard points out that thirty years ago there used to be a lot of carbonic maceration all over the Languedoc, but says that these days people are better at mastering a classic vinification. They have not used carbonic maceration for their Faugères for at least the last five or six vintages.

Nos Racines Rouges, made for the first time in 2005, is another red, coming mainly from Carignan that was planted in 1900 in a 1.89 hectare plot. The plot also includes about 20 per cent of old Terret Blanc, which was planted amongst the Carignan. They are all wonderful old gnarled *gobelet* vines, with a yield of about 15 to 25 hectolitres compared to the usual 40 hectolitres per hectare or so.

Cistus comes from Syrah grown at a higher altitude with some Grenache Noir, Mourvèdre and Carignan. Percentages depend on the vintage and 60 per cent of the *cuvée*, just the Syrah component, is given an *élevage* in *demi-muids*. Their barrels are mostly 500-litre *demi-muids* as they have given up on *barriques*, but they have also tried 400- and 600-litre barrels. The final red wine in their repertoire is Tucade, which was last made in 2009, and it focuses on Mourvèdre which accounts for 80 to 90 per cent of the blend.

Our tasting finished with a cheerful 2012 L'Unique Gaz de Schiste. The name is a play on words: schist is the soil of Faugères and *gaz de schiste* is shale gas, which is also a contentious issue in France. It is a bubbly rosé, 50 per cent Grenache Noir and 50 per cent Mourvèdre, made by the *méthode ancestrale*, and for the first time in 2011. The 2012 has 11 grams per litre residual sugar. The grapes were picked early in September, three weeks early, in order to retain the acidity. Both varieties are pressed and vinified together, and then bottled. There is a light filter at bottling and then the fermentation starts again in bottle. The wine was soft and ripe with some cherry fruit and fresh acidity, and a sweet note on the finish, making a *sympa* finale to an excellent tasting.

Domaine du Causse Noir

La Liquière 34480
Tel : 06 07 23 38 40
jeromepy.caussenoir@gmail.com
www.domaineducaussenoir.com

This is one of the newer estates of Faugères, with a first vintage in 2011. Jérôme Py used to work in the security industry and has come to wine as a second career, 'realizing his dreams'. He has 11 hectares of vineyards in the villages of La Liquière and Caussiniojouls, and they have wonderful views of the Canigou in one direction and the Mont St Claire in the other, with the villages of Laurens and Autignac in the foreground. Jérôme had been wondering about making wine for about ten years and actively looking for vines for five before finally buying from three cooperative members who were retiring. He is now converting to organic viticulture, leaving the grass between the rows and gradually encouraging the fauna to return; his wife has beehives in the vineyards.

For the moment Jérôme rents a simple cellar in the village of La Liquière, but ideally he would like to build his own. The name of the estate comes from the plateau or *causse*, and the black stone is, of course, the schist. And for his labels, Jérôme plays upon his name, with a large ∏, the symbol for pi, on each label. He has no white vines, but makes a characterful rosé from Grenache Noir and Mourvèdre, of which just 10 per cent goes into barrel. It is fresh, but with structure and a touch of aniseed, a rosé for food, or a *rosé de repas,* as the French would say.

There are three red wines. First comes an entry-level ∏ with black fruit. Jérôme used to play rugby and somehow his wines have the physique of a rugby player, with quite solid structure and texture. His wife is Spanish, and although he was born in Sète, his grandparents were Catalan, so it seemed appropriate to name the next *cuvée* Caius, after Caesar's general who invaded Spain. It consists of 20 per cent Mourvèdre, aged in oak, with Grenache Noir, Syrah and Carignan all aged in vat. There is a touch of oak on the palate, with some chunky fruit. Matthias, named after Jérôme's young son, comes from equal parts of Syrah and Mourvèdre with some Grenache and spends eighteen months in new oak, after a three-week maceration, as opposed to just twelve days for ∏. It is very rich, dense and chocolaty with furry tannins and plenty of ageing potential. I enjoyed Jérôme's enthusiasm and admired his courage and energy. He deserves to do well.

Domaine Cottebrune

La Liquière, 34480
Tel : 06 75 87 43 98
domaine-cottebrune@domainespierregaillard.com
www.domainespierregaillard.com

Domaine Cottebrune is an example of interest in Faugères from the Rhône Valley, for it belongs to Pierre Gaillard, who not only produces exemplary Côte Rôtie in the northern Rhône, but also owns vineyards in Collioure at Domaine Madeloc. The first vintage of Domaine Cottebrune was 2006, and Maxime Secher, who runs the estate in Pierre Gaillard's absence, arrived in 2010. His father has vineyards in Muscadet; he trained in the Loire Valley and has worked in South Africa, so the Languedoc was a new *terroir* for him, and he loves it.

Altogether they have 20 hectares of vineyards, with plots in La Liquière, Laurens, Caussiniojouls and, unusually, a vineyard north of the village of Faugères, on the other side of the hills and behind the hamlet of La Caumette. This vineyard is at the northernmost limit of the Faugères appellation. It is an isolated spot, with a little Carignan, half a hectare of Grenache Noir, half a hectare of Syrah, and one hectare of Faugères Blanc, planted with Roussanne, Vermentino and Grenache Blanc. Maxime observed that the vines ripen at least fifteen days later there than in the other vineyards because it is so much cooler, and wild boars are more of a problem there than elsewhere. There are some vines outside Cabrerolles, on very steep slopes, with the vines planted *en eschalas*, with an individual supporting pole for each vine, as in Côte Rôtie.

As for a cellar, they have acquired a partly constructed building on the outskirts of La Liquière. For the moment there is no sign, but they are planning a tasting *caveau*. Vat and barrel samples were tasted. The 2013 white, a blend of equal parts of Roussanne, Vermentino and Grenache Blanc, has spent about eight months on its lees in barrel with some initial *bâttonage*. It was about to be bottled and showed great promise. And the next day I enjoyed the 2012 at the Dame Jane bistro in Faugères; the wine was rich and resinous on the nose with great depth and length on the palate. With his Rhône connections, Maxime has easy access to some second-hand Condrieu barrels.

The rosé, based on Grenache Noir with some Syrah, and partially from pressed juice and partially free-run juice, is fresh and elegant. There are two red wines, Parole de Berger, a blend of Mourvèdre and Syrah, and Transhumance which includes everything else. La Parole de Berger means 'on your honour', *une parole sure*, while transhumance is what sheep normally do, going from winter to summer grazing, and what Pierre Gaillard did in coming to Faugères from Côte Rôtie.

Maxime likes Mourvèdre, but it is not an easy variety; it is often capricious and ripens late, and Pierre Gaillard does not like Carignan. The 2011 Parole de Berger is a selection of different barrels, with fruit, tannin and concentration, and considerable ageing potential. In contrast, Transhumance is a blend of Grenache Noir and Syrah with a little Carignan and is more accessible with some red fruit and spice.

Mas Onésime

Route d'Aigues-Vives, Cabrerolles 34480
Tel : 04 67 93 63 58
olivier@masonesime.com
www.masonesime.com

Olivier Villaneuva's first vintage was 2011 and he shares a cellar with Arielle Demets of Vignoble les Fusionnels. It is a large imposing building on a hill in the middle of the vines outside the village of Cabrerolles. The wind is powerful, but the views are simply breathtaking.

Olivier explains that Onésime was his grandfather's name; apparently it is an old French first name. His grandfather had 5 hectares at the cooperative and then Olivier's father, Emmanuel, took over in 1999, greatly extending the vineyard holding, but he did not want to make wine. Olivier, however, did wish to. He had worked in *travaux viticoles* since 2002, creating vineyards, and covering everything in the vineyard up to and including picking the grapes, but he really wanted to make his own wine. So, in 2011, he took over 7 hectares, including Onésime's original vines at La Liquière, namely 4.5 hectares of Faugères and 0.5 hectares of Chardonnay, and he has 2 hectares of Marsanne and Roussanne coming into production. His first bottling was 2013.

A *mazet*, a typical vineyard worker's
shelter, in the summer heat,
surrounded by old *gobelet* bush vines.

An old Carignan vine, in the defining schist of Faugères.

An impeccably ripe, healthy bunch of Syrah grapes; Syrah is the most widely planted grape variety of the appellation.

The parade of the Confrérie de Faugères in their traditional robes, through the narrow village streets, for the annual Fête du Grand St Jean.

Above: A view from the village of Roquessels over the vineyards of Faugères and beyond.
Below: Vineyards on Jeanjean's Faugères estate, Domaine Fenouillet.

A *capitelle* in the vines. A lovely example of one of the classic dry stone shelters that you find in the Faugères vineyards. Many have been abandoned and fallen into ruin but happily some are being restored.

The church spire of Fos contrasts nicely
with a pallet of wine bottles, that hides
a wine press.

One of the famous windmills that overlook Faugères.

View of the village of Faugères. Spot the windmills on the top of the hill.

His Chardonnay is light and fresh; the rosé, which is mainly Cinsaut with a touch of Grenache Noir, has a pretty pink colour, and some rounded vinous fruit with a dry finish. Olivier makes three *cuvées* of red Faugères. Insoumis is from 60-year-old Carignan with some Syrah and Grenache Noir aged in vat. There is some lovely ripe cherry fruit with a tannic streak and it is mouth-filling and young. Dans le Sillon d'Emmanuel – 'in the footsteps of Emmanuel', after his father – is predominantly Grenache Noir with some red fruit and tight tannins. However, Paradis Caché is more serious, from Syrah with some Mourvèdre, vinified in *demi muids*, with a manual *pigeage* and *élevage* in new wood. The grapes are picked in late October. The wine is intense and rich with an oaky streak of tannin and fruit underneath. It is a promising start.

CAUSSINIOJOULS

Caussiniojouls is another village with a ruined château, dating back to the tenth century, which now houses the cellars of Château Chenaie. There are some attractive narrow streets to explore. The parish church, dedicated to St Etienne, stands right at the entrance to the village, and was built on the site of a tenth-century chapel.

Château Anglade

Montée des Fontenelles, Caussiniojouls 34480
Tel: 06 81 20 80 43
antoine.caussi@wanadoo.fr

Antoine Rigaud's vines at Château Anglade come from his grandparents, while 'Anglade' is his mother's maiden name. His grandfather bought vineyards when he married, mainly around the villages of Cabrerolles and Caussiniojouls, while his grandmother already had vines at Lenthéric. His grandparents also ran the marble quarry in Laurens, and his grandfather still owns the land.

Antoine's main cellar is in *the maison de vigneron* next door to the quarry, but he has a small cellar that was his grandfather's at the back of the château in Caussiniojouls, next to Château Chenaie. He has a house on the edge of the village, right next to one of his vineyards: 'My garden', he quips. His father worked for the petroleum giant Elf and the family lived abroad, so Antoine came here for holidays. Then, in 1998, he started working in the vineyards and took over full responsibility for the family property in 2012.

Antoine would like to make some white wine, but for the moment has no white varieties. His rosé is a blend of 80 per cent Cinsaut and 20 per cent Mourvèdre, all pressed and given a cool fermentation. It is nicely refreshing. And then there are three reds. Cuvée François Galzy, named after his great-grandfather on his mother's side, is a blend of Syrah, Grenache Noir, Mourvèdre and Carrigan. Syrah is usually the dominant variety in each *cuvée*, as he has 10 hectares of it and it tends to be the most productive variety. In any case Antoine likes Syrah because there are so many different aspects to its flavour: it can be floral, or fruity, or more exuberant. François Galzy is easy to drink with some fresh fruit and a balancing streak of tannin. What Antoine wants is '*plaisir et facilité*; when you want a drink, but not a glass of water!' Generally, with his winemaking he does not favour long macerations or heavy extractions, and looks for elegance.

The Cuvée Classique, a blend of Syrah and Grenache, is given twelve months *élevage* in vat, and is ripe and rounded with a satisfying streak of tannin. La Comète is a selection of the best wine. In 2010 the blend was 90 per cent Syrah with some Grenache Noir, again given an *élevage* of twelve months, in large barrels. The oak is nicely integrated, with a firm streak of tannin and some good fruit. In 2011 Antoine acquired a *foudre* and also made a pure Mourvèdre, as it was such a good year for Mourvèdre, with some regular rain. In complete contrast, Mourvèdre produced his worst vat in 2012; such is the character of that most temperamental grape variety.

Domaine Cauvy

3 Montée des Fontenelles, Caussiniojouls 34600
Tel : 06 72 62 23 20
cauvy.pezenas@wanadoo.fr
www.domaine-cauvy.com

I usually have a good nose for a wine cellar or tasting *caveau*, but I had completely failed to notice that as you drive into Pézenas past the yard of the builders' merchants, Ets. Cauvy, there, in the corner, is a small tasting booth. Sophie Cauvy assures me that it has been there for at least three years. Having it there, rather than at their cellars in Caussiniojouls, is easier:

the family business that is the builders' merchants takes up very much more of their time than the vineyards do.

Sophie Cauvy explains that her father-in-law, Pierre, had worked with the large producers' union of Vignerons Val d'Orbieu in the 1980s, and that her husband Philippe had taken over the family vineyards in 1995. He makes the wine, with advice from Mathieu Dubernet, whose father, Marc, was the chief oenologist for the Vignerons Val d'Orbieu, and also a leading exponent of the technique of carbonic maceration as a means of softening the rusticity of Carignan.

The Cauvy family have 20 hectares of vines with the usual five varieties for red Faugères, but mainly Grenache Noir and Syrah. They also make a white Pays de l'Hérault from Grenache Blanc, which is fresh and sappy. Rosie des Causses, a pink Faugères from Syrah and Mourvèdre, is pretty and herbal. And there are five reds, some named after the vineyards and others given fantasy names. Boutinelle is the lightest and simplest, while Baie Violine is a little more substantial. Campauvre implies a poor stony vineyard and the wine is aged in wood for twelve months. Malpas recalls the hard labour of clearing *garrigues* and is a blend of a traditional fermentation and some carbonic maceration, with eighteen months ageing. Pépites Noires, or black nuggets, describing the schist, has also spent eighteen months in oak. The house style seems quite soft and supple, with easy rounded fruit. Sophie Cauvy describes their typicity as supple and ripe, without forgetting the *côté garrigue*.

Château Chenaie

Château de Caussiniojouls, 34600
Tel : 04 67 95 48 10
chateauchenaie@orange.fr
www.chateau-chenaie-vins.fr

Two brothers, Eric and Cyril Chabbert, run Château Chenaie. Their father André originally had his vines in the cooperative, but the brothers began making their own wine in 1993. They have 30 hectares of vines, mainly at Caussiniojouls but also at Laurens and Cabrerolles. In addition they have 400 olive trees and take their olives to the press in Murviel-lès-Beziers. Eric is the brother responsible for the winemaking, rather than the vines, but never the less he is adamant that it is the schist which makes for wine with minerality and notes of the *garrigues*, giving wines with silky tannins after an appropriate *élevage*. The key is to plant each different variety in the most suitable microclimate for it.

They have their *chai d'élevage* in the beautifully restored cellars of the château at the top of the village of Caussiniojouls; it is dominated by an eleventh-century watchtower. They make two *cuvées* of white wine: a Faugères Blanc, Conviction, which is 80 per cent Roussanne with some Rolle and vinified in vat, with some dry peachy fruit; and Les Douves Blanches, which is mainly Roussanne and Viognier with a little Rolle, and spends six months in new oak, with some *bâtonnage*.

Rosé Conviction, from Cinsaut with a little Grenache Noir, is a pretty pale colour, with fresh acidity and a satisfyingly vinous body. Conviction Rouge comes from equal parts of Grenache Noir, Carignan, Syrah and Mourvèdre, all aged in vat. There are black cherries on both nose and palate, with a firm tannic streak and a touch of *tapenade*. Les Ceps d'Emile, which Eric considers to be the most typical Faugères of his wines, recalls the grandfather who planted the old Carignan: blended with a little Syrah and aged in barrel for six months, the wine is nicely characterful and robust. Les Douves Rouge is based on Syrah and with a little Mourvèdre, and is aged for twelve months in barrel; the oak is nicely integrated, with some intense fruit. L'Oblivia is 80 per cent Mourvèdre with some Grenache Noir, given thirteen months in wood. It is firm and intense, with youthful potential, needing more time in bottle, and illustrating Eric's talent as a winemaker.

Domaine de Fenouillet

BP 1, Saint Félix de Lodez 34725
Tel: 04 76 88 81 93
matthieu.carliez@jeanjean.fr
www.jeanjean.fr

This estate belongs to Jeanjean – as previously noted, they are one of the big players of the Languedoc with extensive vineyard holdings. It all started in 1870 with Etienne-Maurice Jeanjean, who lived in St Félix-de-Lodez and made a living selling wine in the Massif Central. Things gradually evolved so that the family now has seven estates in the Languedoc, of which Domaine de Fenouillet is the only one relevant to this book. In addition they produce a range of *vins de négoce* from their cellars in St Félix-de-Lodez, and have the controlling interest in the large Advini group, which includes wine producers from all over France, notably Domaine Cazes in Roussillon and Domaine Laroche in Chablis. The public face of Jeanjean is Brigitte Jeanjean, a lively, vivacious woman of a certain age, a member of the fifth generation. Mathieu Carliez is in charge of the winemaking for all the Languedoc estates.

The vineyards of Domaine Fenouillet were bought in 1993. There are 78 hectares in about seventy different plots, scattered over the four *communes* of Autignac, Laurens, Cabrerolles and Caussiniojouls, offering excellent blending potential. The views as you drive through the vineyards are magnificent, with steep slopes, often north-facing. Faugères contrasts with St Chinian, in that rivers – the Orb and Vernazobre – are more important in St Chinian, whereas in the appellation of Faugères there are numerous small streams.

Jeanjean are converting to organic viticulture, but several of their vineyards are on narrow terraces, which make *enherbement* difficult, and using an *intercep* on a terrace is not easy either: it necessitates a change of equipment.

I tasted the wine at the cellars in the centre of Caussiniojouls. Les Hautes Combes is their Faugères Blanc, a blend of Marsanne and Roussanne made for the first time in 2011. They have just 2.5 hectares of white varieties. These vines are now fifteen years old and are planted on some of their highest vineyard sites at 300 metres, near the village of Caussiniojouls. Essentially the white wine is vinified in stainless steel vats, but just a small amount, maybe 5 per cent, is fermented in barrel, which add a little more substance and texture, but without any taste of oak. The winemaker for Faugères, Damien Guérande, talks about working the lees. The wine is finely crafted: 'If you do too much, the aroma changes. You want to enhance the volume, but not lose the aroma.'

Combe Rouge is a blend of Syrah and Grenache with a little Carignan. Syrah is the base. Damien is considering both Carignan and Mourvèdre, but finds them both more problematic. Somehow it is easier to get the structure of Syrah as you want it. About 20 per cent of the wine goes into wood, so that there is some oak on the palate, but it is restrained and measured, with some peppery flavours and a tannic streak. Combe Rouge is a selection of different plots of varying altitudes and a variety of soils, and takes its name from a small valley where the soil is indeed red.

Grande Réserve includes a higher percentage of Syrah, as much as 80 per cent, with some Grenache Noir, from vineyards closer to Autignac, which ripen earlier, to give the wine depth and concentration. Half of it is aged in oak, but not new oak.

Our tasting finished with 'a surprise', a red wine that did not yet have a name. It was rich and powerful, with new oak and an intense concentration of flavour. The idea was to create something that was very concentrated, a super-prestige wine. It was hand harvested, and the grapes were cooled, hand sorted, destalked and fermented in 500-litre barrels, as well as some 30-hectolitre *tronconique* vats. It was mainly Syrah, with a small yield, the result of a green harvest. The idea was to push the boundaries, to see just what the vineyards could produce if treated very carefully, 'like gardens of schist'. It is undoubtedly an interesting exercise, to see just what can be achieved, but for enjoyable drinkability I favour the more accessible Combe Rouge.

I was later invited to taste a further development, and the first vintage of a new *cuvée*, 2014 Le Père la Minute, marking the culmination of all that research. First the name: it was the nickname of Etienne-Maurice Jeanjean, who was apparently always in a hurry. In contrast, they have taken time to develop this *cuvée*, as Mathieu Carliez explains, working on the selection of vineyards, and in the cellar. They have tried out different fermentation vessels, 500- and 600-litre barrels, and small stainless steel tanks of 20 to 25 hectolitres, and *tronconique* oak vats, which was what they finally opted for. The wine comes from a 1.1 hectare vineyard of 40-year-old Syrah, with half a hectare of 35-year-old Grenache Noir. Mathieu said that they were looking for absolutely ripe grapes, but always with freshness, to maintain the optimum balance. The wine is given a three-week maceration on the skins and the temperature is allowed to rise to 30°C, which makes for rounded flavours. Then the wine goes into barrels, the traditional Languedoc barrels of 340 litres, which are produced by the cooper Boutes in Narbonne. The barrels are new but the toasting is light, to allow for the best expression of the fruit. The wine was bottled in December 2015. You sense that enormous attention is paid to detail, with meticulous care at every stage. When I tasted it in the spring of 2016, it was redolent of ripe spicy black fruit, with some supple but structured tannins, balanced by freshness on the finish and considerable length. It was quite simply a lovely glass of wine that will develop in bottle for several years.

FOS

Fos is one of the prettiest villages of the appellation; on several occasions it has been awarded the accolade of Village Fleuri. Until recently there was just one lone wine estate, but now there are three Faugères cellars, as well as Mas Sibert, an estate with vineyards outside Faugères, which also operates the old village bread oven.

Domaine de l'Arbussèle

Le Moulenc, Fos 34320
Tel : 06 18 07 47 96
contact@domaine-larbusele.com
www.domaine-larbussele.com

Sébastien Louge has taken an interesting path to Fos. He comes from Tarbes in the Hautes-Pyrénées and, after studying agriculture, turned to viticulture and oenology at Bommes in Bordeaux and worked in Ste. Croix de Mont. Then there were more studies in Toulouse, followed by a couple of *stages* at Château Montus in Madiran and Domaine de Montredon in Châteauneuf-du-Pape. He then spent twelve months in the US at Cross Keys vineyards in Virginia, helping them create their cellar. Back in France, he worked at Château Guilhem in Malepère, and then at Domaine de la Grange outside Gabian. However, the idea of doing his own thing had been simmering for a while and he began looking for vines in the appellations of Pézenas and Faugères, and found 10 hectares of vines in Fos and Laurens for sale.

Syrah and both old and new Carignan dominate the vineyards. Sébastien is planning to put all his wine in bottle and, when we first met in May 2014, he had found an old tractor shed which only needed a small amount of work to turn it into a functioning cellar.

Sébastien focuses on the hurdles you have to go through to qualify for financial help as a young winegrower: you must be between 18 and 40, with the appropriate qualifications, and there are forms galore to complete, as your project is checked to ensure that it is viable. He calls it a *'parcours de combattant'*, an obstacle course, but he is keen and eager, and I am sure he will succeed. His first vintage was not the easiest, as things were complicated by the rain. However, when I tasted the wines a few months later, I thought he had made a good start.

There is a crisp rosé, Envol, a blend mainly of Grenache Noir, with some Syrah and a little Mourvèdre. Envol Rouge is Sébastien's entry-level wine, with 45 per cent Syrah, 30 per cent Carignan and 25 per cent Grenache Noir, with an *élevage* in vat. The aim is fruit, and that is just what he has achieved, with a mineral note and youthful freshness. Anthentique comes mainly from old Carignan, with some Grenache Noir and a little Syrah, again aged in vat. The name is a reference to the fact that Carignan was the original variety of Faugères. It is nicely structured with a pleasing rusticity balancing the fruit. And the final red, Révelation, of which there were just two barrels, is a blend of Grenache Noir with 20 per cent Carignan and 15 per cent Syrah. It has some ripe liqueur cherry fruit, balanced with a streak of tannin and would not be bottled for a few months, but promised well.

Domaine Epidaure

Rue de la Condamine, Fos 34320
Tel : 06 25 17 18 10
j.vialla@hotmail.fr

Faugères exercises a powerful attraction: outsiders and even relatively local wine growers are settling in the appellation. Take Jérôme Vialla. His grandfather had a family estate in Mauguio which was sold for inheritance reasons; his father is the *régisseur* at Domaine Valensac in Florensac and make Pays d'Oc, so Jérôme found himself a *fils de vigneron*, but without any family vines. He studied viticulture and winemaking at Carcassonne, and then worked at Domaine de la Pommière, on the plain, which he describes as a factory. They produced 25,000 hectolitres from 200 hectares of vines.

He wanted to get away from the plain, so he bought a small house in Fos in 2012, and met his next-door neighbour, Jean-Pierre Grippal, who was approaching retirement and had no children interested in his vines. And so Jérôme has rented Jean-Pierre's vines on a long-term contract – 20 hectares, mainly of Syrah, Grenache Noir and Carignan, with a little Mourvèdre and Cinsaut, in the villages of Fos and Roquessels. He intends to start gradually, initially making wine for sale in bulk, *en vrac*, and increase the quantity in bottle gradually. But first he had to build his cellar: in spring 2014 he showed me a cleared patch of land with some waterlogged holes for the foundations. He hoped to make his first wine there in 2014, and indeed the cellar was completed just in time for the harvest. With the challenging climatic conditions of September 2014, it was not the easiest of vintages, but Jérôme has made a pink, a white, and three reds. His white is a fresh lively Carignan Blanc, and the rosé a blend of the usual five varieties, but mainly Syrah and Grenache Noir. His entry-level red, again from all five varieties, makes for easy drinking with dry spice. Next comes a blend of Syrah, Grenache Noir and Carignan, with some sturdy youthful fruit, and the barrel-aged wine is a blend of Syrah and Grenache Noir, with some red fruit and a tannic streak.

The choice of the name 'Epidaure' is intriguing. Jérôme's wife is a chemist and the town of Epidaurus was an important centre of ancient Greek medicine.

Domaine Ollier-Taillefer

Route de Gabian, Fos 34320
Tel : 04 67 90 24 59
ollier.taillefer@wanadoo.fr
www.olliertaillefer.com

This is one of the long-standing estates of Faugères. Marcel Taillefer worked to create the appellation or, more precisely, the VDQS, (the category below an appellation) just after the war and, in 1961, his daughter Nicole married Alain Ollier, who was a farmer from Lodève. All the wine was sold *en vrac* until 1976, when Alain took the then pioneering step of putting some wine in bottle, just one pallet's worth. It took a good ten years for them to reach the stage of selling all their production in bottle. Alain began with 7 hectares outside Autignac and then cleared *garrigues* and planted vines in the pretty village of Fos, so that they now have 35 hectares altogether. These include three plots of vines totalling 10 hectares as you come into Fos and above the village on both sides of the valley. That is where they also have their tasting *caveau*, as well as a smart new cellar, used for the first time in 2014.

These days it is the next generation who run the estate. Luc makes the wine and his sister Françoise, who used to run the appellation *syndicat,* is responsible for sales. Together they make a good team: Luc is a thoughtful and sensitive winemaker, while Françoise is bright and vivacious with a keen sense of humour, and always conducts a cellar visit with great enthusiasm. Alain still retains a lively interest in the estate and

*Françoise Ollier of Domaine Ollier-Taillefer, one of the first estates to put
their wine in bottle, and until recently the only estate based in Fos*

is always there to offer a tasting if his children are otherwise occupied. It
was Alain who built the dry stone walls by the cellar; Françoise describes
him as *'un passioné de pierres sèches'* – passionate about dry stone walls.

The new cellar is undoubtedly one of the finest of the appellation. It
is built in porous *pierre du Gard*; each block apparently weighs a ton and
this stone provides excellent natural insulation. The cellar is surrounded
by earth on three sides, complete with *un toit végétal* or green roof.
Thus they save on electricity for insulation and air conditioning, with
further temperature control provided by an ecological *puits canadien*, a
Canadian well. And when you see where they used to make their wine,
you can appreciate the need to move from the cramped conditions.

I have always enjoyed the wines of Ollier-Taillefer, ever since my first
visit to the estate in 1999. They make three red wines. Les Collines is
their entry-level traditional Faugères, for which I have a soft spot; it
is sunshine in a glass, everything that good Faugères should be, fruity
and fresh, but uncomplicated. The blend includes a high proportion
of Grenache Noir with some Carignan and Syrah, and some young
Mourvèdre, all aged in vat. Grande Réserve comes from a selection of
the oldest vines, namely Carignan, Grenache and Syrah, which give
structure, tannin and perfumed fruit, but with more concentration and

depth than Les Collines. It ages very well in bottle. Then there is Castel Fossibus, which is aged in oak and again benefits from some bottle age.

Le Rêve de Noé, a blend of Mourvèdre and Syrah, is a new *cuvée*, made for the first time in 2013. Essentially they have made just one barrel of each variety, aged in new oak, to provide 800 bottles and 60 magnums. It is rich and concentrated, but not heavy, with a harmonious balance between the fruit and oak, and masses of ageing potential. It provides an illustration of how each generation makes its mark.

Les Collines Rosé is a blend of *saigné* and pressed juice, mainly Cinsaut and Grenache Noir, as well as some young Syrah and Mourvèdre, with some fresh raspberry fruit.

Allegro is the white Faugères, a blend of Vermentino and Roussanne. They obtained cuttings of Vermentino from François Guy at Château Coujan in St Chinian and grafted it on to Carignan Blanc in 1991, and made their first white wine in 1994. Roussanne was planted, rather than grafted, at the same time. The Vermentino provides some natural freshness and herbal notes, while the Roussanne fills out the palate with a touch of white blossom. Françoise dismisses Marsanne as uninteresting, and Grenache Blanc as too alcoholic. Altitude also makes for freshness. Allegro develops beautifully with some bottle age – and the local goat's cheese from Mas Rolland in the village of Montesquieu provides the perfect foil.

Baies de Novembre, their dessert wine, comes from Grenache Noir picked in November. They leave one bunch per vine and, if the birds, the weather and the tourists are restrained, the grapes are picked when they are fully raisined. The juice is fermented in oak very slowly until the summer and the wine stays in oak for a couple of years to develop the oxidative character of the Grenache. There are notes of honey and orange with balancing acidity; it is sweet, but with a fresh finish. Needless to say, it is not made every year. And a Fine de Faugères completes their range.

LAURENS

Laurens is one of the more substantial villages of the appellation. It has a château with a highly coloured tiled roof which once housed the offices of the *syndicat*; these days its public rooms are used for exhibitions and other entertainment. The usually dried-up river Sauvanès crosses the village, and it is a short walk to the remains of the abbey of Sauvanès.

Abbaye Sylva Plana

13 ancienne route de Bédarieux,
Tel: 04 67 24 91 67
info@vignoblesbouchard.com
www.vignoblesbouchard.com

The Abbaye Sylva Plana – the name means a plain of trees – is the Faugères estate of the Bouchard and Guy families, and is associated with Domaine des Henrys in the nearby Côtes de Thongue. Cédric Guy's family vines were originally part of the cooperative, but he wanted to make his own wine, and so he began working with Henri Bouchard in 1998; together they developed Sylva Plana with a first Faugères vintage in 1999. Cédric is now responsible for both vineyards and cellar, and works with Henri's son Nicolas. They are one of the larger Faugères producers with 54 hectares, with cellars as well as a restaurant in Laurens. They have been organic since 2008.

Their white Faugères is a blend of Grenache Blanc, with some Roussanne and a small amount of Viognier, with an *élevage* in vat. They have tried barrel ageing but were not convinced because of the loss of acidity. This wine is rounded and honeyed with a firm finish. The rosé is based on Cinsaut which is pressed, while a little Grenache Noir adds some weight, and Syrah accounts for the gentle colour.

They make four different red Faugères. Les Novices is their entry-level wine, based on Le Plant Droit, a variety which Cédric said is a cross between Cinsaut and Carignan which had almost disappeared; it combines the fruit of Carignan with the colour of Cinsaut, and in this instance is blended with some Cinsaut, Carignan and Grenache Noir, all of which are vinified by carbonic maceration. The result is some ripe berry fruit. Le Closeraie comes from older Carignan and Grenache Noir vines, with a drop of Syrah and Mourvèdre. Again they favour carbonic maceration, making for some ripe fruit with a tannic streak. Le Songe de l'Abbaie is mainly Syrah and Mourvèdre with some Carignan and Grenache Noir, with an *élevage* in new oak. The palate is rich with *tapenade* and vanilla fruit. Le Part du Diable comes from a 6-hectare vineyard planted with all five varieties of the appellation, including some very old vines. Carignan dominates. The wine is aged in barrel, and the objective is a wine with greater longevity.

The ruins of the old abbey can be reached along a narrow road out of Laurens, what is described as the '*ancienne route de Roquessels*', and at a certain moment there are views of the ruined castle of Roquessels. The abbey was founded in 1139 and its mother house was the abbey of Sylvanès in the Aveyron. It is a tranquil spot. The monks built a dam in the river Sauvanès to make a small lake for fish, which still exists, but the building itself is now completely overwhelmed by vegetation. Cédric explains that it has been destroyed three times and was rebuilt twice during the Wars of Religion, for Laurens was Protestant. It now belongs to Bâtiments de France (the equivalent of English Heritage), and has never been deconsecrated, but they have left the vegetation to its own devices. There are well-maintained vineyards all around the old abbey, the closest of which is called *le jardin des moines* (the monks' garden), where the vines are particularly vigorous. Cédric has a 35-hectare plot of vines with some gnarled 100-year-old Grenache Noir on the way to the site of the nearby disused quarry which had provided the stone for the abbey; schist would have been too fragile. It is a wonderful peaceful spot with views over the surrounding vineyards and hillsides.

Domaine Frédéric Brouca

10 avenue de la Gare
Tel: 06 58 08 31 59
office@brouca.com

This is one of the newest estates in Faugères. Frédéric Brouca bought 10 hectares of vines from the former estate of Borie Fouisseau in 2012 and is also renting their old cellars in Laurens. He hails from Picardie and used to work for Jean-Marc Brocard in Chablis, but realized that it was winemaking that really interested him and so looked for vineyards of his own. Burgundy or the northern Rhône would have been an option had he been a millionaire; Faugères was a much more affordable proposition. He wanted a cooler site, and organic vineyards. Frédéric spends much of the year in Canada as his wife is Canadian, but manages to be in Faugères at critical moments of the year. In his absence it is Simon Bertschinger from Mas Sibert, a local but not a Faugères domaine, who is now responsible for the day-to-day running of the property, and particularly the vineyards where there is stony clay and limestone as well as schist.

Frédéric considers that he has more of a Burgundian than Languedocien approach to winemaking. He uses a little sulphur in the cellar, but no other chemicals in either vineyard or cellar, and he favours an early harvest, and whole bunch fermentations. He has developed a range of four red wines. The principal one, accounting for 80 per cent of his production, is Champs Pentus, a blend of 40 per cent Syrah, with 30 per cent each of Grenache Noir and Carignan, aged partly in tank and partly in *foudres*. The 2013 still retains a sturdy streak of tannin, with some fresh minerality and fruit. Samsó Seuille is a pure Cinsaut, from 40-year-old *gobelet* vines, aged for ten months in tank, with the delicious fresh cherry fruit typical of that grape variety; this is Vin de France rather than Faugères. Montée la Serre is a blend of 40 per cent Syrah with 30 per cent Grenache Noir, 25 per cent Carignan and 5 per cent Cinsaut, which have spent ten months in 2- to 4-year-old barrels. Fresh red fruit and integrated tannins are the dominant notes, with a refreshing low alcohol of 13.5% abv. The final wine is Clos Sauveplane, a blend of 70 per cent Mourvèdre and 30 per cent Syrah, which has

Frédéric Brouca, who hails from Picardie, is making wine in Laurens

spent twelve months in *foudres* to develop some depth and structure, with firm tannins. It promises to develop beautifully in the bottle. In 2015 Frédéric made his first rosé, a pure Mourvèdre, and he has also ten ares of Terret Blanc with his first white wine planned for 2016.

Mas Gabinèle

1750 chemin de Bédarieux, Laurens 34480
Tel : 04 67 89 71 72
info@masgabinele.com
www.masgabinele.com

I am always intrigued by the paths people take to become wine growers. Thierry Rodriguez studied economics at Montpellier and then worked in the export department of the large group of producers, Les Vignerons du Val d'Orbieu. In 1993 he set up as a *négociant*, concentrating on *vins de cépages*, but had always wanted to make his own wine. His grandparents were members of the village cooperative of Puimisson which made *vin de table* at the time, and his parents-in-law had vines in Causse-et-Veyran. Then, in 1998, he heard of a friend selling some vines and bought just 2.5 hectares. The following year he acquired a further 7 hectares, and now he has a total of 18 hectares, about 20 plots in all, ranging from 2 hectares to 20 ares, with Syrah accounting for 40 per cent. His vines are mainly

Thierry Rodriguez of Mas Gabinèle négociant turned vigneron

between Laurens and Roquessels, a mosaic of plots, one of which is called Gabinèle. '*Une gabinelà*' in Occitan is a *cabane*, a small hut, something rather less solid than a *mazet*, and appropriately his label is an attractive representation of a small hut with a couple of cypress trees.

For his early vintages, Thierry rented cellar space from his friends at Domaine Balliccioni in Autignac, but he has now built a state of the art cellar outside the village of Laurens, which was used for the first time in 2013. Thierry talks about the problems of getting planning permission because he bought the land before it was classified as '*constructible*', and he had to convince the *mairie* in Laurens to revise the Plan Locale d'Urbanisme. That took four years. The building work finally started in April 2013 and was finished just in time for the harvest. There is an attractive internal courtyard, where Thierry is planning a Mediterranean garden. He would also like to plant a small vineyard of *cépages gris*, Pinot, Picpoul, Sauvignon, Carignan, Clairette, Ribeyrenc and other pale-pink varieties. The tasting room is decorated with old photographs, including one of his grandmother as a little girl, with enormous bunches of Aramon.

Thierry talks about the time it takes to restore a neglected vineyard, at least three or four years of careful pruning and feeding the vines with organic matter to restore the balance in the soil. He practises *lutte raisonnée*, and learned his winemaking as he went along, with the help of Jean Natoli. He likes wines that are easily accessible and so he seeks balance in his grapes, wanting grapes which are healthy and ripe, but not over-ripe. He aims for a gentle vinification as he does not want overly concentrated wines; he uses carbonic maceration for some of the Syrah and Carignan, and prefers *remontages* and *délestages* to *pigeage*.

He makes four or five wines, depending on the vintage. His white wine is pure Grenache Gris, a Pays de l'Hérault. About a third of the wine is fermented in barrel and lees-stirred until Christmas, before blending in January; a vat sample is fresh and rounded with good acidity. His rosé is a blend of Mourvèdre with Grenache and Cinsaut, of which a quarter is vinified in barrel to give some weight and body. As a vat sample it is the colour of pink grapefruit juice, with a firm nose, and I could taste some weight as well as fruit. It is definitely a food rosé.

For his Cuvée Tradition, a blend of 40 per cent Syrah, 30 per cent Grenache Noir, 20 per cent Carignan and 10 per cent Mourvèdre,

70 per cent of the blend is given about twelve months oak ageing, but with very little new wood. The result is indeed very rounded and supple, with silky tannins and an elegant finish. It is rather more than an average entry-level wine, and is also significantly more expensive. Le Rarissime, of which the first vintage was 2001, is a blend of Syrah, Grenache Noir, Mourvèdre, and maybe Carignan, depending on the vintage; whatever is best. It spends sixteen months in new barrels, going into barrel immediately after the fermentation, and is blended after the *élevage*. In the 2012, the oak is present but not overpowering, nicely integrated with rounded mouth feel. It is rich but not heavy, and I was very surprised to find the alcohol level reached 15% abv.

In the very best years Thierry also makes Inaccessible. In 2012 just three barrels gave him 800 bottles. It is based on 70 per cent Mourvèdre with 15 per cent each of Syrah and Grenache Noir, with sixteen months in wood. He observes that Mourvèdre has a bad reputation as the appellation decree made it obligatory for Faugères – with the result that the wine growers who did not already have Mourvèdre often planted it in the wrong place, so it performed badly with yields that were too high. Thierry bought a plot of Mourvèdre a while ago and it took several years of hard work to get some good results. The first vintage of Inaccessible was 2010, and the reference is to Jacques Brel's song '*La Quête, Mon inaccessible étoile*', in other words 'The Quest for My Inaccessible Star'. The wine is deep in colour, with smoky fruit on the nose, perfumed with a tannin streak on the palate and a rich finish. The flavours are impressive and the ageing potential certain. Thierry Rodriguez exudes a quiet confidence; he is very committed and highly professional in his approach. This is an estate that deserves to go far.

Château de Grézan

RD 909 Laurens 34480
Tel: 04 67 90 27 46
contact@chateau-grezan.fr
www.chateau-grezan.fr

The history of Grézan goes back to the Romans, who built a villa on the site. Next came a *commanderie* of the Knight Templars, which was connected to the nearby Château de Laurens. And now it is a wine estate.

The Château de Grézan is an extraordinary building. At first glance you might be forgiven for believing it to be a medieval château with its crenellated battlements, but then you look more closely and realize the towers are hollow fakes, *trompe l'oeil* intended to deceive. It was built towards the end of the nineteenth century, during the wealthy period of the Languedoc, when fortunes were made from agriculture – not just from wine, but also from wheat and olives. The *nouveaux riches* of Béziers built houses in the countryside to show off their material success, often choosing the Bordeaux architect Louis-Michel Garosse, but essentially you selected your château from a book of architects' designs. Garosse was inspired by work that he did in Carcassonne in the middle of the nineteenth century, and consequently Grézan has been described as '*la petite cité de Carcassonne*'. The part with the fortified courtyard and wine cellar is now the sole property of the Pujol family, who have been here since 1988. Jean-Louis Pujol bought out his previous partners and now works with his son, Fabien. Adjoining the cellars, across the park, is the habitable château complete with conical towers, which is the property of the Swiss-German Schellenberg family. Jean-Louis was born in Autignac and remembers a tough childhood. His parents had inherited vines, but sold them in the economic crisis of the late 1950s. He recalls horses working in the vines, though his father bought one of the very first tractors so he could work for other wine growers.

Altogether there are 80 hectares of vines, half of which are Faugères. The vines attached to the *château* are *vins de pays* because the land is too flat for Faugères, as it lies to the south of Laurens, towards Magalas. Their Faugères vines are closer to Laurens and in Autignac, as is their vinification cellar. Here at Grézan they have a cellar for *élevage*, complete with a toad who is supposed to bring good luck. The first bottlings of Château de Grézan date back to 1988.

The large barn forms the tasting room. There is an intriguing display of different schist on the wall – *ardoisier*, *gréseux*, *argileux* and *basalte* – illustrating the differences in colour and texture. The Pujols make a pair of Chardonnays, rather than Faugères Blanc. A Chardonnay Pays d'Oc is fresh and clean, and benefits from technological expertise, pressed without contact with air, what they call '*pressurage inert*'. A second Chardonnay, fermented and aged in oak with *bâtonnage*, displays more character. The rosé is also very technological and clean.

There are three red Faugères. Faugères Expression is from 5- to 10-year-old Grenache, Syrah and Carignan vines. It has some stony red fruit, with peppery notes and a fresh finish. Cuvée Heritage includes some Carignan that Jean-Louis's grandfather planted in 1921, à l'ancienne, meaning high-density *gobelet* vines as well Grenache, Syrah and Mourvèdre. It spends twelve months in oak, both *barriques* and *demi-muids*, and is ripe and rounded with an oaky backbone. Cuvée les Schistes Dorés is a reference to the schist *ardoisier*, which has golden reflections in the light. The wine is a blend of Syrah and Mourvèdre that is vinified in *demi-muids*, with a manual *pigeage*, and then aged for two years in wood. It is rich and concentrated.

The Pujols also make a Fine de Faugères; Jean-Louis explains that it is aged in barrel for a minimum of ten years. It is rich, peaty and smooth.

Château Laurens

Domaine de la Grangette, Nissan-lez-Enserune 34440
Tel : 04 67 37 22 36
marketing@montariol-degroote.com

Château Laurens is also known as Château Sun Pool, but the former is the more appropriate name for this estate – the cellars and vineyards are all in Laurens. However, it is a property with a Chinese associate and 'Sun Pool' in Chinese apparently translates approximately as 'great château wines'. The French face of Château Laurens is Stéphane Montariol who is associated with Pierre Degroote, and their consultant winemaker is the Australian, Richard Osborne, who has lived and worked in the Languedoc for a number of years. They have bought vineyards as well as large cellars and farm buildings from Remy Fardel, who used to be involved with the Château de Grézan. The first vintage of Château Laurens under the new ownership was 2013, but the vineyards had already been rented for the previous five years. There are 21 hectares in three large plots, all around Laurens.

They have already done quite a lot of work on the vines, converting them to organic viticulture, but it takes time for the vines to acclimatize and they became fully organic in 2015. The vines to the south of the village, towards Grézan, are on schist while those in a 14-hectare block near the quarry, planted in 1970, are on sandstone and *galets roulées*. Those vines ripen a week to ten days later than the others, as they are in a much windier position and about 40 metres higher. The altitude allows for some wonderful views towards the nearby villages.

The cellars, which are more like a large barn, conform to the classic Midi model. They were built in the early nineteenth century with a high ceiling and solid walls. There are concrete tanks and new stainless steel vats, and swallows have nested on the rafters, which apparently augurs good luck.

This is Richard's first experience of Faugères. He had previously worked with Pierre Degroote at Domaines Virginie, and now also works in the Minervois and in Limoux. He has a down-to-earth Australian approach to winemaking: 'Wine is all about fruit. You must keep the fruit.' He vividly remembers a criticism at a Pays d'Oc tasting: 'This wine is too fruity.' For the 2013 vintage they used cultured yeast as an insurance, because they had no experience of the cellar and needed to check that the environment was healthy.

Stéphane talks about typicity. With schist, he says, you obtain good levels of ripeness, especially with Syrah, with lots of red fruit and the warmth of the *terroir*. Faugères retains freshness, like the higher

A sign on the wall of the old stables, which roughly translates as: It is firstly expressly forbidden to smoke in the stables or barns and secondly to ride either the horses or the carts, or to let anyone else do so.

vineyards of the Terrasses du Larzac around St Jean de Blaquière. *Les anciens,* the old local wine growers, appreciated the fresh nights and hot days of Faugères, making a wine that was rich, but not heavy.

Amongst the 2013 vat samples there was a fresh juicy Cinsaut, prompting Richard to observe that this was the first Cinsaut he had ever really liked. The Syrah was peppery with supple tannins; it had been picked as late as 15 October. A potential blend for 2013 consisted of 55 per cent Grenache Noir, 30 per cent Syrah, 15 per cent Mourvèdre and 5 per cent Cinsaut, but no Carignan, with a small percentage in wood for six months; it would be blended in late May for bottling in January. It was spicy with ripe red fruit and a tannic streak. In contrast, the 2012 was spicy with an explosion of rich liquorice on the palate, supple tannins and just a touch of wood. Richard favours supple tannins, which is apparent from the 2011 wine. It will be interesting to observe the progress of Château Laurens as they find their way.

Domaine de Sarabande

14 ancienne route nationale, Laurens 34480
Tel : 06 74 30 43 28
pauldouglasgordon@gmail.com
www.sarabande-wines.com

Paul Gordon, who comes from Sydney, first discovered wine while working in London for Terence Conrad. When he went back to Australia he found a job with the Australian Oddbins and studied winemaking through a correspondence course at Charles Sturt University. He then worked a vintage at various estates – Brokenwood, Domaine Chandon and Hardy's – and then became a flying winemaker in the department of the Gard, in Spain and also in New Zealand, at Isabel Estate in Marlborough. Isla, who became his wife, had left Ireland and was backpacking in New Zealand at the time; she turned up at Isabel to earn some money. They spent five years in New Zealand and then it was time to come to Europe. They first looked in Spain but the land was too expensive, so they shifted their attention north of the Pyrenees and realized that Faugères ticked all the boxes: 'It's close to the mountains, close to the sea, has very good soil and great wines, nice villages and it is not too busy.' They looked for vineyards to rent and someone offered them 5.5 hectares, in two blocks just outside the village of Autignac. Then they found a house in Laurens with a large garage that was perfect for some small vats and a few barrels. Paul and Isla took over their first vines in March 2009, just in time to prune them. They now have 8 hectares and work organically, with minimal use of sulphur and copper.

Paul bottles all his wine with a screw cap as most of his sales are overseas and, even more revolutionary for a French appellation, he puts the grape variety blend on the front label, rather than on a discreet back label. Paul likes experimenting with his rosé. The 2013 is Grenache Noir with just 10 per cent Mourvèdre. He uses only natural yeast and fermented it at 16° to 18°C. A malolactic fermentation of the Mourvèdre rounds out the palate nicely in the vat sample, so that there is restrained acidity, balanced by fresh fruit from the Grenache Noir.

Paul says 2013 was a tough year to harvest as everything was so late; they were the only ones picking in mid-September. A vat sample of the Grenache Noir is an explosion of liqueur cherries on the palate. The Mourvèdre is ripe with savoury notes and the 80-year-old Carignan has some ripe rustic fruit. Syrah, from a new barrel, was perfumed and peppery. Paul talks about typicity; above all, he wants freshness in his wine: 'You get very good acidity from the soil in Faugères. In other parts of the world, if you wait until the grapes taste ripe, you need to add tartaric acid. Natural acidity is so important for the fresh fruit character.' He does not use any cultured yeast or malolactic culture, nor does he fine or filter. He makes his wine as naturally as possible, but does use some sulphur.

Moving on to the 2012s in bottle, his 2012 Misterioso Pays d'Or, a blend of Grenache Noir and Syrah, is ripe and perfumed. It is called Misterioso as it is the surprise *cuvée*, a blend which can change from year to year. The 2012 Faugères, from 65 per cent Grenache Noir aged in vat plus 25 per cent Carignan and 10 per cent Syrah aged in barrels, has acidity and tannin with lovely fresh fruit. And 2012 was the last vintage of his Vin de France, which included Aramon from a vineyard he no longer has. The Aramon was blended with Carignan, making what would have once been a typical blend of the region. This last vintage has some lovely ripe rustic fruit for its swansong. In its place Paul will probably make another Faugères, from Carignan with some Syrah.

Their aim is to make serious wines with ageing potential, but Paul is not afraid to experiment. This estate has evolved enormously since its beginning in 2009, and you sense that things will never stand still.

Chateau Sauvanès

Avenue de la Gare, Laurens 34480
04 67 96 64 06
contact@vallat-languedoc.com
www.vallat-languedoc.com

The Vallat family bought Château Sauvanès from a *bordelais* company in 2003, with 42 hectares, mostly in Laurens, as well as one plot in Cabrerolles. They already owned Château Mondagot in Montpeyroux and Château les Thérons in St Saturnin. It is very much a family business: the father, Jean-François, runs the vineyards, while one son, Camille, makes the wine, and the other, Vincent, is responsible for the commercial side of things. Vincent says that the previous owners had invested in the cellar, but had rather neglected the vines, so that they have had to do a lot of replanting and rewiring.

There are wonderful views of the Caroux in the distance. They have 38 hectares of vines all together in one large plot in Laurens, including some old Grenache Noir and Carignan; such a big plot is most unusual. They have also taken on another estate of 10 hectares, *en fermage,* as the owner does not actually want to sell it, so the vineyards of Mas Colombier will be incorporated into Château Sauvanès.

They make a straightforward range of Faugères. There is a fresh rosé based on Syrah, and a white from Grenache Blanc with some Roussanne, for which the winemaking is very simple, though they are wondering whether some oak ageing might give the wine more body. The basic red is a blend of equal parts of Syrah, Grenache Noir and Carignan with 10 per cent Cinsaut, all aged in vat for six months. It is fresh and fruity. In contrast, the more serious Château de Sauvanès is mainly Syrah with some Grenache Noir and Carignan, with two-thirds of the wine aged in barrel.

Vincent enthuses about Syrah. They have two particularly good plots, and with Mas Colombier – for which the first vintage was 2013 – they are considering a pure Syrah, or almost pure. He thinks those vines will make for more powerful wines, whereas those of Sauvanès produce more *fraicheur*. Indeed, for Vincent the typicity of Faugères is *fraicheur*.

He makes a comparison with Montpeyroux, describing that as hotter, more *viandé*, while Faugères is liquorice and *fruits noirs*.

Domaine Schisterelle

27 bis avenue de Béziers, Laurens 34480
Tel : 06 03 22 16 56
celine-cabanel@orange.fr

Céline Cabanel is bright and vivacious with a winning smile. She lives on the edge of Laurens, with an old barn serving as her cellar. She has 6 hectares of vines, half Faugères and half *vin de table*, which came from her grandparents, from whom she took over in 1999. In 2008 she took the decision to leave the cooperative and make her own wine. Her parents work in civil engineering and her husband is a salesman, so the vineyard is very much her personal project. She calls it *'une jolie aventure'*, a lovely adventure, and as for the name of the estate, it is the combination of *'elle'*, or 'she' and the schist of Faugères.

There is a white Vin de France from Chardonnay and Muscat, which is soft and ripe; a pink Faugères from pressed Grenache Noir with some dry fruit. The first red wine is a *vin de table* from Cabernet Sauvignon and Grenache Noir. Faugères Coup de Coeur is a blend of Syrah with some Grenache Noir and Mourvèdre, aged in vat. The vinification is simple with no carbonic maceration and the result is lightly spicy and cheerful. Omage, a homage to her grandparents, is mainly Grenache Noir with a little Mourvèdre, which spends ten to twelve months in barrel. When asked about projects for the future, she replies 'a new cellar and a barrel-aged Syrah', that she would probably call L'Imprévu.

Domaine Valambelle

25 avenue de la Gare, Laurens 34480
Tel : 04 67 90 12 12
domaine.valambelle@outlook.fr
www.domaine-valambelle.com

The Abbal family, who own Domaine Valambelle, have been in Laurens since the Revolution. The father, Michel, worked his first vintage in 1954, the year he left school. At that time the VDQS was just about to be recognized, but, as Michel remarks, Faugères never produced the large yields of other areas. The family vines were in the Laurens cooperative, which Michel left in 2002 to make his first wines in 2003. His son Thierry went to agricultural college and feels it is now time to go it alone, while his daughter has done computer studies and helps with sales.

Michel has 23 hectares of vines. The name of the estate means 'a beautiful valley' and that indeed is where his vines are, in a valley between Faugères and Laurens. To reach them you drive through the middle of Laurens and up the concreted river valley of the Sauvanès; sometimes there is a trickle of water, but more often it is used as a road or for parking (though Michel remembers two metres of water in the village square in 1967). A dirt track leads up into the vines. His father had planted vines here in 1921, when he married. Michel planted the vineyard of Mourvèdre, on the plateau, in 1982, while he was still a *coopérateur*. He talks of the need to *défricher* in the 1970s, clearing the *garrigues* with a bulldozer, and it is hard to imagine that these slopes of neatly tended vines were once covered with dense vegetation. Michel has always worked organically, but has never bothered to register with any of the relevant organizations.

His cellar, which he built himself, adjoins his house. There are concrete vats, which are easy to clean and make for stable fermentation temperatures, and there are some barrels for just one *cuvée*. Altogether he makes as many as five red wines, depending on the vintage, as well as a pink and a white. The white Faugères, L'Angolet, is a blend of Roussanne and Grenache Blanc – '*angolet*' is an Occitan term for the cool wind that comes down from the mountain. The rosé is predominately Grenache Noir, and mostly *saigné*, with some opulent ripe strawberry fruit. Faugères Tradition is called Millepeyres, 'one thousand stones' in Occitan – a reference to the very hard stony schist. Then there is red L'Angolet and Le Florentin, as well as Caprices des Schistes, which is predominantly Mourvèdre with some Grenache Noir and was made for the first time in 2011. Grande Cuvée, of which 70 per cent is aged in wood for twelve months, completes the range. Le Florentin recalls family history, for Florentin Abbal was an artist who died too young at the age of 20, and Michel and his wife are both descended from Florentin's brother. This is the wine I like best of all, with some gentle spice. And I appreciate the attractive design of Michel's labels, which include the words 'Artisan Vigneron'.

ROQUESSELS

Roquessels is a maze of narrow streets, dominated by the ruins of a tenth-century castle, from which there are wonderful views of the surrounding countryside and villages, looking south towards Gabian and the coast. There are just a handful of wine growers.

Château des Adouzes

Tras du Castel, Roquessels 34320
Tel: 04 67 90 24 11
adouzes@orange.fr
www.adouzes.com

Jean-Claude Estève has a tasting room and office in his father's house in the centre of the village of Roquessels. It is a rather sombre building dating from 1939, built by his grandfather. The name Adouzes comes from a *lieu-dit*: the tiny hamlet on the road between Faugères and Gabian, now called Castelsec, was once known as Adouzes. They have vines nearby.

Jean-Claude explains that he is the fourth generation of wine growers in Roquessels. His great-grandfather arrived from La Croix de Mounis, in the northern part of the Hérault, where the family had been sheep farmers, and stayed in Roquessels, marrying a girl from the village whose family had a little land, with vines and olives, and also some arable land to provide fodder for their horse. The young couple kept hens and rabbits, and were self-sufficient. Their son, Jean-Claude's grandfather, started his three-year stint of military service in 1911 and then managed to survive the First World War and create an estate which Jean-Claude's parents subsequently enlarged. Originally they were cooperative members both at Laurens, which they left in 1985, and in Faugères, from which they resigned in 1990, in order to make and bottle their own wine from 42 hectares of vines. In 1985 they were the twentieth independent wine grower to set up in Faugères. Jean-Claude says that in 1985 bulk wine was selling well: 'The *négociants* used to call us, but these days we need to call them and they name their price.' Jean-Claude still sells a little *en vrac*, but that market is shrinking. Wine in bottle now forms the bulk of his sales.

I tasted their full range of wines. The white is a blend of Roussanne, Grenache Blanc and Rolle, made for the first time in 2009; Jean-Claude planted white varieties when the appellation was created in 2005. The vinification is simple, the wine fresh and light. Château des Adouzes rosé is a blend of Syrah and Grenache, made by the *saigné* method, with a cool fermentation, and includes grapes from 50-year-old vines, while Domaine Estève Rosé is lighter.

In addition there are several red wines. A common theme is lack of oak, with just one wine '*vieilli en fûts de chêne*', in *barriques* including some American oak. Jean-Claude believes that American oak makes an impact much more quickly than French oak. His winemaking is uncomplicated. He does not always destalk everything, as the stalks, he says, can provide a useful filter for *remontages*, but Grenache Noir stalks are usually green, so those he does remove.

Domaine Estève red is ripe and fruity, an easy-drinking wine resulting from a simple vinification. Domaine Thibault – named after Jean-Claude's son – is a blend of Syrah, Carignan and Grenache Noir, with the Syrah fermented by carbonic maceration, something that Thibault really wanted to try. Château des Adouzes is a Carignan-Syrah blend, including Carignan vines that are over fifty years old. Cuvée Elegance, a blend of Syrah and Carignan, made for the first time in 1998, attempts to be just that, with soft tannins and some ripe fruit. Finally, Plô de Figues is named after *a lieu-dit* of 5 hectares on a nearby plateau, appropriately one with fig trees. It is a blend of Syrah, made by carbonic maceration, with equal amounts of Carignan and Grenache, and a low yield of just 18 hectolitres per hectare, and some of the vines are as much as eighty years old. *Élevage* is in vat and the wine is ripe, fruity and supple, typifying the style of Château des Adouzes.

Domaine Bois de Rose

Route de Pézenas
Tel: 06 34 99 22 08
jeanluc.maraval@orange.fr

Jean-Luc Maraval has a tasting booth on the road between Faugères and Gabian. I had driven past it previously and had wondered why there was a tasting booth there, but the answer is quite simple: Jean-Luc's vineyards are right by it. He has 6 hectares that he bought in 2005. They represent a mid-life career change: he had worked in insurance for twenty-five years. He proudly declares that he is '*le fils d'un vigneron*' as his father used to have vines in Olargues. Bois de Rose is the name of the plot, and there is a different flower on the label of each *cuvée*, changing with each vintage.

Jean-Luc made his first wines in 2007, after spending two years with the cooperative. He now rents space at Vino-Tec in Autignac, owning his vats and sharing an oenologist who does the analysis. When tasted, the weather was rather chilly, and it must be said that the wines were also rather chilly – not the ideal tasting temperature. The rosé is mainly Cinsaut with some Grenache Noir and, given a couple of hours' skin contact in the press, has some fresh acidity. There is one vineyard dedicated to rosé and the two varieties are co-fermented. The red wine is half Grenache Noir with a quarter each of Syrah and Mourvèdre, which represents the composition of the vineyard. It is aged in vat, and has some liqueur cherry fruit.

Jean-Luc works hard, with cheerful enthusiasm, selling his wines at village *fêtes* and local markets; he is a regular at the Saturday morning market in Pézenas.

Château des Peyregrandes

11 chemin de l'Aire, Roquessels 34320
Tel : 04 67 90 15 00
chateau-des-peyregrandes@wanadoo.fr
www.chateaudespeyregrandes.com

Marie-Geneviève Boudal is a cousin of Jean-Claude Estève from Château des Adouzes. When her father died, she and her architect husband decided to take over their share of the family vines. She was brought up in Bédarieux and used to come to Roquessels as a child at the weekends. Marie-Geneviève is bright and vivacious, petite and elegant, and that is the character of her wines. The estate comprises 25 hectares. She talks of having converted to organic viticulture, for which she was certified in 2015: 'It has not been difficult to adapt. I was fed up with using chemicals, and the wines are so much better.' And why the name Peyregrandes? It is a play on words: '*peyre*' is the Occitan for stone, and her father's name was Pierre.

Her entry-level wines are labelled Domaine Bénézech-Boudal, as she used to be Mademoiselle Bénézech. The white Faugères is a blend of Roussanne and Marsanne; the vines were planted in 2007 and the wine undergoes a classic vinification with some *bâtonnage*. Marie-Geneviève makes two rosés. Domaine Bénézech is a blend of Cinsaut which is pressed, and Grenache and Syrah which are *saigné*. It is quite simple and fresh. More characterful is Château des Peyregrandes, from a selection of Syrah and Grenache that are pressed. A quarter of the blend spends four months in wood, which gives some weight and richness. It is a *rosé de repas* as opposed to a *rosé d'apéritif.*

The entry-level red, Domaine Bénézech-Boudal, is easy and fruity with black cherries; Château Peyregrandes has more structure and depth; while the Cuvée Prestige is a blend of oak-aged Syrah with Carignan and Mourvèdre. It is a more substantial wine, but Marie-Geneviève is adamant that she does not want the taste of oak. Cuvée Marie-Laurence, named after her grandmother who bought some of the family's original vines, is a blend of co-fermented Syrah and Grenache. The Syrah is a little riper and the Grenache Noir less ripe, with an *élevage* in vat. It is not made every year, and I found it quite rich and less elegant than the other wines. Cuvée Charlotte, named after her grand-daughter, is a blend of 80 per cent Syrah with 10 per cent each of Grenache Noir and Mourvèdre, all aged in oak for twelve months, including one third new oak. Not surprisingly oak is the dominant characteristic of the young wine.

Marie-Geneviève feels that south-facing slopes are the key to typicity here. She explains that she wants to bring out the schist, particularly the minerality of the schist, with a balance between power, finesse and elegance. She certainly achieves that in her Cuvée Prestige.

Domaine des Trinités

6 chemin de l'Aire, Roquessels 34320
Tel: 04 67 90 23 25
simon@trinites.com
www.trinites.com

The appellation of Faugères does seem to attract more than its fair share of foreigners. One of the rising stars amongst the newcomers is Domaine des Trinités in Roquessels. Simon Coulshaw is British and his wife Monica comes from Barcelona. Simon's father was brought up in Paris and kept a family home in France; he instilled a love of wine in his son, and wine was part of everyday family life. Simon did quite a bit of winemaking early on and then worked in IT until 2004, when he elected to do the two-year course at Plumpton in East Sussex. He even thought about buying land in

*Simon Coulshaw of Domaine des Trinités, one of the outsiders, who has
contributed much to the energy of Faugères*

Sussex, but southern reds are his real passion and so he began the search for
vineyards and a cellar in the Mediterranean, looking in Spain as well as in
the Midi. The Rhône valley was out of the question because he could not afford anything more than Côtes du Rhône, but good vineyard land was still
affordable in the Languedoc. However, he had very precise ideas as to what
he wanted – and with the one-hundred-and-seventh property he visited, he
found it. It was in the village of Roquessels, in the heart of Faugères.

There were so many rejects because he wanted an interesting *terroir*,
not vineyard land on the plain. He was also looking for unrealized
potential, believing that there was nowhere to take an estate which was
already doing well. What is now called Domaine des Trinités fulfilled
these criteria. The vineyards now comprise 17 hectares of Faugères
around the village of Roquessels, and 9 hectares of the newer *cru* of the
Languedoc, Pézenas, around the village of Montesquieu. The previous
owner had produced much more bulk than bottled wine, so there
was enormous scope for development and improvement. The cellar
was already well equipped with stainless steel vats and a very efficient
basket press from 1928, which has now been replaced by a streamlined
pneumatic press. Simon's first vintage at Domaine des Trinités was 2007.

Simon is full of ideas and opinions, which he expresses with articulate enthusiasm. When asked about the typicity of Faugères, he is in no doubt: 'It is freshness that sets Faugères apart. There is a natural lift, you get wonderful aromatics, notes of the *garrigues*, with fruit and spice from the schist. It is not heavy or concentrated. Faugères is about schist. Do not mess around with it.'

Simon's range of wines has evolved over the years, and he has, as the French say, also '*relooké*' some of his labels. As well as Faugères and Pézenas, he also makes white Pays d'Oc. Viognier L'Invité is whole-bunch pressed and given a cool fermentation, so that the flavours are lightly peachy, but not oily. The vineyards are on cooler north-facing slopes of schist and basalt. Roussanne now enjoys a little skin contact, thanks to the new press, so that the 2013 vintage is much more exuberant than the more restrained 2012. Simon is particularly enthusiastic about his Roussanne: 'It is so much more than a blending wine, which is how it's often used in the Midi.' His rosé is fresh, taut and as mineral as possible, with good acidity and some fresh strawberry fruit.

A new addition to the range in 2013 was L'Etranger, which is mainly Cinsaut with a splash of Syrah, given a long maceration with a daily *pigeage,* making for gentle extraction. The result is some lovely perfumed fruit on both nose and palate. Essentially Simon makes two *cuvées* of Pézenas, Le Pech Mégé and la Devèze, and three Faugères, Le Portail, Les Mourels and occasionally Cuvée 42. Le Portail is the entry-level Faugères and a blend of 60 per cent Syrah with some Grenache Noir, Carignan and a little Mourvèdre, while Les Mourels is mainly Mourvèdre with 20 per cent Grenache Noir, with an *élevage* in vat. Simon wants ripe grapes and gentle handling. His Mourvèdre is particularly successful as it is planted on a good south-facing slope. He is not alone in observing that people often have Mourvèdre in quite the wrong place.

His flagship wine, produced in tiny quantities, is Faugères, Cuvée 42. Why 42? It's from *The Hitchhiker's Guide to the Galaxy*: 'It's the answer to the ultimate question of life, the universe, and everything,' explains Simon. In this instance it represents a serious labour of love, the production of three different biodynamic vineyards, a hectare each of Grenache Noir, Syrah and Mourvèdre, which are co-fermented and then spend eighteen months in 500-litre barrels. The first vintage was 2009 and Simon subsequently made it in 2010, but not since. The wine is rich and concentrated, but with a fresh finish. 'Cinnamon and spice and all things nice', comes to mind. I wonder how it will age.

GABIAN

Gabian is a village that does not feature within the appellation of Faugères. However, as previously described, had the right decision been taken when the VDQS of Faugères was first discussed in the 1950s, Gabian – or at least some of the vineyards of the village – would today be part of the appellation of Faugères. This makes Gabian the Faugères that might have been, and that is why it is included here.

Gabian was a relatively wealthy village. It has a good supply of water, to the extent that in Roman times it sent water from the *source de la Rasclauze* to Béziers. At the same time oil was discovered, accounting for the name of the road called chemin du Pétrole. Petrol also gave the nearby village of Pouzolles its name, for Pouzolles means literally 'puits à l'huile', or oil well. In the seventeenth century there were references to a fountain of oil from Gabian being used for medicinal purposes and valued for its therapeutic qualities. In the early twentieth century the oil was transported from the train station of Gabian; production lasted from 1924 until 1950. The Espie family at Clos des Carolines have vineyards by the old oil well.

The Château de Cassan is another important landmark, a magnificent building on the outskirts of Gabian, which is said to have 365 windows. The land originally belonged to the monks of the Prieuré de Cassan, dating from 1080, and the château, as it exists today, dates from the eighteenth century. These days its public rooms are used for concerts and exhibitions, but the chapel is deconsecrated. It deserves to return to its former splendour.

In 1955 it was suggested that Gabian should be grouped with the other villages of Faugères when the VDQS was being considered, as the northern part of the village shares the same schist. But, as detailed in Chapter 1, the director and *conseil d'administration* of the cooperative decided that they did not want to bother with the constraints that the implementation of the VDQS would impose on yields and the choice of grape varieties. The cooperative, appropriately named Le Carignano, the Occitan name for Carignan, closed down in 2006 following some bad financial and sales decisions. The large buildings still stand – some defunct cooperatives have been demolished – but for the moment its future is rather uncertain. The remaining members of the cooperative send their grapes to the nearby village of Roujan.

Meanwhile the viticultural fortunes of Gabian have flourished, for the village has attracted several talented newcomers. More recently Gabian has been included in the new *cru* of Pézenas, a *cru* delimited mainly by administrative boundaries to include most of the villages around the picturesque town of Pézenas. Gabian is the most northerly of these, but in practice few of the wine growers of the village label their wine as Pézenas. You will also find simple AC Languedoc, as well as IGP Pays d' Oc or Hérault, or indeed Vin de France.

Gabian is included here as it provides a fascinating example of what happens to a village that is not part of an established appellation, and which also provides a dramatic contrast to that appellation. In an appellation you have to conform to the regulations of that appellation and your choices are limited; in Gabian things have developed without those constraints, with the additional benefit of a wide diversity of soil types. There are three extinct volcanoes nearby, accounting for basalt soil. There is also clay, limestone and sandstone as well as schist in the northern part of the village. The unhampered possibilities have attracted outsiders and make for original interpretations of grape varieties, as will be seen in the following profiles of the various estates. There are also, of course, a couple of producers who have followed the more traditional and conventional approach.

Domaine de Cadablès

Chemin du Pétrole, Gabian 34320
Tel: 04 67 24 76 07
cadables@free.fr
www.cadables.com

Bernard and Christine Izarn had been very successful potters in Corsica near Ajaccio for about ten years, but they had married in Faugères and wanted to return to the Languedoc. They did not know much about making wine but fell in love with a ruined *mas* outside Gabian and bought it in 2004. It is indeed a beautiful spot, with a view of the Château de Cassan in the distance. Bernard explains how they bought 30 hectares of

Bernard Izarn, of Domaine de Cadablès, potter turned winemaker

land around the *mas*, all on old terraces, with 5 or 6 hectares of vines: Syrah, Grenache, Carignan, Terret and Cinsaut. They vines had been pretty much neglected; there were even trees growing in the middle of the vineyards. The first summer they camped while making the *mas* habitable, and for the first couple of years they sent their grapes to the nearby Neffiès cooperative.

The vineyards are mainly planted on volcanic basalt, as they are on the extinct volcano of Cadablès. They now have 7 hectares of vines, in about ten different plots, mainly south facing, with old *gobelet* vines of Carignan, both red and white, Terret Blanc and some Syrah which is trained on wires. They work organically, and are fervent believers in the concept of *agro-ecologie*, or ecological agriculture, whereby they encourage the biodiversity of their vineyards and land so that everything is in balance. A friend has beehives on their land and another grazes cows in the vineyards in winter; the cows keep the grass at bay and also provide manure. Plump black hens roam through the vines, and they also have horses and a donkey; as Bernard puts it, they want to create *un petit paradis*. The Roman aqueduct that took water to Beziers ran close by and there is a high water table, with plenty of water in the subsoil, and consequently no problems with water stress.

After a couple of years as members of the Neffiès cooperative, Bernard and Christine realized that what they really wanted to do was make their own wine. They met Karen and Manu from Domaine Turner-Pageot (page 163), who encouraged this and allowed them to use their cellar in Gabian for the 2008 and 2009 vintages of Cadablès. By 2010 the cellar at Cadablès was renovated and useable – 'the fulfilment of our dreams', enthuses Bernard. Their first vintage comprised 15,000 bottles, which they began selling in 2011.

Bernard has a robust attitude towards French bureaucracy. Some of his wines are mere Vin de France and some Pays de l'Hérault, but he is not at all interested in the appellation. Their range of wines has gradually evolved. There is a white Pays de l'Hérault, from two thirds Terret to one third Carignan, fermented in vat, with the wine staying on its lees until December to give it some weight. The rosé is a Vin de France, a blend of Cinsaut with 10 per cent Grenache Noir. And there are three reds; Chemin à l'Envers, Pays de l'Hérault is a blend of Syrah, Grenache and Carignan, given twelve months ageing in old barrels, with some rounded spicy fruit. Bernard talks of being in the cooperative and told that he should pull up some vines which were worthless: '*mais je prends le chemin à l'envers*', he says, and did not follow the advice. Champs de Pierre, Pays de l'Hérault is a blend of 90 per cent old Carignan, planted in the 1960s, with 10 per cent of the best Syrah, again kept in old wood for twelve months. This has the lovely freshness of Carignan, with the minerality of the volcanic soil. Terre Promise is the newest addition to the range, a blend of 90 per cent Mourvèdre with 10 per cent Grenache. Mourvèdre was the first variety that they planted at Cadablès, and this wine amply demonstrates the elegant flavours of Mourvèdre – and Bernard's growing talent as a vigneron.

Domaine Cardet

3 impasse des anciens écoles, Gabian 34320
Tel: 04 67 89 52 43
chr.cardet@orange.fr
www.domainecardet.com

Christian Cardet was brought up on the outskirts of Paris and his parents come from Normandy, so he came to wine by a rather roundabout route. He first picked grapes in Champagne in 1993 and did some other work in the vineyards. In 1996 he was considering going to work in London when friends asked him why he didn't go back to school and get into wine. So he did, to the *lycée viticole* in Beaune, and then worked in Oregon and California, picked grapes at Clos du Tart and went to Chile and then South Africa in 2000. He was considering what to do next and wondering about the Languedoc when he heard that Bernard Nivollet, the owner of Château Haut-Blanville near Pézenas, was looking for an assistant *régisseur*. By 2003 Christian had acquired a house in Gabian and in 2006 he bought 4 hectares of vines from cooperative members who were retiring. By 2015 he had converted to organic viticulture, with Ecocert.

He has eight different plots in his 4 hectares, of Syrah, Grenache and Carignan, and the soil includes clay and limestone, sandstone and also schist for some Grenache Noir in the northern part of the village, closest to Faugères. His small tasting *caveau* was once the old stable of his house in a cul-de-sac just off the main street of Gabian. For the moment he has no white grapes; that is a project for the future. He makes a rosé from Grenache Noir, Carignan, and Syrah that are *saigné*, but the colour is light and delicate, a pretty salmon pink, with herbal notes on the nose and palate and a dry finish. His entry-level red is a blend of Syrah and Carignan from his young vines. The aim is fruit, without too much extraction, and that is what he has achieved: a fresh peppery red, with a streak of tannin. Other red wines are named after places with a particular association. Osorno, after a volcano in Chile near Curicó, is mainly Syrah with some Carignan, aged in vat. This is the heart of the range, and has fresh black fruit on the nose and palate, with a streak of supple tannins. Christian, following his Burgundian training, believes that *pigeage* gives better extraction. Tahaa, the name of the vanilla island near Bora Bora in French Polynesia, is from 50 per cent Grenache Noir, with equal parts of Syrah and Carignan, and spends at least twelve months in wood, depending on the vintage. It is quite firm and peppery on the palate, with more weight and structure. Cap Agulhas, which takes its name from the southernmost point of South Africa, is 95 per cent Carignan with 5 per cent Syrah, part aged in vat, and part in barrel. The Carignan is mostly from 50-year-old vines planted on slopes of clay and limestone near the Château de Cassan. There is firm red fruit, with balancing tannins, and a very satisfying freshness on the finish.

Eventually Christian would also like to make a white wine, maybe from Marsanne and Roussanne. *Viticulteurs* are retiring in Gabian, people without anyone to take over their land, and so he is optimistic about the availability of suitable vineyards.

Clos des Carolines

22 avenue de Faugères, Gabian 34320
Tel: 04 67 24 66 48

The cellars of Clos des Carolines are behind an imposing eighteenth-century house on the avenue de Faugères, the main street of Gabian. Asked about the name, Lionel Espie explains that the street was called Avenguda de la Carolinas in Occitan, and 'caroline' is a variety of poplar tree. As for clos, there are also three small walled vineyards adjoining the cellars, behind the house; you would never suspect their existence from the road. Altogether the Espies have 26 hectares of vines, scattered around the village, including some of the highest vineyards, at 250 metres, planted on volcanic basalt. They have also have clay and limestone, and some marly sandstone (*marnes grèseuses*), but no schist. And they have vineyards on chemin du Pétrole, where oil was produced early in the last century. Their oldest vines are Carignan, planted in 1947, but the average age is only about twenty.

Lionel Espie is the fourth generation on the family estate. His first job involved the production of false teeth but in 2001 he decided to return to the family property, and worked with his parents until they retired. His first bottling was the 2003 vintage, a rosé. However his grandfather, Jean Montels, had bottled small quantities of a late-harvest Clairette in the 1970s, but in tiny quantities for friends and family. These days they grow the usual quintet of Languedoc varieties, as well as some Pinot Noir, and for white wine, Chardonnay, Viognier and Chasan, and make just three wines to sell in bottle, quite simply a red,

Lionel Espie of Domaine des Carolines, one of the more traditional estates of Gabian

a white and a rosé. The white is a blend of 75 per cent Chardonnay with Viognier; the rosé a *saigné* of Grenache, Syrah and Cinsaut, for which the grapes are picked early in the morning, and the juice run off the skins before they go to bed. The red is predominantly Syrah, with some Grenache, Mourvèdre, and Carignan. A small part of the blend spends a little time in barrels of Tronçais oak, some recent, some older, just to give a little oxygenation and a hint of richness. All three wines are Pays d'Oc and sold under the name L'Equilibre des Sens. Lionel observes that wine must be balanced – and your wallet too, he adds as an aside – and hence the name; there is tightrope walker on the label. In his white wine he looks for freshness; the rosé is quite crisp and the red has a touch of pepper and oak. However, wine in bottle represents just 10 per cent of the production of the estate; the rest is sold *en vrac*.

Ultimately Lionel would like to extend the range, but for the moment he is content to satisfy current demand.

Domaine La Grange

Route de Fouzilhon, Gabian 34320
Tel: 04 67 24 69 81
info@domaine-lagrange.com
www.domaine-lagrange.com

Domaine La Grange is on the road out of Gabian going towards Fouzilhon, and is yet another example of outside investment in the Languedoc. The property was bought in 2007 by Rolf Freund, who already had a successful business in Germany as a wine shipper. The previous owner has stayed on as *chef de culture*, running the vineyards, relieved that he no longer has the full responsibility for a family estate. In Mr Freund's absence the estate is very capably managed by Sandrina Hugueux. A new cellar was built for the 2015 harvest, and they have recently changed winemakers; Sebastien Louge has moved on to make his own wine at Domaine de l'Arbussèle in Fos, and was replaced in 2014 by Thomas Raynaud, who has an impressive CV and has worked largely in Roussillon at Domaine Lafage.

Altogether Domaine La Grange comprises 40 hectares, in about twenty-five different plots, half in appellation Languedoc or Pézenas, and half Pays d'Oc; they have also taken over the management of the 15 hectares belonging to the Château de Cassan. The soil is quite varied, *un peu de tout*, as Sandrina puts it. There are extinct volcanoes close by and in the same plot of vines they can have red and yellow soil, limestone and clay and basalt, and they also have about 5 hectares of schist in their vineyards on the edge of the appellation of Faugères. There is plenty of underground water so drought is not a problem. Their oldest vines are some Carignan from 1956; Cabernet Sauvignon was planted in the 1980s, and they have other international grape varieties, especially Sauvignon and Chardonnay for white wines. In the vineyard they follow the principles of *lutte raisonnée*, using a minimum of products, and are members of Terra Vitis. The key to *lutte raisonnée* is observation, rather than action, with minimal chemical intervention, using organic products wherever possible. Sandrina talks about how their work has evolved in the vineyard. The former owner accepts their ideas and since

Sandrina Hugueux, the very able manager of Domaine la Grange

2007 they have really focused on the vineyard, reducing yields. The *palissage* has changed; canopy management has improved and they have analysed the soil before any replanting. Rolf Freund may be an absentee owner, but he does visit every six weeks or so.

There are four levels to their range of wines. The entry level is Classique, comprising a red, white and rosé Pays d'Oc. The white is a blend of Chardonnay and Sauvignon; the rosé comes from Syrah, Cinsaut and Mourvèdre, and the red from Syrah, Merlot and Carignan. Next come six different varietal *terroir* wines, based on different soils, and then four Tradition wines. Sélection is a blend of Syrah and Merlot, from some of the best plots, with the Merlot softening the Syrah to make a rounded, supple glass of wine. Grande Cuvée Blanc is a blend of oak-aged Chardonnay and Sauvignon, with some satisfyingly leesy fruit, while the Grande Cuvée Rosé is a blend of Syrah and Mourvèdre.

Prat Bibal, after the name of the vineyard and an AC Languedoc, is a blend of Grenache Noir, Syrah and Mourvèdre.

Most serious of all is the Castalides range (Castalides are nymphs who live in a well, and inspired a poet who drank the water from that well; we are meant to be inspired by the wine). The Réserve is AC Languedoc and a blend of oak-aged Grenache Noir and Mourvèdre. For Edition they use the Pézenas label, and it is a blend of some of the best plots of Syrah and Grenache Noir, from hillside vineyards with an altitude of 250 metres. Most of their vineyards are on undulating rather than steep slopes. Each plot is vinified and aged separately and then blended shortly before bottling. They favour several different coopers, Seguin Moreau, Boutes and François Frères amongst others. And finally there is Icône, another Pézenas, and a blend of Syrah and their best Mourvèdre, given eighteen months in oak, with some rich concentrated fruit and oak. There are notes of tapenade from the Syrah while the Mourvèdre gives backbone and notes of the *garrigues*. Sandrina observes that Mr Freund likes concentrated wines; however, the fruit must dominate the flavour, not the wood, and there must be some freshness too. She sums up the style of the wines of La Grange, describing them as modern wines, with fruit. They certainly illustrate some of the new trends of the Midi.

Domaine des Pascales

20 av. Roujan, Gabian 34320
Tel: 04 67 24 16 91
ljdomainedespascales@wanadoo.fr
www.domaine-des-pascales.fr

This is the largest estate in Gabian, owned by the Lavit family, Jacques and his son Frédéric, yet in the general scheme things it has a rather low profile. The company's sales are mainly in central France, with Peugeot factories its most important customer. The greater part of their production is sold in bulk, and also in BIB, what the French call bag in box, rather than in bottle. However, Domaine des Pascales does have a range of twelve different wines in bottle, including various varietal IGPs and some Coteaux du Languedoc.

Jacques is the sixth generation of this family of wine growers. He notes that an ancestor had fought in Napoleon's army at the beginning of the nineteenth century, though he does not know whether he was at Waterloo, or not! Pascales was the name of the first plot of land that the family bought in the area, when they came south from Aveyron. In their 60 hectares they have quite a range of grape varieties, including the usual five red varieties of the Languedoc, as well as Cabernet Sauvignon and Merlot, and for whites, Grenache Blanc, Sauvignon and Muscat à petits grains. They have also planted, with a note of originality, some Nielluccio which comes into production in 2016. When asked, Why Nielluccio?, Jacques replies that it copes well with drought and performs well on hillside vineyards. The land is divided into roughly four main plots, with the half in the northern part of the village being schist. Everything is mechanically harvested and their winemaking methods seem pretty straightforward.

The decision not to participate in the development of the VDQS of Faugères took place when Jacques was a young man. It was the decision of the village cooperative and the independent *vignerons* of the village were not consulted, but his family has never belonged to the cooperative – 'we don't have the cooperative mentality', he remarks. He bottled his first wine in 1983, and his son, Frédéric, who studied at Montpellier, is continuing the family business.

Jacques Lavit of Domaine des Pascales, a large and
traditional estate in Gabian

Jacques and Frédéric built their large cellar themselves and are rightly very proud of it, no longer using the cellar that you might spot in the main street of Gabian. The proud owner of a 1958 Mercedes, Jacques' other love is *la chasse*, as wild boars are such a pest in the vineyards, and his hunting dogs each have a kennel made from an old wine barrel. Housed in the drive approaching the cellar, each dog has its own pen, bearing its name, and most of the dogs are named after grape varieties, such as Mauzac, Aramon and Négrette.

The simple rosé, is a pure Grenache Pays de l'Hérault, with some delicate fruit and a firm finish. Their oaked red, a Coteaux du Languedoc called Château Lavit, is a Syrah, Grenache, Mourvèdre blend, while the semi-sweet Muscat is also Pays de l'Hérault. The fermentation is stopped by chilling and then the wine is filtered, so that the fresh grapey taste of the fruit is retained.

Domaine Senti Kreyden

Rue des Violettes, Gabian 34320
Tel : 06 42 47 17 91
erna.senti@bluewin.ch
www.sentikreyden.com

Erna Senti Kreyden comes from Switzerland, where her parents made wine, Pinot Noir and Riesling, in the Graubünden or Grisons region of Switzerland, and her brother has now taken over Weingut Senti. She worked in the financial industry before rediscovering her viticultural roots. She explains how she and her husband, Olivier, would come on holiday to the South of France; they did not want to spend all day on the beach, so they explored the countryside. One thing led to another – in the form of some olive trees and a tiny vineyard of old Counoise, which they bought in 2005. That is one of the thirteen grape varieties of Châteauneuf-du-Pape, but is found less often in the Languedoc. Things have taken off from that. Erna made her first two vintages in Verena Wyss's cellar (see page 166) and studied, and in 2008 she gave up the day job to concentrate on wine.

She now has 9 hectares, in ten small plots. She wants to remain small. You sense that she pays great attention to detail; everything is finely handcrafted; she believes that if you work hard in the vineyards, the work in the cellar will be much easier. However, for the moment, space is a problem; she has a tiny vinification cellar in the back streets

Erna Senti Kreyden, from Domaine Senti Kreyden, who bought her first vines after enjoying holidays in the area

of Gabian and is hoping to get planning permission for a new one on a hill outside the village, but that is taking its time. Meanwhile she also rents cellar space at Cazillac, an old property dating back to the twelfth century with a tower built in 1137, between Pouzolles and Magalas. There is plenty of space for barrels and bottles but currently the cellar has neither electricity nor water, so visits are made by candlelight.

Erna focuses on single varietals, with her main market being Switzerland. Consequently her wines are either Pays d'Oc or Pays de Cassan, after the nearby château. She has an eclectic range of grape varieties. If you want to know what Aramon, one of the old and much-decried varieties of the Languedoc, tastes like, this is the place to come. It is sold as Vin de France and has some rounded ripe fruit, balanced with quite firm tannins. There is some Merlot, but Erna is not sure how successful it really is in the Languedoc. Clos d'Eve is a pure Grenache, aged in old wood for twelve months. It is ripe and rounded with some cherry fruit. Octopus is a pure Counoise, from old *gobelet* vines that look just like an octopus, and the taste is redolent of fresh cherry fruit. Carignano, the Occitan name for Carignan, was planted in 1962 and has fresh red fruit and elegant tannins, a lovely example of another decried variety. Amata Syrah is rich and concentrated with firm peppery fruit. The last in the range is Mourvèdre, just one barrel. The tiny quantity makes the printing of the labels disproportionately expensive, so Erna has numbered the bottles by hand with smart gold paint. It is a lovely example of the grape variety.

Domaine de la Tour Penedesses

2 rue Droite, Faugères 34600
Tel : 04 67 95 17 21
domainedelatourpenedesses@yahoo.fr
www.domainedelatourpenedesses.com

Alexandre Fourque is the one wine grower of Faugères who also has vineyards in Gabian. As explained (see page 85), Alexandre does not come from the region. He has gradually developed an estate, initially in Gabian and then in Faugères, so that he now has 25 hectares in Gabian and 15 in Faugères, in thirty-seven different plots, and all within about half an hour of each other by tractor. His vineyards in Gabian include several *terroirs*, taking into account the diversity of the village, and with at least 7 hectares on schist in the northern part of the village, towards Roquessels.

Reaching Alexandre's vineyards also takes in some of the history of Gabian. There's the Roman aqueduct near Domaine de la Grange and a very narrow road, chemin des Moulins, which goes past the remains of five old watermills which were used for milling flour; the *mairie* of Gabian is slowly buying and restoring them. Alexandre has a terraced vineyard above the old railway line, with Syrah on schist, and Grenache on the lower terrace. Towards Pouzolles, he has a hectare of Pinot Noir, planted at a density of 6000 vines, with just 80 centimetres between the vines, although the rows themselves are quite wide. Close by is a spring where oil lingers on the surface. There is a particularly stony vineyard off the road to Vailhan; when Alexandre planted it, he had to remove enormous quantities of stones – he calls it '*un travail de dingue*', a madman's labour. But really it is a series of vineyard gardens: *des jardins de vignes*.

Alexandre talks about the different soils of Gabian. There are three extinct volcanoes, Ste Hilaire, Ste Marthe and Cadablès, and on their lower slopes, some very stony soils, *villefranchien* and *galets roulées*, and then in the northern part of the village there is schist. Faugères, he says, is definitely cooler and with more rain than Gabian, making the wines of Faugères more elegant, with interesting tannins. The volcanic soil is hotter, and the vines tend to suffer from more drought stress. The harvest is usually a week later in Faugères. He has done a lot of replanting, and tends to have lower vines in Faugères, at 40 centimetres, as opposed to 70 centimetres in Gabian.

Since the development of the *cru* of Pézenas, all Alexander's wines from Gabian are Pézenas, including Les Moulins, Cuvée Antique, Les Volcans, Clos Magrinon and Clos Penedesses. Cuvée Antique is a blend of 65 per cent Grenache Noir, with 15 per cent Syrah and 5 per cent Mourvèdre, and then 15 per cent from a vineyard planted in 1906, *en foulé*: in other words, with a crowd of different varieties, Terret Noir and Terret Gris, Counoise, Cinsaut, Carignan Noir and Alicante Bouschet – an extraordinary fruit salad of different grapes. The nose is light and spicy with a touch of spice on the nose, and the palate has some supple tannins and a touch of liquorice, with quite a fresh finish.

Les Volcans comes from vines planted on basalt, with 60 per cent Syrah, including fruit from vines planted in 1962 making it some of the oldest Syrah in the Languedoc, as well as Grenache Noir, Mourvèdre and Carignan. The colour is deep with some firm, leathery, smoky fruit on both nose and palate. It is definitely hotter and riper than his Faugères, illustrating the differences between the two villages.

The name of the estate comes from a vineyard near Gabian, Clos Penedesses, with 75-year-old Grenache Noir and some Counoise, which is more commonly found in Châteauneuf-du-Pape. The grapes for this *cuvée* are picked two months later than usual, at the end of October, resulting in a yield of about 15 hectolitres per hectare, 'after the wild boars, the blackbirds and the *vendangeurs du dimanche* have all had their share'. The aim is a wine rather like a Valpolicella Amarone. The grapes ferment very slowly in oak and the flavours are dense and sweet – just like an Amarone – making an original note.

Domaine Turner-Pageot

3 avenue de la Gare, Gabian 34320
Tel : 04 67 00 14 33
contact@turnerpageot.com
www.turnerpageot.com

Where does an Australian winemaker, Karen Turner, meet a French winemaker, Emmanuel Pageot? In this case, the answer is working for Hugel in Alsace. They travelled the world, working two vintages a year in South Africa, Australia, Tuscany and Portugal before settling in the Languedoc. They returned to France with a new baby in early 2004 and it

Emmanuel Pageot, the most innovative and original winemaker in Gabian

was initially very difficult to find jobs, despite their impressive CVs. Then Karen was offered the post of winemaker at the Prieuré de St Jean de Bébian outside Nizas, in time for the 2004 vintage, and that is where she still works. Meanwhile Karen and Manu, as his friends call him, began looking for vineyards in the area that matched Manu's strict criteria of north-facing hillside sites. They now have 10 hectares in seventeen different plots, fifteen of which are north-facing, and with a tremendous variety of soils. There are two hectares of schist, but also limestone and clay, soils which can cope with water stress and provide a decent yield. They made their first vintage in 2008, from 3.75 hectares bought from seven different *viticulteurs*. They have worked biodynamically right from the very beginning.

Their newly extended cellar is behind their house in the centre of Gabian. Manu takes delight in going against the mainstream; he firmly asserts that his aim is to make atypical wines, and he does, very successfully, with a range of intriguing and challenging wines. Le Blanc, AC Languedoc, is a blend of 70 per cent Roussanne and 30 per cent Marsanne. Contrary to the usual practice of a cool fermentation for white grapes, Manu lets the temperature of the fermentation rise to over 20°C. The Roussanne is pressed in the normal way and given plenty of lees contact, while the Marsanne is destemmed and crushed and then the juice, to which the skins and stems are added, is left in an open-top vat for the beginning of the fermentation, and then put into barrel. The two varieties are blended three or four months before bottling, and the wine exudes character. It is golden in colour and on the palate there is a wonderful freshness, with some firm tannins as well as acidity, with white blossom fruit, and some salinity. The texture and mouth feel are very satisfying, with length and depth.

Rupture is their pure Sauvignon, which is vinified in vat, with a small amount kept in barrel on its lees, and with some *bâtonnage*. The length of time depends on the vintage and the ripeness of the grapes; a warmer vintage will make for more weight. It is labelled merely Vin de France, but these days, in the hands of a talented winemaker, Vin de France is likely to indicate a wine of considerable interest, rather than basic table wine. Rupture has firm minerality on both nose and palate; the juice was fermented at over 20°C which means that the thiols which are responsible for the very pungent flavours of Sauvignon evaporate to leave more subtle flinty mineral notes.

Depending on your point of view, 48H is a light red or a dark rosé, and it is so-called as the juice spent forty-eight hours on the skins. The blend is 70 per cent Grenache Noir, grown on schist, and 30 per cent Syrah from clay and limestone vineyards. Some of the Grenache is pressed immediately. The colour is a bright deep pink and on the nose I found raspberries and strawberries with some spice, and on the palate more fruit and some light tannins. As Marie Folz, who has been working with Manu since the beginning of 2016, observes, it has the nose of a rosé and the palate of a red wine. That sums it up very nicely.

Le Rouge, AC Pézenas, is a blend of Grenache Noir on schist and Syrah on clay and limestone, of which one third is aged in wood. The flavours are fresh and peppery; Manu is working on fine-tuning this wine as it is his largest production and he wants more fruit-driven flavours – and he is succeeding. Carmina Major, also a Pézenas, is a blend of equal parts of Mourvèdre and Syrah, grown on basalt, which spends twelve months in wood over two winters. It has more depth and structure than Le Rouge, with some smoky notes from Mourvèdre and some spicy fruit, with some ageing potential.

Named after the number of the plot on the *cadastre*, as the French call the land registry, B815 is a blend of 90 per cent Grenache Noir with 10 per cent Mourvèdre. This is AC Languedoc rather than Pézenas, as the blend does not confirm to the requirements for Pézenas. It has a lovely deep colour and a rounded spicy nose, but not the immediate fruitiness of Grenache. The Grenache character comes out more on the palate, with fresh cherry notes, and a firm tannic streak from the Mourvèdre. Again there is considerable ageing potential, and barrel samples of the 2015 exploded with fresh fruit in the mouth. Manu is particularly enthusiastic about Grenache Noir on schist, describing it as very Burgundian, with wonderful aromas, finesse, elegance and freshness, while on limestone it is riper and richer.

Les Choix, a pure Marsanne, Vin de France is what you might call an orange wine, as the colour is orange-golden after spending six weeks on the skins and two years in wood. Curiously it does smell of orange, and the tannins from the skins give a firm streak to the palate, but there is freshness too, balanced with a saline quality and some intense minerality.

Manu has a lively and enquiring mind. Some large glass jars along a wall in the garden are jars of vinegar maturing, and he has made *verjus* too, for the kitchen. The next project is a new tasting area, with the old manger from the stables, and a hen house in the garden.

Domaine Verena Wyss

Lieu-dit Canteperdrix,
Chemin du Pétrole, Gabian 34320
Tel: 04 67 24 77 63
contact@domaine-verenawyss.com
www.domaine-verena.wyss.com

Fortuitous circumstances brought Verena Wyss to Gabian. She and her husband, Jean-Pierre, ran a successful architect and interior design business in Zurich, but a friend had bought a wine estate in the nearby Côtes de

Verena Wyss of Domaine Verena Wyss, with a reputation for delicious vins de pays, notably Roussanne

Thongue and they came to visit; Jean-Pierre enjoyed helping in the cellar. Then, a few months later, their friend invited them back. 'I have something to show you', he said. So they came, and saw, and succumbed. This is a beautiful spot, with the Languedoc hills undulating into the distance. Neither Jean-Pierre nor Verena had any previous thoughts of escaping from civilization, as Verena put it, but they were instantly captivated by the possibilities at Canteperdrix, as the estate was then called in the late 1980s. Unfortunately a cooperative in Provence was already using the name Canteperdrix and Verena was obliged to change the name, much to her disappointment (there are partridges – *perdrix* – in the vineyards). She still retains an emblematic partridge on her labels.

She has nearly 14 hectares of vines, not on schist but on *argilo-calcaire*, clay and limestone. Over the course of thirty years she has extensively replanted the vineyards. When she first arrived there were Aramon, Terret and Carignan, and now there are Viognier, Roussanne, some *bordelais* varieties and some Grenache Noir and the related Lledoner Pelut, all for a range of IGP Pays d'Oc rather than an appellation. Unusually the vineyards are concentrated all around the house and cellar, and now they are all farmed organically. Verena has no training in winemaking apart from a course on pruning, so she has learned from experience. For the last twenty years she has been helped by her very able cellar master, Patrick Goma. Viognier was her very first wine, made in 1994.

These days her range comprises a pair of Viognier, one aged in vat and the other including an oaked component, which makes for a fuller, richer wine. There is a convincing Roussanne; a refreshing rosé from Cinsaut, Grenache and Lledoner Pelut. A pure Lledoner Pelut, which is related to Grenache Noir but has the advantage of ripening more slowly, has some fresh cherry fruit, while Bel Canto is a blend of Cabernet Sauvignon, Merlot and Petit Verdot, and makes a delicious expression of the grape varieties of Bordeaux.

For a number of years Verena and Jean-Pierre managed two lives, in Zurich and Gabian, but now Verena is widowed and feels very much at home in Gabian, returning just occasionally to Switzerland.

6

FINE DE FAUGÈRES

Surprisingly it was Fine de Faugères that gave the name Faugères its reputation outside the Languedoc. Noël Salles ran a distillery in Faugères at the end of the nineteenth century that was unique in the Languedoc, as his alembic was an *alembic à repasse*, or a *charentais* Cognac still, whereas all the other stills in the Languedoc at that time were *alembics à colonne*, like those used in Armagnac. This was at the time when many of the villages of the Languedoc had a distillery as well as a cooperative, and the quality of the wine was rated for its suitability as a *vin de chaudière,* a wine for distillation. *Eau de vie du Languedoc* is not so different from Fine de Faugères, for *fine* means alcohol *issu de vin.* It all depends on the quality of the wine. For Fine de Faugères this depended on the clearest juice which came from Carignan Blanc and Terret Blanc. I tasted an 1895 Fine de Faugères with Claude Caumette, and it was rich and spiry.

In the first half of the twentieth century Fine de Faugères was exported all over the world, and in 1948 it was recognized as an appellation. The distillery continued to function until the end of the 1960s, by which time its reputation and quality had declined and Fine de Faugères was not selling so well – to the extent that much of the stock was sold off at auction in the early 1970s.

Fast forward to 1999, when the INAO was doing some spring cleaning. Fine de Faugères had been recognized as an AOP, an *eau de vie réglementé,* but none was actually being made, so something had to be done if they wanted to keep the appellation. Consequently various *vignerons* got together and found a distiller who had the right type of still: he was Mathieu Frécon, who came from Montpeyroux. Fine de Faugères needs to be distilled within the appellation of Faugères, and therefore the first were initially made in a barn in Caussiniojouls. Françoise Ollier describes how growers not only took their wine, but also the wood to heat the still. Then Mathieu Frécon was installed at the old distillery in Autignac. He has now moved on; the new distiller, Martial Berthaud, is young and enthusiastic, and with his colleague Quentin Le Cléach makes Fine de Faugères for twelve *vignerons.*

Martial heats the wine by gas in a copper container of 300 litres. It takes six hours and the wine gently evaporates. The alcohol with the aroma evaporates before the water does, and then condenses when it touches the copper. It cools, going through copper pipes chilled by cold water. The result is clear liquid, *le brouille,* which is then distilled again. This time both the first and last parts – the *tête* and the *queue,* the head and the tail – are discarded. The head contains some bad aromas, such as methanol, and the tail is too bitter. The heart, the *coeur,* is kept. The first distillation gives 100 litres from 300 litres of wine, which is then reduced to 30 litres in the second distillation. Great care and skill is needed to just retain the *coeur*; the nose decides. If the wine is of high quality, without any additional chemicals – it must not have been treated with sulphur – less head and tail have to be removed. If the wine is high in alcohol, it gives more liquid. Usually, according to Martial, there are no quality issues in Faugères.

Differences in taste come from the various grape varieties and the quality of the wine, as well as the length of ageing. Fine de Faugères requires a minimum of five years ageing, but ten is even better. Usually you can start to taste the *fine* when it is five years old, and the *vigneron* decides when to bottle it. At ten years of age it is an XO, meaning Extra Old. Grape varieties that are not included in the appellation of Faugères can be used, but they must be grown on appellation land. Didier Barral, for example, makes a special blend for his *fine* and Martial says that the quality of Didier's wine is very high, giving great results. Domaine Ollier-Taillefer uses the fine lees for its *fine*, again with delicious results, as the lees round out the *eau de vie*. The choice of barrel is another quality consideration, but the jury is still out on what is best. Ollier-Taillefer uses red wine barrels so that the *fine* takes on colour more quickly, while Château La Liquière prefers new barrels. I was allowed to sniff a barrel, with a note of vanilla.

The distillery has a separate ageing cellar which is controlled by the *douanes,* or Customs and Excise. No tax is paid until the *fine* leaves the distillery. One essential difference between ageing wine and ageing *fine* is that *fine* requires changes of temperature like a *rancio,* or oxidized wine. It would age in an attic, whereas wine normally needs to age in a cool cellar. It also needs humidity, so water has to be sprayed if temperatures get too high during the summer.

Everyone has the right to ferment fruit for distillation, on condition that they give their fruit to somebody who is authorized to distil. They are allowed 10 litres of pure alcohol per annum, on which they pay a lower tax provided it is only for family consumption. Consequently Martial also distils some fruit brandy, including some rather delicious-smelling apricot, and in 2014 they distilled an organic *fine* – but it will not actually be on the market for another few years.

The distillery itself, which was used by the previous incumbents until 1970, has a slightly shambolic air about it. It is a large building with the remains of the original enormous still, which Martial describes as not especially big. There is a stash of bottles from an order that was never collected, labelled Brandy Symphony 1982, which Martial says is not particularly good. He is full of plans to streamline the distillery and create a small museum.

Fine de Faugères

Martial Berthaud and Quentin le Cléach
L'Atelier du Bouilleur
9 Avenue de Béziers, Autignac 34480
Tel: 06 51 69 68 68
contact@atelier-du-bouilleur.fr
www.atelier-du-bouilleur.fr

7

FAUGÈRES TODAY

Today Faugères is a flourishing appellation, but it is not without its problems. One of them, sadly, is its cooperative, which dominates the appellation, accounting for 1000 hectares of Faugères – in other words, about half the surface area of the appellation. It is responsible for the biggest brand of the Languedoc, Mas Olivier, which sells a million bottles a year. This is no mean achievement, but the retail price is currently a mere €4.95 (for the 2014 vintage) and the quality simply does not deliver the excitement and flavour which I would expect from a Faugères. The wine is perfectly correct and well made, but I certainly would not rush to buy it as an example of Faugères if there were other bottles available; I expect a little more excitement. That French retail price of €4.95 drags down the average price of Faugères, which creates other problems on the market, causing an imbalance of prices and depreciating the public perception of the appellation. Many people who know Mas Olivier do not necessarily realize that it is a Faugères, only that it is a large Languedoc brand with maybe a rather tenuous link with Faugères. Or, if people do realize that it is Faugères, it merely serves to diminish the overall image of Faugères. Why not sell Mas Olivier as a simple 'appellation Languedoc', where a price of €4.95 is not out of line, and put the quality emphasis on the better *cuvées* of Faugères?

The other thing for which I reproach the cooperative is its name, Les Crus Faugères, which is conspicuously displayed outside their tasting *caveau* on the main D909 close to the village of Faugères. It is grossly misleading. Any innocent tourists seeing that sign would imagine that they would be able to taste the wines of several producers. Not so; the only wines available for tasting are those of the cooperative. For the biggest selection of wines for tasting, go instead to Les Amants de la Vigneronne, where Régine and Christian Godefroid run a very welcoming tasting *caveau* and shop, representing most of the *vignerons* of the appellation. But that is just one *vigneron's* initiative; it is a great shame that there is no collective effort by the official body of the growers' *syndicat* to showcase the full range of the wines of the appellation, as they do in the Maison du Vin in St Chinian.

Faugères needs to be seen in the context of the whole Languedoc. It was one of the first appellations, created in 1982, along with neighbouring St Chinian. Then, in 1985, when the Coteaux du Languedoc was created, as well as Minervois and Corbières, Faugères was incorporated into the Coteaux du Languedoc, together with several other *crus*, the original VDQS of the region, that stretched from the outskirts of Narbonne almost as far as Nimes. As Faugères and St Chinian were already appellations in their own right, they have never been obliged to add the mention Coteaux du Languedoc to the label, which gives them a certain autonomy.

The Coteaux du Languedoc has undergone numerous changes over the last thirty years, not least that the appellation 'Coteaux du Languedoc' is due to be replaced by simple 'Languedoc' in 2017. Meanwhile new areas are coming to the fore. The notable example here is the Terrasses du Larzac, which covers the hills of the Languedoc from Octon to Aniane, incorporating the original *crus* of Montpeyroux and St Saturnin. Grès de Montpellier is a rather more fluid area around Montpellier, with less precise identity, and Pézenas covers vineyards around the historic town of Molière.

Currently the powers that be are intent on creating a system of what they call *hierachisation*, a kind of quality pyramid rather like that which you find in Bordeaux or Burgundy. However, some of the terminology is the prerogative of the *bordelais* and Burgundians, with the result that the original idea of a series of *grands crus* was firmly squashed by the INAO. These days some of the more dynamic *crus* of the Coteaux du Languedoc are working towards individual appellations within the context of the Languedoc and some are succeeding, such as Picpoul de Pinet and La Clape. Some appellations, such as St Chinian and Minervois, have achieved the recognition of a *cru* for their most qualitative areas. In the case of St Chinian this means Berlou and Roquebrun, and for Minervois the village of La Livinière, and for Corbières, Boutenac.

Faugères, however, is really too small to single out a particular village or subzone as a *cru*, so consequently the whole appellation has been recognized as a *cru du* Languedoc.

Nathalie Caumette, the bright, energetic and very determined president of the *syndicat*, explains the permutations. As president, her aim is to *valorise*, to enhance the value and develop the image of Faugères; she has absolute faith in the *terroir* of Faugères, stating that the *délimitation parcellaire* was well done, so that less interesting plots are merely *vins de pays*, or Indications Géographiques Protegées (or IGP) as they are now called. Faugères itself is very coherent. She explained that '*cru*' is *un mot libre*, a free word, so that anyone can use it. But the same does not apply to '*premier*' or '*grand*' *cru*. Furthermore, Faugères was never a denomination of the Coteaux du Languedoc because it was already an appellation in its own right, *une appellation communal,* covering seven villages and identified by its schist. But things are not carved in marble and can be contested, and so Nathalie was able to obtain the elevation of Faugères to *cru* status. As she puts it, 'Faugères shouted and was heard.' Apparently there was some discussion about prices, with a suggestion of a minimum price, but Nathalie said 'non' to that. As yet the position of Faugères as a *cru* is still rather fluid. It is unclear how much actual difference it will make, and so far there has been no clear communication about it.

However, in order to raise the profile of Faugères further, the *syndicat* is promoting the identity of Faugères as a 'Grand Terroir de Schiste', to emphasize the link between great wine and schist. There was a previous attempt with an earlier marketing concept of the Cuvée des Trois Tours, taking its name from the three windmills which dominate the skyline above the village of Faugères. This lasted for about five or six years. The participating wine growers conformed to certain quality criteria with a stricter *cahier de charge*, entailing lower yields, older vines, *palissages* and specific grape varieties, as well as an internal tasting. There was also a special bottle, which was expensive to produce, with the insignia of the three towers. But the concept really needed unanimity amongst the growers, and that was not forthcoming: for one, and despite being the largest producer, the cooperative did not participate.

Hopefully Faugères Grand Terroir de Schiste will be more successful. The objective is to stimulate the wine growers, including those of the cooperative, to emphasize their very individual *terroir*. It is up to the wine growers themselves to decide which wine will be labelled *grand terroir de schiste*. There are no specific quality criteria, simply a recognition that the wine in question should be something good, and the wording will only feature on the label of the better and more expensive *cuvées*. The suggestion of a minimum price of €10 was rejected, with most growers considering that to be an unsatisfactory criterion. Frédéric Albaret thinks the concept of Grand Terroir du Schiste should improve the image of Faugères, remarking that a *grand vin* needs time, so there should be a minimum length of *élevage*, followed by a tasting as a control of quality. Above all, the *terroir* must be emphasized, because that is the whole point. As things stand at the moment, the onus lies with the individual growers and, although Faugères is a small appellation, Frédéric sees enormous variety within it, not least amongst the personalities of the various wine growers.

The appellation is run by its *syndicat*, and Valérie Desblancs is the new young director. She explains that the *syndicat* is now an ODG. The French like acronyms and this one stands for the Organisme de Défense et de Gestion, so – in other words – the *syndicat* protects the name of Faugères and checks that the *cahier de charge* is followed. The *cahier de charge* lays down the regulations for the production of Faugères, covering grape varieties, pruning, yields and work in the vineyard. The wine growers have to accept a growing amount of paperwork in order to control traceability. You cannot produce Faugères unless you are a member of the *syndicat*, and you have to pay to be a member in order to contribute to its running costs. The annual fees are calculated on the basis that a *vigneron* pays a yearly subscription per hectare and per hectolitre for both bulk and bottled wine. In addition there are fees payable to the Conseil Interprofessionnel des Vins du Languedoc, the interprofessional governmental body that is responsible for the overall organization of the appellations of the Languedoc, and the promotion of the wines of the region.

There used to be regular tastings to ensure consistent quality, the so-called *labelle* tastings that gave a wine its appellation, but these have been discontinued. However, there are numerous other checks, so that minimum quality is assured. All Faugères must be vinified within the area of the appellation. The *syndicat* asked for Faugères to be bottled within the appellation as well, but that suggestion would create problems for the cooperative as they regularly sell about 4000 hectolitres *en vrac* to Belgium every year. There is other *négociant* activity, but the bulk market for Faugères is very limited and the price is low compared to, for example, Pic St Loup.

With, at the last count, fifty-eight wine growers, including the cooperative, there is not a lot of money to spend on publicity and communications. The main projects is the annual *fête*, the Grand St Jean in the middle of July, which is a great showcase for the appellation and much appreciated by the many wine enthusiasts who visit it. Sadly by no means all the wine growers participate. As a regular visitor for the last ten years or so, I would like to see some other faces and wines there, not just the same faithful and public-spirited *vignerons*. The now annual wine fair of Vinisud, which is a fantastic showcase for the whole of the Languedoc, if not for the Mediterranean, is another important vehicle for Faugères and well supported by many of the growers. There are also a good number of Faugères *vignerons* at Millésime Bio, the bi-annual wine fair specializing in organic wine. And then there are other smaller events, with a local slant.

Michèle Solans, who has been responsible for PR for Faugères for the last six years – she has recently retired – describes how Faugères used to be seen as a rather sleepy appellation compared to some of the better known areas such as Pic St Loup, but says that things are definitely beginning to change. The creation of a new association, L'Association des Terroirs de Schiste du Monde, may bring a broader, more international dimension to Faugères. There are currently fifteen member *terroirs*. All but two are French, with several appellations from the south, namely Faugères, St Chinian, Cabrières and Fitou from the Languedoc; Maury, Collioure and Banyuls in Roussillon; Côte Rôtie and Seyssuel in the northern Rhône Valley; Savennières in the Loire Valley; Kastelberg, which is a *grand cru* of Alsace; and Morgon, which is one of the ten *crus* of Beaujolais and remarkable for its granitic schist, plus the Valais in Switzerland and Priorat in Catalonia. Bernard Vidal is the president of the organization; he admits that for various reasons they have not been very active and are taking their time to get it effectively established.

These days nobody can deny that there is a palpable energy in Faugères. There are new estates created by people from outside the appellation as well as the succession of a younger generation, the children of the people who created the appellation. The 2014 harvest alone saw the creation of four new estates, some growers with roots already firmly established in Faugères, but others from further afield. They are young people who have bought or rented land from retiring *vignerons* who were either cooperative members or sold their wine in bulk, and include Nicolas Maury, the son of the president of the cooperative.

The international mix of Faugères helps gives the appellation an exciting energy and there are not just foreigners coming to the area, but French people from other parts of France, including Bordeaux, Normandy and Alsace. You will find people from Australia, Ireland, England, Spain, Canada, Belgium, Switzerland and Germany. All of them have chosen Faugères because they recognize its enormous potential. As noted earlier, Simon Coulshaw had been looking for an estate he could grow because there was no point in buying something that had already reached its pinnacle. Paul Gordon sums it up when he says quite simply that Faugères ticks all the boxes: 'It is close to the sea and close to the mountains; it has a great *terroir* and some great wines, nice villages and vineyard land is both affordable and available.' These newcomers question some of the traditional and accepted practices. Paul, with his Australian outlook, has had no hesitation in using screw caps or in putting the grape varieties for each *cuvée* on the front label, albeit discreetly: both things that the more conservative French wine grower would hesitate to do. Gwenaël Thomas, who works with Jean Natoli, observes that the new people attract journalists who are looking for new talent. The newcomers also bring the benefit of experience in other fields of activity and other countries, all of which makes for a vibrant and energetic appellation. Amongst the old-established estates, such as Domaine Ollier-Taillefer and Château La Liquière, the children are successfully taking over as their parents stand back. The new generation inevitably brings new ideas, and also new wines.

Prices for vineyards within the appellation of Faugères are still affordable whereas in other parts of the Languedoc they are becoming more expensive, notably in areas closer to Montpellier where there is pressure on land for housing. In 2012 you could find vineyards in Faugères for €10,000 per hectare, rising to €20,000 for better quality vineyards, with an average price of €16,000. Compare that with the Pic

St Loup, just to the north of Montpellier. In 2012 prices there ranged from €30,000 to €46,000 per hectare, with an average price of €37,000. By way of comparison, in neighbouring St Chinian the average is €12,500 with a low of €9000 and a high of €18,000. Minervois is significantly cheaper with an average price of €9000, while Fitou averages €14,000, but descends to €6000. As for *vin de pays* or IGP vineyards, prices in the Hérault range between €8000 and €18,000 with an average of €13,000. For prices in bottle, the lowest would be Mas Olivier at €4.95, while prices for some of the *cuvées prestiges,* such as Mas Gabinele's Inaccessible, are serious or, at €85 for the 2012 vintage, well nigh inaccessible indeed. However, there is a great selection of Faugères in the middle-price range, around €10 to €12 a bottle.

Is Faugères becoming better known? Simon Coulshaw comments that *cavistes* in Montpellier are now prepared to expand their horizons a little further west and consider wine from Faugères, which they had rejected only a few years ago. As for the export market, as noted, the Chinese have discovered Faugères. Luc Salvestre, the director of the cooperative, spends several weeks a year there, selling about 10 per cent of the cooperative's total production, mainly at the higher-priced end, for the gift market. Jean-Michel Mégé from Domaine de la Reynardière feels that the Chinese want mature wines and the French market is polluted by Bordeaux. None the less, the domestic market is by far and away the biggest market for Faugères; the most recent figures available give exports representing just 11 per cent of total sales. The French market concentrates on supermarkets, at 34 per cent, and the combination of wine shops, restaurants, and cellar door accounts for 50 per cent of total sales. Françoise Ollier hazards an informed estimate that *vente directe* at the cellar door represents about 15 per cent of the total. As for exports, the most important markets in Europe are Belgium, Holland, Germany, Denmark and the United Kingdom, and further afield the United States and Canada, as well as the cooperative's successful business with China. Faugères generally provides a very acceptable price/quality relationship; fortunately, because there is no doubt that the most expensive Languedoc wines are difficult to sell.

Most of the wine growers are relatively optimistic. Gwenaël Thomas feels that Faugères has a very positive *dynamique*: 'Perhaps in the past it was a bit slow to communicate, as it was rather a timid vineyard with less powerful wines, but now it is making up for lost time.' He praises Nathalie Caumette as president, suggesting that she has some effective new strategies, and declares that Faugères is an appellation with some strong personalities; their differences of attitude and opinion need to be respected.

Frédéric Albaret thinks Faugères has a very strong identity of *terroir*. He sees it as a young appellation which needs to take the time to evolve; basically it is an agricultural community of farmers, making just one vintage a year. Bernard Vidal feels strongly that Faugères needs to create its own identity, to distinguish itself from the rest of the Languedoc. That, of course, is where schist comes into play.

There is some pessimism too. Marc Roque feels that the wine industry is becoming more of a business and less of a farming community. Nor is Jean-Louis Pujol of Château de Grézan very optimistic. He notes that a lot of money has been spent in the region, in the Languedoc, but that it is still in crisis. There is still a lot of *arrachage*, with vineyards within the appellation being abandoned, and there is no economic stability. He would prefer a more stable region. The established appellations allow for so many different grape varieties, so he would like to see a policy concentrating on *terroir* to differentiate between the various wines, and that of course is what Faugères is doing with Grand Terroir de Schiste. Nathalie Caumette pertinently says that 'the weakness of the Languedoc is the mixture of appellations and *vins de pays*, but that could also be our strength. Faugères is very homogenous, with a high level of quality. The critical mass is going in the same direction, towards quality.'

Corine Andrieu from Clos Fantine observes that 'the appellation decree must not block our liberty or our creativity'. She is something of a free spirit and sells some of her wine as Vin de France, which allows her *une liberté totale*. She feels an appellation can lose its authenticity if it does not let nature express itself.

But I would like to finish with two pertinent observations. The first is from Françoise Ollier. As she effectively expresses it: 'Faugères is a *marque collective*, a brand that we all own. If our grandparents had behaved as the *vignerons* do today, there would be no appellation, and we would all be making *vin de pays*. Everyone should support the appellation, for that is where the future lies.' However, some of the newcomers are more dispassionate about their adopted appellation. They feel that a lot of the wine growers do not appreciate that they are sitting on a gold mine and, while they are working well, they are merely maintaining the status quo, without any appetite for change and improvement. Quite simply, they do not realize just how great Faugères is and that it has the potential to be one of the best appellations in the Languedoc, if not in the whole of France.

8

VINTAGES

The Mediterranean climate is generally temperate, so vintage variations are less extreme than in northern France, but there are differences none the less, with varying amounts of sunshine and, more significantly, varying amounts of rain, affecting the *stress hydrique* of the vines. In an ideal world the water reserves are replenished in the winter; spring is mild, the summer warm and sunny, with a couple of storms, usually around 14 July and 15 August (which are public holidays in France), to refresh the vines. September should be warm and sunny for the harvest, with the weather beginning to break around the equinox. But each year brings its own particular variations. As Pierre Jacquet from Domaine Binet Jacquet notes, the typology of each vintage is determined by climate, while the *terroir* remains constant. '*Une millésime; une verité; on ne change rien*,' which might translate as 'one vintage; one truth; nothing changes'.

Each wine grower has a personal view of the harvest and opinions can vary, so what follows is a distillation of conversations and comments, with welcome help from Françoise Ollier in her capacity as a previous secretary of the *syndicat*. Nathalie and François Caumette of Domaine de l'Ancienne Mercerie hosted a marvellous vertical tasting of La Couture, back to their very first vintage in 2000, which also gave some helpful insights, with the occasional deviation into the climate of the potato patch. I also spent a morning with Bernard and François Vidal, with some contrasting bottles. Bernard pertinently remarks that the wine growers in the Languedoc are very much less concerned by specific differences than they would be in Bordeaux or Burgundy; generally there were harvests without any surprises. And the year which really stood out in Bernard's memory was the hard winter of 1956, when he was still at school. These days he is concerned about the impact of global warming making for less refreshing wines; the harvest date is generally earlier than it was even ten years ago and, although he does not think the amount of rainfall has changed significantly, what has changed is *when* it rains. The heavy rainfall of September 2014 is an obvious example of this.

2015

This is generally seen as a very good vintage. Certainly the vat and cask samples that I have tasted recently have shown plenty of promise. Catherine Roque at Mas d'Alezon has produced some deliciously peppery Syrah and some fragrant Cinsaut, as has Simon Coulshaw at Domaine des Trinités. The summer was hot, good, with a couple of advantageous rainstorms in August. Paul Gordon of Domaine de Sarabande described 2015 as 'yet another year where the elements threw everything at us. It was a scorching hot southern French summer with temperatures often hitting 40°C', but the end of August brought some beneficial rain, and there was a further rainstorm in early September. That did not adversely affect the quality.

2014

This was one of the challenging harvests of recent vintages. The spring was unusually warm, with July weather in May, and at the beginning of July the rainfall of the year was 50 per cent below average. But then things changed: the summer was not so hot, thus with May weather in July, making it *'une année à l'envers'* or a back to front year. The first couple of weeks of September were warm and sunny, and then came the rain, which caused problems for the later-ripening varieties and for those who favour a later harvest. However, Faugères did not suffer as much as some other parts of the Languedoc.

2013

The Languedoc fared very much better than the rest of France with 320 days of sunshine. Paul Gordon at Domaine Sarabande described 2013 as 'spectacular'. It was a tough year to harvest because everything was so late, but the wines are turning out very well. For Brigitte Chevalier of Domaine de Cébène, 2013 was 'even better than 2012, with elegance and power'. The summer arrived late and, with a cool spring and temperamental weather at flowering, the crop – particularly of Grenache – was reduced through *coulure*. Michel Abbal at Domaine Valambelle obtained just 50 hectolitres from 5 hectares of Grenache Noir, instead of the usual 150 hectolitres. For Pierre Jacquet, it was the *millésime du viticulteur*; you needed to understand your *terroir*.

2012

This was a year with water, with a cool spring and a rather grey summer. September was overcast, but there was no rain. While people asked where the sun was, the rain did not come until October. The difficult decision was the date of the harvest. Syrah performed well in 2012, as there was no water stress, but was none the less slow to ripen, whereas Grenache Noir and Carignan ripened more easily. Domaine de Cébène found the wines lighter and more elegant, more *aerien,* and generally the wines are fruity, but with no great concentration. On the whole the wines have good acidity but are less ripe than some other vintages.

2011

Frédéric Albaret at Domaine St Antonin found the wines more concentrated; generally it was a much hotter year, with some very ripe Grenache Noir. François Vidal would agree: it was a sunny year with more concentration of flavours and higher alcohol levels, and initially less expressive than 2012, but with good potential. The enthusiasts of Mourvèdre, such as Christian Godefroid from Les Amants de la Vigneronne, consider 2011 with its regular rain to be a Mourvèdre year.

2010

A wetter year, so the vines did not suffer from water stress. The spring was wet and there was even, very unusually, snow in March. The warm weather arrived at the end of June; August was hot, and the harvest was relatively uncomplicated, making for wines with elegance, concentration and balance.

2009

A lot of wine growers enthused about this vintage. The grapes were healthy, but quantity was fairly low because the vines were still recovering from the effects of the hail of 2008, but that meant good concentration in the wines. May and June were hot, and the rainfall was normal: 'as we want it' observes Nathalie Caumette. A hot August led to some irregular ripening and water stress for some. Brigitte Chevalier was very pleased, even though there was only a small *sortie de raisins* after 2008 hail. Jean-Michel Alquier's vineyards benefitted from a light storm in both July and August.

2008

This was the year it hailed on 4 September, a week before the harvest was due to start. The hail swept through the southern part of the appellation in the course of a few minutes early in the evening; the noise of hailstones landing on a paved terrace was deafening and the vineyards next morning looked as though a herd of goats had shredded all the leaves. Amongst those affected by the hail, Domaine Ollier-Taillefer was fairly average, with 20 per cent less red and 60 per cent less white wine. Their *cuvée* Les Collines certainly had a *gout de grêle*, a taste of sour cherries which lingered in the mouth. Otherwise the spring was wet, with a particularly wet May, and storms in July and August. Some people had problems with mildew, as well as suffering from the hail, but those who escaped the hail produced some nicely balanced wines.

2007

This was another year when the Languedoc fared very much better than the rest of France for weather. There was a good-sized crop and the wines have that attractive Faugères freshness. Françoise Ollier enthuses: '*J'adore* 2007, because it is so fresh'. Brigitte Chevalier's 2007 Ex Arena combines freshness with a lovely note of maturity. As Brigitte smilingly observes: 'It hasn't got a wrinkle.' The spring was wet, but there was no summer rain and very little rain in September. François Vidal describes it as a very balanced vintage, with neither too much rain nor sunshine. The harvest was an easy one and his Cistus has elegant concentration and minerality.

2006

A hotter year than either 2007 or 2005. There was no rain from mid-March until mid-October, but happily the previous autumn and winter had been wet, so there were no serious problems of water stress. The wines tend to be quite rich and concentrated, with some sturdy tannins.

2005

Wines with a similar character to 2007. There was an average amount of rain during the spring, with a storm in April and no rain during the summer. Nathalie Caumette recorded 110 millimetres of rain on 6 September, when they started the harvest the previous day, and 35 millimetres for 7 September. La Couture was drinking beautifully in the summer of 2014.

2004

A dry May with a little rain in June and none in July. Some rain fell in August, 'providentially' says Nathalie Caumette, but when 48 millimetres fell at the beginning of September she felt that providence had its limits as the rain caused rot in some places. Happily there was sufficient wind to have a drying effect and the best of the 2004s are drinking very nicely, with soft tannins and supple fruit. For the Vidals 2004 was a 'complicated year', with a lot of rain before the harvest, making things difficult for the earlier-ripening grapes, but Cistus has turned out beautifully and was drinking very elegantly in January 2015.

2003

The year that is remembered for the heatwave, but there was no drought as there had been heavy rainfall during the winter, with 600 to 700 millimetres of rain between October 2002 and March 2003. The spring was fairly dry, and the summer very dry and hot. A heatwave is defined by a daytime temperature of more than 35°C and a night-time temperature above 20°C for three consecutive days: between 1 and 14 August the temperature on several occasions reached as high as 40°C. A little rain mid-August refreshed the vines. Inevitably the harvest was early with very ripe grapes, and the later-ripening varieties performed particularly well. Nathalie Caumette would have expected her Grenache Noir to survive the heat better than it did; they threw away withered grapes. But a heatwave is relative in a southern climate.

2002

This is remembered by Nathalie Caumette as *une année terrible*, a very wet year. Some wines are fairly light and mature, and have developed quite fast. There was indeed rain at the end of August and in September, which complicated the harvest. However, the *syndicat* report is more positive, describing it as a year for the Mediterranean varieties, Carignan, Grenache and Mourvèdre. Despite the rain the berries were quite small and yields low.

2001

This was a dry year with a warm spring and a dry summer apart from two good storms, making for a small quantity of very good wine. Cool nights and a drying north wind further helped the ripening process and contributed to the quality. Michel Louison, who created Château des Estanilles, reckons that his 2001 Clos du Fou is the best wine he ever made;

I was lucky enough to drink it with Catherine Roque and compare it with 2001 Les Bastides from Jean Michel Alquier. Clos du Fou was fresher and riper, while Les Bastides was rich, leathery and beautifully mature, and both exhibited considerable ageing potential.

2000

A mild and wet spring after a dry winter. A hot August with a little rain, while September was relatively warm and dry. Nathalie Caumette remembers her first vintage as a year of regular rain with no water stress, and La Couture from that vintage is drinking beautifully, with some elegant leathery notes and mature fruit. It is generally considered to be a very successful vintage.

1999

Some regular rainfall during the spring, so no water stress during the summer. *Entrées maritimes*, damp sea breezes, caused some concern over the condition of the grapes, but the wine growers who worked well in their vineyards produced some lovely spicy wines, such as Cuvée Gaëlle from Château Haut Fabrègues, which has aged better than the sturdier 1998. For Bernard and François Vidal it is one of their favourite vintages of Cistus, and in January 2015 it was drinking beautifully with some elegant balsamic and tapenade notes and a long silky finish.

1998

Considered to be an excellent vintage. A dry year with a hot summer and even some drought conditions, so that the grapes were healthy but lacking in juice, making for ripe, concentrated wines.

1997

A very wet year with an extraordinary 1800 millimetres of rain, but happily September was hot and dry, which helped the quality and produced some fruity elegant wines.

1996

Quite a wet year and quite a large crop, making fruity wines without much staying power.

1995

A dry but not especially hot year, resulting in low yields of concentrated wines. A fine vintage.

1994
Rain in the latter half of the harvest created problems, but fortunately the *ban de vendange,* allowing the start of the harvest, was earlier than usual. A low yield, the result of hail in 1993, and relatively light wines.

1993
Healthy grapes until hail struck on 9 September, the day before the harvest was due to start. Michel Louison lost 80 per cent of his crop: 'We were like zombies, picking everything with the help of friends, and it turned out much better than expected.'

1992
A difficult vintage. It has been compared to 1996, with a fair amount of rain, making supple wines that were ready fairly quickly. The rain also demanded a strict selection of the grapes, what Jean-Michel Alquier calls '*extra cuisine en cave*'. However, a bottle of 1992 Château des Estanilles was far from fading when drunk in December 2014; it lacked the warmth of Faugères and tasted quite structured. Michel Louison must also have achieved some successful *cuisine en cave.*

1991
A cool summer with a wet September, making quite elegant wines that are overshadowed by 1990.

1990
A good year. Jean-Michel Alquier considers it the best vintage he ever made, a finer wine than 1991, and he draws comparisons between 2000 and 2001, and indeed 2010 and 2011, with the first vintage of the decade in each case overshadowing the following wine.

1989
A good vintage. No particular climatic problems.

1988
A small crop, the result of a very dry year.

1987
A very wet year, with rain causing considerable problems during the harvest. A lot of wine was declassified into *vin de table,* and even the *syndicat's* official rating was damning – mediocre.

1986

Jean-Luc Saur from Château Haut Fabrègues remembers a lot of rain in September, but they had nearly finished the harvest by then. The summer was quite cool and made for wines with *finesse*.

1985

A very cold winter and a very hot summer. Alain Ollier talks of a great vintage, '*un très grand millésime*'.

1984

Rain at the harvest. Quite a hot year, with quite drying tannins.

1983

A hot year, resulting in rich wines that tended to lack acidity.

1982

The year of the appellation. The harvest started on 16 September. A beautiful vintage, with fresh but concentrated wines.

APPENDIX I: PRODUCTION FIGURES

Vintage	Hectolitres	Hectares	Number of wine growers
2014	66,531	1,896	59 + 1 cooperative
2013	62,058	1,858	57 + 1 cooperative
2012	63,695	1,890	57 + 1 cooperative
2011	70,591	1,939	58 + 1 cooperative
2010	59,948	1,979	56 + 1 cooperative
2009	59,188	2,052	55 + 2 cooperatives
2008	64,300		
2007	62,500		
2006	72,501		
2005	74,728		
2004	74, 649		
2003	69,112		
2002	70,806		
2001	78,703		
2000	80,611		
1999	79,731		
1998	73,708		
1997	78,075		
1996	68,374		
1995	47,012		
1994	60,708	1,712	
1993	47,082	1,623	
1992	60,539	1,348	

1991	64,425	1,592
1990	70,692	1,555
1989	60,000	1,224
1988	55,000	1,214
1987	57,000	1,043
1986	50,000	1,028
1985	53,380	998

APPENDIX II – DATES OF THE BANS DE VENDANGES

Dates	Picking date at Ollier-Taillefer
2015 – 27 August	7 September
2014 – 28 August	8 September
2013 – 29 August	17 September
2012 – 30 August	6 September
2011 – 26 August	5 September
2010 – 3 September	9 September
2009 – 3 September	7 September
2008 – 15 September	
2007 – 30 August	10 September
2006 – 11 September	
2005 – 14 September	
2004 – 17 September	
2003 – 2 September	
2002 – 6 September	16th September
2001 – 13 September	
2000 – 21 September	

And then there's a gap until 1982: – 16 September

Francoise Ollier's grandfather, Marcel Taillefer, made a note of everything. Here are his picking dates back to 1962. I think they are worth noting; as Françoise says, there would have been much more of the later-ripening Carignan in the vineyards then, and the climate was probably a little different so, for historical interest:

1981 – 25 September
1980 – 5 October
1979 – 27 September
1978 – 7 October
1977 – 1 October
1976 – 30 September
1975 – 3 October
1974 – 5 October
1973 – 23 September
1972 – 4 October
1971 – 4 October
1970 – 30 September
1969 – 6 October
1968 – 30 September
1967 – 24 September
1966 – 17 September
1965 – 22 September
1964 – 14 September
1963 – 25 September
1962 – 24 September

APPENDIX III: CLIMATIC DATA

Average annual rainfall (mm) between 2000 and 2015

Jan	Feb	Mar	Apr	May	Jun	Jul	Aug	Sep	Oct	Nov	Dec	Annual
45.9	48.7	62.2	69.3	43.4	40.7	21.4	40.4	67.4	97.2	75.5	58.3	670.4

Average temperatures (°C)

	Jan	Feb	Mar	Apr	May	Jun	Jul	Aug	Sep	Oct	Nov	Dec	Annual
Average	7.4	7.5	10.8	13.6	17.3	21.6	23.7	23.3	19.6	16	11.3	8.0	15.0
Average minimum	3.0	2.6	5.6	8.2	11.4	15.2	17.1	16.7	13.7	11.2	6.9	3.6	9.6
Average maximum	11.8	12.3	16	19.1	23.1	28	30.3	29.9	25.6	20.8	15.6	12.4	20.5

Source L'ACH – L'Association Climatologique de l'Hérault

APPENDIX IV: BREAKDOWN OF GRAPE VARIETIES FOR 2016

RED

Syrah	32%
Grenache Noir	28%
Carignan	21%
Mourvèdre	11%
Cinsaut	8%

WHITE

Roussanne	44%
Marsanne	20%
Vermentino	17%
Grenache Blanc	14%
Clairette Blanc/Viognier Blanc	5%

APPENDIX V: AN APPELLATION SUMMARY

If a wine grower has vineyards in the appellation of Faugères, then that is what he or she makes. Until the white appellation of Faugères was created, white wine was labelled Coteaux du Languedoc. As Faugères was recognized as an appellation before the Coteaux du Languedoc, there needs be no mention of the word Languedoc on the label.

Growers in the village of Gabian, outside the appellation, have much more flexibility. Their best wines are likely to be part of the new *cru* of Pézenas, for which they must conform to strict regulations, particularly relating to grape variety percentages. Otherwise wine from appellation land, and planted with the appropriate grape varieties, will be labelled Coteaux du Languedoc, or Languedoc. The Coteaux du Languedoc appellation is set to disappear in 2017.

If growers have grape varieties that do not conform to the appellation, they may make *vin de pays*, which are now called IGP or Indication Géographique Protégée. They can choose between the broadest category, namely Pays d'Oc, the departmental delimitation of Pays de l'Hérault, or the local zone, Cassan. And if they want the barest minimum to do with bureaucracy, they can opt for Vin de France, which has replaced the previous term of 'vin de table', with differences. They can now include a vintage and a grape variety and, while Vin de France may lie at the bottom of the pyramid of quality, in practice and in the hands of a talented winemaker, it can indicate something worthwhile that simply does not conform to accepted practices.

GLOSSARY

Some French winemaking terms are so much more precise and less clumsy than the equivalent English terms, and the same goes for wine descriptions too. If you are talking to French winemakers, inevitably some French words creep into the notes and the subsequent text.

Amarone – a style of Valpolicella, made from raisined grapes so that the wine is rich and sweet

Are – a historical unit of measurement, equivalent to 100 square metres

Arrachage – pulling up of vines; in the past growers were paid a subsidy to do so with *primes d'arrachage.*

Assemblage – blend

Ban de vendange – the date for the official start of the harvest, before which the wine growers may not pick

Barrique – barrel of 225 litres

Bâtonnage – lees stirring

Bonbons anglais – English boiled sweets

Cahier de charge – the document that lays down the regulations of the appellation and what the wine grower may or may not do

Capitelle – little dry stone building, looks like an igloo

Carbonic maceration – a method of fermentation, whereby whole bunches are put into a vat filled with carbon dioxide, and left to ferment. Contrary to a usual fermentation, the pressed juice is better than the free-run juice.

Cépage – grape variety

Circulade – a traditional village of the Languedoc, built in a circle around a central point for reasons of defence

Commune – village in the context of Faugères, but also the unit into which French departments are divided

Coulure – a disorder of the vine which can occur if flowering takes place in unsatisfactory climatic conditions, so that the berries fail to develop, adversely affecting the yield

Cru – literally a growth, and part of the French wine hierarchy

Cuvaison – time in vat with grape skins in contact with the juice

Défricher – clear scrubland or *garrigues*

Délestage – rack and return is the best English translation. The juice is run out of the vat, so the cap of grape skins sinks to the bottom and then, when it is returned to the vat, rises up again through the juice.

Délimitation parcellaire – the precise delimitation of vineyard plots within an appellation

Demi-muids – usually about a 500 to 600-litre barrel

Effeuillage – leaf plucking

Égrappé – destalked

Élevage – literally the rearing, the educating or ageing of wine

Enherbement – leaving grass, etc., in the vineyard

Entrée de gamme – entry level

Fermage – term for renting a vineyard

Finesse – tasting term that implies elegance, and even more

Flavescence dorée – one English translation is 'grapevine yellows'. A disease of the vine, spread by leaf hoppers, which kills young vines and severely impacts the yield of older vines. A potentially serious problem.

Foudres – large barrels, anything from 5 to 500 hectolitres

Fraicheur – freshness, but even more so, with a certain refreshing quality

Gobelet – bush vines

Grand cru – literally a great growth, above premier *cru* in the pecking order

Gras – literally fat; a wine with some weight

Gris – a term used to describe a grape variety that has a pale pink skin when ripe, such as Grenache Gris as opposed to Noir or Blanc

Guyot – method of cane pruning not dissimilar to *cordon de Royat*

Haut de gamme – top of the range

IGP – Indication Géographique Protégée, the term which has replaced *vin de pays*

INAO – Institute National des Appellations d'Origine; the government body that controls all the details of an appellation

Intercep – piece of vineyard equipment that enables you to weed mechanically between the vines within the row

Labelle – term used for the tasting session which that ensures that a wine is of acceptable quality for an appellation

Lieu-dit – small plot of land on a map, literally 'place named'

Lutte raisonnée – Sustainable viticulture; you think before you spray, rather than spraying irrespective of climatic conditions

Matière – literally 'matter'; implies a wine with some substance

Mouillage – to dampen the cap of grape skins

Négociants –merchants who buy grapes, juice, wine in varying stages of preparation and then make their own blends

Occitan – the *langue d'oc*, the original language of the Languedoc, also spoken in other Mediterranean areas and today enjoying something of a revival

Ouillage – topping up of barrels, when wine has been lost naturally by evaporation

Palissé / palissage – describes vines that are trained on wires

Pigeage – pushing down

Premier cru – a first growth, and usually below grand cru in the hierarchy

Rafle – grape stems

Remontage – pumping over

Rolafaca – a Brazilian machine which flattens the grass, partially cutting it, so that it turns into mulch and compost

Saigné – term used for making rosé, literally means 'bleeding' the vat, and running off juice

Souplesse – supple character

Stagiaire – a trainee student, doing work experience

Surface foliaire – ratio of leaf area to grapes

Syndicat – union, as in the growers' union that runs the appellation

Terroir – a French term impossible to translate directly into English. It includes soil, but also aspect and altitude, and encompasses the overall environment of the vine.

Tonnelier – cooper

Tronconique vat – a large tapered vat that may be in wood or stainless steel or concrete and which is used for fermentation or *élevage*

VDQS – Vin Delimité de Qualité Supérieure, the category beneath *appellation contrôlée* and now virtually defunct

Vendange verte – a green harvest, carried out in July if there are too many grapes

Vers de la grappe – larvae from two insects, cochylis and eudemis, that can do considerable damage to vines

Viandé – literally 'meaty', a certain farmyard note in the wine

Vigneron – wine grower; they make their own wine as well as grow grapes

Viticulteur – grower of grapes; does not make wine

En vrac – wine in bulk

METRIC MEASURES – US EQUIVALENTS

1°C = 33.8°F
1 centimetre (cm) = 0.39 inches
1 gram   = 0.03 ounces
1 hectare = 2.47 acres
(an 'are' is 100 square metres, and a hectare is 100 ares)
1 kilometre = 0.621 miles
1 litre = 1.75 pints
(a hectolitre is 100 litres)
1 metre = 3.28 feet
1 millimetre (mm) = 0.04 inches

BIBLIOGRAPHY

Berry, Charles, *In Search of Wine*, London, 1935, republished 1987

Boissieu, Jean et al., *Les Vins du Rhône et de la Mediterranée*, Editions Montalba, 1978

Bousquet, Jean-Claude, *Terroirs viticoles, Paysages et géologie en Languedoc*, Editions Ecologistes de l'Euzière, 2011

Caumette, Claude, *Images de Faugères*, Éditions Lo Sauta Ròcs, Faugères, 2010

Dion, Roger, *Histoire de la Vigne et du Vin en France des Origines au XIXème siècle*, Flammarion, Paris 1959

Guyot, Jules, *Etudes des Vignobles de France*, Paris, 1868

Healy, Maurice, *Stay Me with Flagons*, London, 1949

Jefford, Andrew, *The New France*, Mitchell Beazley, London 2002

Jullien, André, *Topographie des Tous les Vignobles Connus*, Paris 1866

Lachiver, Marcel, *Vins, Vignes et Vignerons: Histoire du vignoble français*, Fayard, Lille, 1988

Pomerol, Charles (ed.), *Terroirs et Vins de France*, Total-Edition-Presse, Paris 1984

Rendu, Victor, *Ampélographie Française*, Paris 1857

Wilson, James, *Terroir*, Mitchell Beazley, London 1998

Woon, Basil, *The Big Little Wines of France*, London 1972

ACKNOWLEDGEMENTS

This book would never have happened without the initial help and encouragement of several friends, in no particular order, Alex MacCormick, Wilf Healy, Lits Philippou, Jenny Curra and Monique Dorel. Simon Coulshaw kindly cast an anglophone *vigneron's* eye over my text.

Michèle Solans exercised skills of diplomacy and tenacity making appointments with sometimes elusive wine growers; she undoubtedly simplified my life. Gary MacDonald has taken some wonderfully evocative photographs of the Faugères scenery as well as perceptive portraits of some of the *vignerons*. The old postcard photographs come from Domaine St Martin d'Agel, Brigitte Barreiro from Jeanjean helped with other photographs, and Charlotte Habit supplied a photograph from Château Laurens. Valerie Desblancs, the director of the Faugères syndicat answered my seemingly endless questions with enormous patience and provided the maps of the area.

But books about wine are above all about the people who make the wine, in this case the fifty or so *vignerons* and *vigneronnes* of Faugères, who were happy to open bottles and generously share their wines and talk about their challenges and their achievements. Nor should I forget the nine wine growers of Gabian. Without them all there would be no book.

Thanks are due to Richard Burton for his courage in agreeing to publish a book about one small vineyard in the Languedoc.

And last but certainly not least my husband, Christopher Galleymore, deserves appreciative thanks for living with the trials and tribulations of a gestating book.

INDEX

Note: the prefixes de, des or d' are ignored in the alphabetical sequence.

Index created by Meg Davies